"A triumph of a maturing biblical counseling movement. Elyse Fitzpatrick, a counselor with uncommon insight into common problems, teams with Dennis Johnson, a seminary professor with a firm fix on justification and the centrality of the gospel, to produce a cross-centered counseling tool. Expect to find the refreshing intersection of the liberating truth of the cross and the power of the gospel to move counselees and impart hope. This book is a major contribution not only to biblical counseling but also to the person in the pew."

—TEDD TRIPP, Pastor, author, international conference speaker

"Broken people remain so because they never truly understand the nature or extent of God's love. Following the pattern of Paul's letter to the Ephesians, this book triggers worship and hope with exhilarating descriptions of the gospel of Christ and shows us how to live out the love and freedom of the gospel in the relationships and struggles of everyday life. May God use this book to bring a wholeness and joy to believers that is irresistibly attractive to everyone around them."

—KEN SANDE, President, Peacemaker Ministries

"Fitzpatrick and Johnson teach that effective counseling for broken and hurting people does not mean walking *beyond* the gospel into some modern form of psychotherapy, which ultimately provides no solutions. All Christians, especially pastors, counselors, and church workers who yearn to see genuine healing and transformation in their families and churches, should practice the principles of this book personally and use it to help others. This book is biblical counseling at its best; absorbing its teaching will make us all better counselors."

—DR. JOEL R. BEEKE, President, Puritan Reformed
Theological Seminary

"A treasure of gospel-proclaiming, biblical, and practical help for every person striving to grow in grace and help others to do the same. Professional counselors, church leaders, and laypeople will all benefit from the accessible case studies drawn from the authors' decades of experience ministering to real people in real situations. This is no mere how-to manual. If seemingly hopeless cycles of sin and immaturity are tempting you to wonder if real change is even possible, *Counsel from the Cross* is just the book to encourage you and help you to remember both what the gospel declares about us and what it demands of us."

—TARA KLENA BARTHEL, author, *Living the Gospel in Relationships*; coauthor, *Peacemaking Women*

"Elyse Fitzpatrick and Dennis Johnson present a compelling case for the very radical and eminently practical power of the gospel in helping counsel broken people. One will not find here the usual Scriptures taken out of context or mere proof-texting approach that so-much of Christian counseling has offered the evangelical community. Instead, Johnson's exegetical insights and Fitzpatrick's case-wise counsel show how and why we must apply the love and grace of Christ at each stage of our counseling. They are to be praised for mining the riches of the gospel and offering a real model for and recovery of Christ-centered counseling."

—REV. DR. ALFRED J. POIRIER, author, *The Peacemaking Pastor*

"I've learned more about biblical counseling from Elyse Fitzpatrick than from anyone else writing in the field today. I tear into her new books and return repeatedly to them for inspiration in my own work. Elyse's collaboration with Dennis Johnson has produced a volume that is both theologically astute and full of practical wisdom. I'm already applying the principles I've learned from it in my counseling."

—DR. LAURA HENDRICKSON, author, psychiatrist, biblical counselor

COUNSEL FROM THE CROSS

Crossway books by Elyse Fitzpatrick:

Because He Loves Me:
How Christ Transforms Our Daily Life

Comforts from the Cross:
Celebrating the Gospel One Day at a Time

Crossway books by Dennis Johnson:

Heralds of the King:
Christ-Centered Preaching in the Tradition of Edmund P. Clowney
(editor and contributor)

COUNSEL FROM THE CROSS

connecting broken people to the love of Christ

Elyse M. Fitzpatrick and
Dennis E. Johnson

CROSSWAY

WHEATON, ILLINOIS

Trade paperback ISBN: 978-1-4335-3413-3

Library of Congress Cataloging-in-Publication Data
Fitzpatrick, Elyse, 1950–
   Counsel from the Cross : connecting broken people to the love
of Christ / Elyse M. Fitzpatrick and Dennis E. Johnson.
      p. cm.
   Includes index.
   ISBN 13: 978-1-4335-0317-7 (tpb)
     1. Counseling—Religious aspects—Christianity. 2. Bible—Psychology.
I. Johnson, Dennis E. (Dennis Edward) II. Title.
BR115.C69F58   2009
253.5—dc22   2008049984

Crossway is a publishing ministry of Good News Publishers.

VP		21	20	19	18	17	16	15	14
14	13	12	11	10	9	8	7	6	5	4

To our children and their spouses,
Eric and Susanne, Christina and Julien,
Peter and Mandi, Laurie and Daniel,

*with the prayer that the Lord will continue to give them
grace and wisdom as they nurture our grandchildren from the cross.*

DENNIS

To pastor Mark Lauterbach and his wife, Rondi,

*with thanks for their friendship and for consistently
reminding me of our Savior.*

ELYSE

Contents

Preface

IT IS NO SECRET THAT COUNSELING—whether for-mal-ized under terms such as *psychotherapy*, *life coaching*, *intervention*, *personal empowerment*, or some other new-and-improved label—is big business in North America, and it continues to burgeon. As Western culture drifts away from the Creator's design for human life and community, the intrapersonal and interpersonal effects of our first parents' original rebellion against God, the one who made them for friendship with himself and gave them everything they could possibly need and more, are becoming more overt all the time. These effects include depression; burnout; international conflict; intergenerational conflict; interracial conflict; marital conflict; class conflict; church conflict; anxiety; fear; behavioral patterns that are simultaneously self-centered and self-destructive; pornography and other forms of sexual exploitation; senseless cruelty and wanton violence in war zones, urban streets, and suburban school cam-puses; and the list could go on.

As this list implies, the need for counseling—for what older generations of pastors called "the cure of souls"—is as evident in the contemporary church as it is in the culture at large. The shelves of Christian bookstores groan under the weight of publications that promise a religious solution to a wide spectrum of dysfunctions, addictions, and distresses, from anorexia to obesity, from timid insecurity to brash abrasiveness, from chaotic disorder and lack of self-discipline to paralyzing inhibition and driven rigidity. Church staffs expand to include caregivers with specialized education and credentials that evoke confidence in those who limp, wounded or

11

wayward or both, to Christ's people and their shepherds in search of relief—sometimes even at the cost of repentance.

So why add one more counseling book to your local bookstore's shelves or (we hope!) to Amazon.com's seemingly infinite online inventory? Whether you are a pastor shepherding a congregation of a hundred or a thousand, a layperson to whom others look for spiritual guidance with personal problems and growth in godliness, or simply a follower of Jesus seeking his grace to persevere in faith and faithfulness in a miserable situation, Elyse Fitzpatrick and I want to lay before you a provocative claim: the cross of Christ and the gospel that proclaims it really are "the power of God for salvation [comprehensive rescue] to everyone who believes" (Rom. 1:16). In that cross, on which occurred the execution of God's Son, lies hidden "the power of God and the wisdom of God" (1 Cor. 1:18–24). And in that cross lies the power both to liberate hearts that have been caught in seemingly unbreakable cycles of defeat and to instill hope that *change can actually happen* in us, in our relationships, and in those whom we love fiercely and resent intensely at the same time.

We believe that the cross of Christ exposes both our own and our counselees' utter helplessness and unworthiness. Each of us rightfully deserves the guilty verdict and divine wrath that Jesus bore in our place on that cross. Therefore, when we take the cross seriously, we find our pride, our self-satisfaction, and our smug resentment toward or contempt for others shattered into a thousand pieces.

But the cross also exposes another very surprising truth: the holy sovereign Lord whose authority we have defied and whose glory we have deflected to unworthy rivals *was willing to endure the judgment* that his own impeccable justice pronounced upon us. The cross declares that we are loved with an intensity that defies our capacity to comprehend, not because we are intrinsically lovable but because God is intrinsically love. These are the twin messages of the cross—brutal honesty about our guilt and impotence and the glorious assurance of our welcome by the Father in his beloved Son.

Together they pack divine power, through the Holy Spirit of God, to pry our affections loose from enslaving patterns of self-defense and self-indulgence and to set our hearts free to run, by grace alone through faith alone, toward the goal, "until we all attain to the unity of the faith and of the knowledge of the Son of God, to mature manhood, to the measure of the stature of the fullness of Christ" (Eph. 4:13).

Does it sound too simplistic to claim that in the cross of Christ and in the surprising combination of ego-smashing humility and despair-smashing confidence that trust in the gospel produces lies the power to set struggling people free? Can the cross really free men and women from addictive appetites, whether physical or mental, cut through hearts hardened and turned poisonous by long years of bitter grudge-bearing and blame-shifting, and "turn the hearts of fathers to their children and the hearts of children to their fathers" (Mal. 4:6)? Can it make self-absorbed husbands into sacrificial servant leaders (Eph. 5:25–33)? Can it make defiant or untrusting wives into daughters of the King, set free to glorify their Lord through "respectful and pure conduct," adorned in "the hidden person of the heart with the imperishable beauty of a gentle and quiet spirit" (1 Pet. 3:2–4)? Is the gospel *really* a panacea—a cure-all—or is it just one more "medicine show" product, hyped by claims that no elixir could ever fulfill?

We believe that when God the Creator provides a cure-all, it really cures all, and that when he sent his eternal Son as redeemer, he set in motion a new creation power that will eventually eradicate both the sin-twisted self-centeredness of our hearts and the sin-infected wounds that we have inflicted on one another. We believe that the church's pastors, elders, spiritual caregivers, and members must embrace and rest in the truth that Christ is the one "in whom are hidden *all* the treasures of wisdom and knowledge" (Col. 2:2–3)—yes, all! And we believe that this reality is profoundly relevant to the way Christian counselors address the struggles of those who come to them for help.

So we invite you to join us in a venture of exploration to discover the power to defeat sin and sadness, conflict and bitterness, and self-pity and self-contempt, not by walking *beyond* the gospel that first brought us into the favor and family of God but rather by moving more deeply *into* that same gospel. And we invite you to notice the many ways in which the inspired human authors of God's inerrant Word, the Bible, bring their readers back, again and again, to what Jesus has done for us through his obedient life and sinless sacrifice. They address a whole spectrum of interpersonal conflicts and intrapersonal captivities. Our prayer is that you will join us as we point hurting, guilty, trapped people away from ourselves and toward the only Savior who can rescue them not only from sin's condemning guilt and penalty but also from its tyrannizing, paralyzing grip.

Dennis E. Johnson

Acknowledgments

GLIMPSING IN RETROSPECT hints of God's sovereign design of the path that has led to *Counsel from the Cross*, Dennis would like to thank:

Elyse, for the invitation to participate in this project with her, for her and Phil's friendship, and for her always-insightful, faithful, and fresh contributions as a lecturer in my elective on the role of women in the family, the church, and society.

Pastor Jim Newheiser of Grace Bible Church who, as director of the Institute for Biblical Counseling and Discipleship, invited me to speak at IBCD's 2007 Summer Institute on the relationship of the gospel doctrine of justification and pastoral counseling. At that same institute Elyse taught on the power of the gospel to motivate and instill hope in counselees, and it was the delightful intersection of our presentations and perspectives that week that led to our collaboration on this book.

My faculty colleagues at Westminster Seminary California for their united stand on behalf of the biblical and Reformational articulation of the astonishing good news of justification by grace alone through faith alone on the grounds of Christ's sacrifice and righteousness alone. I'd particularly like to thank R. Scott Clark, editor of our faculty volume that pertains to these essential issues,[1] for his invitation to address the interface between the biblical way—the only way—for sinful people to be declared right with God and the daunting challenges of pastoral counseling. This assignment pulled me out of my comfort zone, but the pain of that stretching did me good spiritually as well as ministerially. It was Pastor Newheiser's reading of my essay in the faculty volume that led to my invitation to participate in the 2007 IBCD Summer Institute.

My pastor, *Ted Hamilton*, who counsels us from the cross week by week from the pulpit as he unfolds the Bible's consistent witness to Christ and his gracious rescue work for us. Thanks also go to all my fellow elders, shepherds of God's flock at New Life Presbyterian Church, for seeking to apply the gospel consistently in our leadership of the church and our care for Jesus' beloved sheep.

My beloved wife, *Jane*, who loves and encourages me though I don't deserve it, thereby reflecting the gospel of unmerited grace in our marriage even as she, like Moses, cannot see how the glory of the King shines through her (Ex. 34:29; 2 Cor. 3:18).

The Lord Jesus, who loved me and gave himself for me, setting me free not only from sin's condemnation and penalty but also from its heart-enslaving tyranny.

Elyse would like to thank:

Dennis Johnson, who surprised me by being willing to work on this project and then continued to surprise me throughout the year with his deep insight, lucid precision, gentle correction, profound scriptural knowledge, and great love for our Savior.

Iain and Barbara Duguid—and through them the work of Tim Keller—for opening my eyes to the wonders of the gospel for believers.

George Scipione, David Powlison, Paul David Tripp, Ed Welch, Jim Newheiser, and *Randy Patten* for teaching me how to apply the powerful truths of Scripture to all of life.

John Piper and *Desiring God Ministries* for teaching me of the supremacy of God in all things.

The wonderful people at Grace Church San Diego and especially those in our small group for their prayers and support through this process.

My husband, *Phil*, who has demonstrated God's love for me for so many years and has created an environment for me to learn, grow, and flourish. Your humility and gentle leadership have taught me much about the gospel and my Savior.

And all our children, and their children who love to see their names in a real book: *Wesley, Hayden, Eowyn, Allie, Gabe, and Colin.* "Take up and read!"

Introduction

NINETEENTH-CENTURY Princeton theologian B. B. Warfield wrote:

> There is nothing in us or done by us, at any stage of our earthly development, because of which we are acceptable to God. We must always be accepted for Christ's sake, or we cannot ever be accepted at all. . . . This is not true of us only when we believe. It is just as true after we have believed. It will continue to be true as long as we live. Our need of Christ does not cease with our believing; nor does the nature of our relation to Him or to God through Him ever alter, no matter what our attainments in Christian graces or our achievements in behavior may be. It is always on His "blood and righteousness" alone that we can rest.[1]

What did you think when you read the preceding quotation? Let us suggest a couple of possibilities. Did you think, "Of course I believe that it's only because of Christ that I'm accepted! Why bring that up again?" Or perhaps you think, "Yes, justification is wonderful. But I'm looking for a book about sanctification. Perhaps this isn't the right one for me." There's even a possibility that you were a little uncomfortable about the words "blood and righteousness," and you're wondering what they have to do with the brokenness you are feeling today.

In this book, we have collaborated to bring you a book that will take the truth of our acceptance before God by Christ's righteousness alone and make it practical as you live your everyday life. We know that there are already literally thousands of books on counseling topics, so why write another one? Is there anything to say that hasn't been said countless times over? Why talk about the gospel again when what people need is concrete advice for living? There are several reasons.

First, many Christians love Jesus and the gospel but just don't know how his incarnation, sinless life, substitutionary death, bodily resurrection, ascension, and reign ought to impact them in the "real world." When I (Elyse) asked a friend of mine how the resurrection should impact troubles she was facing, she replied, "I suppose that it should but I just don't know how." We've written this book for everyone who can echo that thought, for those who say, "We know that Jesus should matter more than he does; we just don't know how to make that happen."

Some of you are feeling weak and broken right now and you are wondering if what you need will indeed be found in hearing the gospel message again. We can tell you with greatest assurance that the answer is a resounding yes! Everything we need is found in Jesus Christ, in some aspect of grace or beauty or suffering or glory that he demonstrates for us.

"But," you might be thinking, "I've heard that message before, and I'm still struggling." Yes, perhaps you have heard and believed the message before, but can you tell us how his ascension thrills and comforts you right now? If you can't answer that question, don't be discouraged. Most of us have never even considered it. But there is great hope in the ascension, and we will show you why.

Second, we focus on gospel truths for the sake of Christians involved in helping ministries who want to see how the Bible and, in particular, the gospel of Jesus Christ can help others who are suffering. For instance, does the Bible address the blight of pornography or the darkness of depression? If so, how? Does the gospel speak to men and women with broken hearts and broken marriages? What does Jesus' sinless life mean when your friend discovers that her husband has filed for divorce?

Third, restating gospel truth is vital for brothers and sisters who identify themselves as "biblical" counselors and who are already convinced of the sufficiency of Scripture to answer life's problems. To these dear friends we are issuing a gentle call to remember Jesus and the declarations of the gospel. Biblical counselors have fought a long and difficult battle to call the church back to her confidence in the Word of God in order to effect change in the lives of God's people. This is a great good. But in our desire to bring Scripture to our friends and counselees, have we overemphasized the imperatives or obligations of Scripture but neglected the declarations or indicatives? This is a question every biblical counselor should ask him- or herself. Only you know if, in your desire to help others grow in godliness, you have left Jesus behind.

And finally, we tread again the ancient gospel paths as a gift for all believers who love their Savior and want to spend time savoring him. Many of us are so caught up living the Christian life that we are in need of a little visit with him. So here you are. Go ahead; remember how much he loves you.

CHAPTER ONE

What Do You See?

Therefore be imitators of God, as beloved children.
EPHESIANS 5:1

I (ELYSE) HAVE LIVED less than a quarter of a mile from Interstate 15, one of the busiest freeways in California, for about eight years now, and because of that I've had firsthand experience with what is commonly referred to as "white noise." Although this busy freeway is so very nearby, I'm rarely aware of it; its persistent hum has become background noise to me. Of course, if there is a semi rolling down the stretch near my home and the driver lets his foot off the accelerator, I'll hear the popping of his engine, but generally speaking I don't even know that the freeway is there. It has become white noise, and I'm glad that my brain tunes it out, because at my age I don't need any more distractions.

While I am thankful for this innate ability to ignore unimportant, repetitive sound, I'm afraid that we don't do a very good job differentiating between what we need to pay attention to and what can be safely ignored. To be more specific, I fear that familiarity with certain biblical concepts is liable to make them seem insignificant to us. I'm afraid that we unintentionally strip certain concepts of importance and prominence and relegate them to the category of white noise —we recognize they are there, but we just don't pay much attention to them.

WHAT ARE YOU AWARE OF?

Please look again at the verse with which I opened this chapter, Ephesians 5:1. Now, let me ask you a question: What do you see? When you read those eight words, what were you most impressed by? Close your eyes for a moment and try to recall its message.

If you are familiar with the New Testament, you might have recognized the passage and were probably most aware of the command to imitate God, both because a command to imitate God is astonishing and because it's not something most of us would think we have mastered. Of course, we realize that there are other words in the verse—"therefore" and "as beloved children"—but because we think we have already understood or mastered the truth that God forgave us (4:32, to which "therefore" points), and that we are his beloved children, we gloss over them. The "therefore" and "as beloved children" are white noise to our spiritual ears. We filter these words out; they have become irrelevant. And when that happens, it changes the message of the verse and, ultimately, of the entire Bible.

When all we see in Ephesians 5:1 is the command to imitate God, our thoughts will turn inward onto ourselves, our efforts, and our record. If we fancy ourselves serious Christians and all we see in this verse is our duty, then we will probably spend a few moments thinking that we need to be more conscientious about obedience. *Oh, yes, yes, I can see that I need to try harder at imitating God.* Or, if we are painfully aware of our ongoing failure to be godly, despair will flood our hearts and we will feel confused and overwhelmed by such a command. *Imitate God? How could I ever possibly do that? I'm already such a failure!* However, if you are someone who helps others apply Scripture to their lives, you might immediately think, "Now, there's a verse I could use with so-and-so!" thereby deflecting the command off of yourself.

You see, if certain concepts in Scripture have become white noise to us, it will be all too easy to read a verse like Ephesians 5:1 and see only its obligations. I, too, can see myself using the verse to develop a list of the attributes of God and then making a plan to implement those attributes in my daily life. *God is holy, merciful, righteous and just. This month I will concentrate on being holy. I'll research what it means and then I'll try to implement it in my life. Next month I'll* . . . Because I'm like you, if you asked me what I saw in that verse I would tell you, "We're called to imitate God."

Our propensity to disregard the familiar can be so very detrimental to our faith. When the rest of the verse, "therefore" and "as beloved children," has become white noise to our spiritual ears, we will quickly gloss over it without stopping to consider why it's there or what it's meant to tell us. We won't think to ask why the Holy Spirit positioned such a daunting command in the context of such familiar words. Instead, we will be quick to strip out the familiar and boil down Scripture to a tidy little take-away list of do's and don'ts.

What actually gets relegated to this position of irrelevance is nothing less than the glorious gospel of Jesus Christ, nothing less than Jesus' accomplishments through his incarnation, sinless life, death, resurrection, and ascension. Because we are so familiar with the gospel message, it gets shoved to the periphery of our spiritual consciousness and becomes nothing more than words to be remembered at Christmas and Easter. The truths represented by "therefore" and "as beloved children" are like the constant din of the Interstate 15—unless someone draws your attention to them, they just don't register.

When we lose those truths, what takes center stage in our awareness? We do, of course. When we lose the centrality of the cross, Christianity morphs into a religion of self-improvement and becomes about us, about our accomplishments, and about getting our act together. We become people who ask WWJD (What *would* Jesus do?)[1] without ever considering the gospel or WDJD (What *did* Jesus do?). Although most of us recognize that Jesus' work is somehow tied to our work, we don't know quite how or why. For instance, if I asked you how the ascension informs and impacts your life today, would you be able to tell me?

To illustrate how detrimental it is to push gospel declarations out to the margins of our awareness, let's see what "therefore" and "as beloved children" from Ephesians 5:1 tell us.

YOU ARE FORGIVEN

Ephesians 4:32, the verse that immediately precedes Ephesians 5:1, reminds us of a wonderful truth: *God in Christ has forgiven us*. When Paul commands Christians to imitate God, he does so in light of a very specific divine action: "God in Christ forgave you." What he is saying is this: *because* you have already been forgiven, you can and should imitate God. *Because* God has already declared that he will not hold your sins against you, you can adopt this attitude of grace with others. That's why Ephesians 5:1 begins with "therefore": "Therefore be imitators of God, as beloved children." The "therefore" is a gospel declaration, meant to comfort, encourage, and inform you *before* you get to the gospel obligation, "be imitators of God."

You might be wondering why it is so important to hear yet again what Jesus has already done. After all, haven't we heard that message before? Why would we need to hear it again? We need to hear it again because if we have forgotten his work on our behalf, it will skew the way we think of him, the way we think of ourselves, and the way we think of others. In addition, we will miss the emphasis on imitating God's forgiveness that this verse is meant to communicate, not just a generic imitation of Godlike qualities but a specific imitation of his forgiveness.

HOW WE THINK OF HIM

If we forget God's generous, overwhelming grace in forgiving us, we will think of him as a "hard man, reaping where [he] did not sow, and gathering where [he] scattered no seed" (Matt. 25:24). We will have low thoughts of him. We will see him as a harsh taskmaster, exacting rigorous, impossible obedience from us and being disappointed and angry with us when we (predictably) fail to meet his expectations. We will assume that God continues to hold our sins against us and that he is tallying up all the ways in which we fail. When we fail to savor his astonishing mercy, he will morph into a satanic caricature in our minds, a Pharaoh, demanding that we make bricks without straw. In response, we will be bound to hide our talent in the ground for fear of greater failure or harsher rebuke and then grudgingly return it to him when we have to (Matt. 25:25).

HOW WE THINK OF OURSELVES

If we forget that we are forgiven by God because of his Son's sacrifice, we will see ourselves as slaves trying to earn his goodwill and make up for past miscues rather than as forgiven children. We will be afraid to try to obey because we know we are bound to fail. If God is like Pharaoh, he won't be touched by our halting efforts at obedience. We will be afraid to persevere because we'll know that we are doomed from the start. Why bother trying? We will be void of the love for him that is meant to motivate and fuel all our attempts at obedience. We will become lazy, unbelieving servants (Matt. 25:26).

HOW WE THINK OF OTHERS

If in our sight God becomes a caricature of Pharaoh, then our brothers and sisters in Christ are nothing more than fellow slaves who had better pull their weight. If God seems harsh and demanding, unforgiving and exacting, then that is exactly how we will treat others. Forgive them for sinning against us? Well, maybe, but only after we've gotten our pound of flesh, and they have proven that they are really sorry and have really changed. Why would we be generous toward them when God has been so demanding of us?

When we forget about God's lavish forgiveness, we will hate our Master, and we will oppress our fellow slaves. After all, it certainly wouldn't be right for them to get away without meeting Pharaoh's quota like we have to! We will demand strict obedience without forgiveness because that's what we imagine God has demanded from us. Forgetting that we are already forgiven will rob us of those Christlike qualities of kindness, generosity, gentleness, and longsuffering. It will also rob us of the only acceptable motive for obedience: love. The gospel declaration embodied in the "therefore" makes all the difference in the world.

YOU ARE BELOVED

After reminding us of God's mercy and forgiveness, Paul writes that we are to imitate God as *beloved children*. It is important that we remember that we are beloved children because beloved children function differently from houseguests or foster kids. Although guests or foster children may be welcomed into a family home for a time, everyone knows that they aren't really part of that family. A guest or foster child knows that he doesn't have the same access, inheritance, freedom, or assurance that a son or daughter has. He can't just run and jump on the father's lap and kiss his cheek and ask for treats. He knows that his position is tenuous and can change at any moment. He knows that he has to earn love and a place in the home.

God's disposition toward us is entirely different because we are beloved. He isn't simply tolerating us, regretting that he opened the door to the likes of us. No, we're *beloved*. This is the same word that the Father employed to describe his disposition to his Son; he referred to him as beloved or as his Beloved (see Matt. 3:17; 17:5; Eph. 1:6), and because of Christ's work on our behalf, so are we. Jesus himself said that his Father loves his people as he loves his Son (John 17:23). This is an astonishing truth. You are his beloved. *Beloved* is what your heavenly Father thinks of you. Does that make you want to be near him, to learn of him, and to be like him? Of course it does. If you are in Christ, he calls you his beloved.

Not only are we beloved, but we are also beloved children. All Christians have been irrevocably adopted and given full rights as God's sons. (In the grace of Christ, both women and men enjoy the privileged status of sons.) All the riches of grace and blessings of relationship with him are ours now; all that he has is ours by inheritance. We can rest securely knowing that he won't ever abandon us. He is a good and faithful Father. He is devoted to our soul's safety and complete sanctification. Because he has adopted us and made us his children, he is determined that we *will* be like him. We are his children; we will ultimately resemble him. He is shaping us into his image (Rom. 8:29; Eph. 4:24).

In light of these blessed declarations, we can boldly pursue godliness. His Spirit is in us, and he has guaranteed our eventual transformation. Because of the Son's ongoing incarnation and the indwelling of his Spirit, we are "bone of his bone and flesh of his flesh." The Son has been made like us; we are being made like him. He is the firstborn among many brothers. We are family!

HOW COULD THESE TRUTHS BECOME WHITE NOISE?

If Christianity is about Christ, how does it happen that he becomes marginalized in our daily lives? How do the truths of the gospel become nothing more than insignificant white noise? Why does John 3:16 bore us? It bores us for at least two reasons, one more insidious than the other.

We naïvely press the gospel out to the margins of our faith because we have never really been taught how it's meant to connect with our daily lives. One day I had a conversation with a dear friend who told me about struggles she was having in a relationship. I asked her, "How do you think the resurrection impacts this circumstance?"

She replied, "I know that it should but I just don't know how."

I think that we all have a sneaking suspicion that the truths of the gospel ought to mean something more to us than they do, but we don't know how to make those connections. Yes, the incarnation, perfections, death, resurrection, and ascension of Jesus Christ ought to have a practical impact on our daily walk, but just how those dots connect isn't really clear.

More insidiously, I think that we relegate the gospel to the back of our religious bus because, although we may admit our spiritual impotence with our lips, deep in our hearts we remain convinced of our own ability to live a moral life.

We also fear loss of control. It is unsettling and humiliating to realize how utterly dependent we are on having Someone Else do for us what we cannot do for ourselves: change our heart's affections and desires. As long as I have a "list to work on," I can keep my hands on the reins of my life and on my struggle against sin. So even though the gospel shouts to us that we are depraved, that we deserve a shameful death and an eternity in hell, that we must be given someone else's righteousness in order to stand before a holy God, we continue to think that if we could just find the key to holy living, we'd be able to work it out. *Just give me a list! Teach me the right prayer! Introduce me to the right counselor!*

It's no wonder that self-help books top the charts in Christian publishing and that counseling offices are overwhelmed. Our pride and our neglect of the gospel force us to run from seminar to seminar, book to book, counselor to counselor,[2] always seeking but never finding some *secret* to holy living.

Most of us have never really understood that Christianity is not a self-help religion meant to enable moral people to become more moral. We don't need a self-help book; we need a Savior. We don't need to get our collective act together; we need death and resurrection and the life-transforming truths of the gospel. And we don't need them just once, at the beginning of our Christian life; we need them every moment of every day. Let's take a moment to think about how these truths might help a Christian sister facing a difficult crisis.

APPLYING ALL OF SCRIPTURE TO LIFE

Madeline is a hardworking, homeschooling mother of five who has faithfully worked to educate her children and train them for the Lord.[3] She loves God, loves serving in the church, and loves her husband and children and their home. But the unthinkable has just happened: her eldest daughter, who is seventeen, is pregnant.

Madeline is crushed when she discovers that Hannah has been living a double life. While Hannah openly professed faith and appeared to acquiesce to all her parents' demands, she had actually schemed to arrange trysts with a Christian boy down the street.

To say that Madeline is devastated and disillusioned would be a momentous understatement. Every day she vacillates between giving up in defeat and humiliation or giving full vent to her fury at Hannah's betrayal and lack of appreciation for all Madeline's years of sacrifice for her daughter. Madeline is also wondering why God hasn't upheld his part of the bargain. After all, she trained her daughter up in "the way she should go." Why didn't God keep her from departing from it, as he contracted to do in Proverbs 22:6? She feels betrayed, deserted, confused, disappointed, angry, and ashamed.

How would you help Madeline? What does she need to remember? Madeline needs a healthy dose of gospel truth. The gospel tells Madeline about the Lord, about herself, and about Hannah, and it also tells her about the methods and motivations of obedience.

First, the gospel informs Madeline about God's nature. He isn't surprised by either her own sin or her daughter's; in fact, God is more aware of it than she ever will be. His plan to overcome evil with good was set in place long before Hannah was born, long before this world was born. Because of the gospel, Madeline can be assured that God will overcome all evil, even Hannah's sin, with good.

But overcoming sin cost God dearly. He sent his Son from heaven to be born as a baby, to be wrapped in rough cloth, to suffer cold and hunger, to be schemed against and betrayed, and finally to be hung in humiliation on a tree, defiled by our sin (despite his own flawless innocence) and drinking down the cup of his Father's wrath. Although Madeline feels overwhelmed by her daughter's sins against her, she needs to remember that Jesus had to suffer for her sin, too. At the same time, Madeline needs to remember that full atonement has been made. God no longer holds Madeline's sin against her, and if Hannah is truly his, he doesn't hold her sin against her, either.

Madeline also needs to remember what the gospel tells her

about herself. God's love for her isn't based on her performance or on her children's performance. His love is based solely on the performance of his Son. She can rejoice that God doesn't operate on a quid pro quo basis, like a cosmic vending machine that spits out treats for those who perform flawlessly. By grace alone she has been given the complete righteousness of the Son. She is his beloved child because she is in the Beloved One. The gospel tells her that her Savior, who took on flesh like hers in order to redeem her, is ruling sovereignly from heaven, never forgetting about her for one moment, never neglecting to cause all things—even her sin—to work for good. He will sanctify and keep her, even though it feels like she has been set adrift on a dark and stormy sea.

The gospel reminds Madeline that she is more sinful and flawed than she ever dared believe. She is to remember that because of indwelling sin, all people, even children who live in a perfect home, like the prodigal's home in Jesus' famous parable,[4] can and do rebel. Our children are more sinful and flawed than we ever dared believe. They are just like us: willful creatures with souls that resist humble submission. No amount of external training, protection from worldly influences, or classical education will change that fact.[5] Only the Spirit of God can change a human heart. Only God's love in Christ can make us grow in love and delight in him.

Only the gospel can change how Madeline feels about Hannah and consequently how she treats Hannah. When she is tempted to wrath, self-pity, and self-righteousness, she needs to remember that the Savior had to die for her, too. As she humbles herself before the cross, she will be able to mourn over her sin as well as the sins of her children, and she will know God's comfort (Matt. 5:4).

By faith she can war against anger, self-pity, and self-righteousness because she trusts that her struggle against sin isn't in vain. On Calvary it seemed as though all had been lost, but Calvary isn't all there is. There is an empty tomb. The empty tomb assures her that even though she feels hopelessly trapped by anger and self-pity, the power of sin has been broken in her life.

Then, as she experiences the enveloping comfort of the Spirit, she will be humble enough to seek to comfort Hannah, to see Hannah's sin as no more morally repugnant than her own, and much of her self-justifying wrath will be drained. As she sees how Jesus washed the feet of sinners just like her, she will be encouraged to pick up the basin and the towel with her children again. As she seeks to imitate God to her family, she can rest in the truth that her sins are already forgiven.

The gospel will remind Madeline that she is a beloved child. Although Hannah's sin is grievous and the ramifications of it will last for the rest of Madeline's earthly life, Madeline can remember that when the Father looks upon her he says, "Beloved." While walking through this earth she may never understand why God's plan in her life had to include this humiliating trek through what, at times, feels like the valley of the shadow of death (in part because of her pride and concern about her appearance), but she can know one thing: she is more loved and welcomed than she ever dared hope. God's love for her has determined that this sorrow is a good. She can be assured of this because she trusts that God loves her and is for her. "If God is for us, who can be against us? He who did not spare his own Son but gave him up for us all, how will he not also with him graciously give us all things?" (Rom. 8:31–32).

When Madeline begins to doubt God's love for her or his wisdom in bringing this trial into her life, she can remember this precious truth: the Father gave his Son to make her his own. He, too, knows what it's like to be betrayed by his children, and yet he has made her his own. Jesus Christ has suffered with her, and although she was, in part, a cause of his suffering, still she is beloved. Madeline has been adopted. She is her heavenly Father's child. He will never leave her nor forsake her, and even though the road she is traversing seems terrifying and gloomy, she can be assured that because of the ascension, this trial isn't all she will ever experience. She will know light and joy and comfort and rest and everlasting love. Because this is her future, she can have the faith to persevere today.

After she has warmed her soul by the fire of the gospel, she can seek to imitate God in her home. She and her husband can extend mercy to Hannah and to her boyfriend. She can lovingly talk with her other children about sin's folly and God's grace. She can openly confess her own sin and talk about how God's grace has assured her. She can even face the question of whether her own treatment of her children over the years might have tempted Hannah to secretive hypocrisy or to mistaking sexual intimacy for the genuine love Hannah's heart hungers for.[6]

As Madeline continues to humble herself before God's mighty hand and trust that in the exaltation of Christ, she will be raised up over all the enemies of God's kingdom, sin and rebellion will ultimately be squelched by his mighty power, and Madeline can be assured of this because Jesus is ruling right now at the right hand of her Father.

What does Madeline need? She needs the song of the gospel to take center stage and drown out all other voices of revenge, despair, works-righteousness, fear, and self-trust. She can have faith that through Jesus' glorious power, the gospel will captivate her heart because she has been forgiven, beloved, and adopted.

HEARING THE SONG

I'm thankful that I rarely hear the freeway that runs by my house, as I filter out its constant hum, but I am grieved that I so frequently ignore the gospel my Savior is singing so sweetly to me. Like you, I need to hear that gospel song over and over again because my soul is a sieve and the gospel leaks out of it, leaving only the husk of Christianity—my self-righteousness and obligations.

Do you need to hear his gospel song, too? Why not take a few moments now to enjoy these precious truths again: God has forgiven you because of Christ's precious death in your place; you are his beloved child because of Christ's precious life credited to you. Can you hear him singing this never-ending theme to you, his bride?

PURSUING COUNSEL FROM THE CROSS

1) We all know what white noise is. Have the gospel truths of salvation by grace alone in Christ alone become white noise to you? How long has it been since you were enthralled by the thought that God so loved the world that he gave his only Son? Do you remember that God so loves *you* that Christ died for *you* (Gal. 2:20)?

2) What reactions do you have to your own or others' sins and failures that might signal when your heart has grown deaf to Christ's song of grace?

3) When you read Ephesians 5:1, what were you most aware of? How did you respond to the command to "imitate God"? Were you self-assured, thinking that you were already doing a pretty good job at it, or were you crushed and despairing? Were you sure that if we just told you how to do it, you'd be able to do it?

4) Aside from the command to imitate God, did you see anything else in Ephesians 5:1? If so, what?

5) How does a fuller appreciation of the gospel change the way you view

- God?
- Yourself?
- Others?

6) Summarize in four or five sentences what you have learned from this chapter. What was new? What was most important to you?

CHAPTER TWO

Seeing Your Savior

And we all, with unveiled face, beholding the glory of the Lord, are being transformed into the same image from one degree of glory to another.

2 CORINTHIANS 3:18

IT'S PART OF THE LIFE CYCLE of every living thing to grow and mature. It's also natural for us to hope that we will be better people today than we were yesterday and that the things that trouble us at present will somehow be resolved in the future. No matter where we turn in the world—to radio talk shows and daytime television, the Internet, and particularly our e-mail inbox— snake-oil salesmen are touting the latest cure for whatever problem or impediment we might face. No matter if our problem is acne, anger, ever-increasing debt, impending divorce, shyness, depression, or unruly children, there is someone right around the corner telling us how he will make our life better.

We frantically search through a myriad of solutions; our eyes are drawn in a thousand differing directions. And while there is no end to these pseudo answers to our difficulties, it is apparent from their mere proliferation that none really effects change, at least not over the long haul. Sure, we might have some temporary successes, but after a while we find ourselves right back where we started. Nothing that the world has to offer can change the human heart. Yes, of course we can learn to rearrange the furniture of our lives so that we seem tidier, more together, but no merely human means can ever free us from ourselves.

We are all hoping for change and progress, Christian and non-Christian alike. In contrast to our culture's unabashedly self-exalting approach to personal perfectibility, serious Christians are intent on something more than merely "getting it together." We are hoping instead for growth in godliness, or what is commonly referred to as sanctification. Rather than seek a quick fix, we look inward, at our own sinfulness. We diligently practice confession and repentance. We are encouraged to examine ourselves, to search out sin and unbelief.

Although we are commanded to tackle sin in this way, there is a problem here too. If we focus too narrowly on our failures and never take our eyes off ourselves, we can become mired in endless navel-gazing, and, even as Christians, simply looking at ourselves doesn't have the power to transform us. If we keep our eyes riveted on ourselves, even as we routinely practice confession and repentance, we will stay bogged down with the same old sins. We need to set our eyes on something beyond ourselves or our failures. We need to glimpse something that is more powerful. We need to see Jesus Christ and the transforming glory of God.

BEHOLDING THE GLORY OF THE LORD

As we do, the Corinthians longed to be more like their Savior. They, too, needed grace to battle the materialism that infected their culture, faith to fight the idolatry and impurity that had marked their own lives, and wisdom to know the difference between an outward show of goodness and true inward holiness. They needed to know how to be effective witnesses for Christ. So Paul pointed them toward the true locus of change. He wrote, "We all, with unveiled face, beholding the glory of the Lord, are being transformed into the same image from one degree of glory to another" (2 Cor. 3:18).

In light of the Corinthian context, Paul's counsel is astonishing. As an orthodox Jew speaking to Gentiles, he could have said that they would be transformed by looking at God's law. The message of moral improvement through strict law keeping was certainly a popular one among his contemporaries, including both observant Jews and ethically sensitive Gentiles. Instead he called this use of the law a ministry of death (2 Cor. 3:7). Paul might have told them to look to teachers who were outwardly religious, powerful, successful, or popular. Instead, he called such teachers insincere, boastful peddlers of God's Word (2 Cor. 2:16).

Although advertising his past achievements in Jewish law keeping and his present accomplishments in Christian ministry might have helped Paul to look good outwardly and given him a leg up in pastoral prestige, he intentionally humbled himself and refused to lean on any sort of self-made righteousness. He didn't want the Corinthians to look at him. In contrast to the false teachers, he regarded his good reputation and former blameless law keeping as dung (Phil. 3:8). Instead of boasting about his accomplishments, Paul boasted about his frailty, his unpopularity, and his weakness and persecutions (2 Cor. 11:30; 12:9–10). He deliberately humbled himself and refused to boast in his abilities so that the Corinthians would not be drawn to focus on him. He wanted them to know that the power to transform heart and life belongs to God and not to man (2 Cor. 4:7–11; 13:4).

Paul's one all-encompassing passion was to preach, honor, and exalt Jesus Christ, and so he counseled the Corinthians (and us) to look away to the glory of the Lord. He knew that they weren't going to be transformed by gazing at their own glories or the glory of any other mere human. He knew they wouldn't progress in sanctification by observing their sin and failure. He told them how true transformation takes place: by beholding the glory *of the Lord*.

In one sense, Paul's insight—that we can be transformed only by the glory of the God on whom we gaze—should have been familiar to any Jew or Gentile who knew the Old Testament Scripture. After all, Paul was simply echoing, unpacking, and applying the ancient account of Moses' experience at Sinai, when he beheld God's glory on the mountaintop and then descended to the Israelites, his face radiating glory, reflecting the splendor of the Lord who had spoken to him (Ex. 34:29–33). Paul insisted that Moses' and Israel's experience of the visible display of God's glory foreshadowed Christians' spiritual experience of our "beholding" God's glory in an even deeper, life-transforming, longer-lasting way.

That's all well and good, you might be thinking, *but exactly how can we behold God's glory? After all, he's invisible, and we can't see into heaven.* Where will we see unseen and eternal things (2 Cor. 4:18)? Should we head out to the beach and watch a sunset or perhaps wander into a cathedral to gaze upon beautiful stained glass representations of him?[1] How can we see what is invisible and thus experience the transformation we so desire? Where will we see his glory? We will see it in the gospel, of course.

THE GLORY-DISPLAYING GOSPEL

If we want to see God's glory, if we long for ourselves and others to be transformed into godliness, we must dwell on the gospel, where his glory is most clearly seen. It is the gospel into which we are to look, and it is by the power of the gospel that we will be changed.

Paul informs us that by his grace God has shone the "light of the gospel of the glory of Christ" (2 Cor. 4:4) into our hearts. It is in this light that we see everything else: who he is, what he has done, who we are, and how we can change. It is this light that first enabled us to see our glorious Savior, and it is this light that continues to transform us. Unlike unbelievers, who have blinded minds, we have received from God eyes to see "the light of the knowledge of the glory of God in the face of Jesus Christ" (2 Cor. 4:6). The knowledge of God's glory is revealed to us as we look upon the face of the Son. And it's this knowledge that will transform us.

But still, we might ask, where is he, that we might see his face? How are our hearts and minds informed and illumined by the gospel? Has God promised to use specific means to reveal this glory to us? Yes, of course. We are invited to look upon the face of Jesus

Christ and God's glory in the gospel in several ways, each of which can be found in the local church.

We are going to refer to these glimpses into God's glory as "the means of grace." Although God could directly inform our minds and hearts, he usually uses ordinary measures (or means) to accomplish this goal and to impart grace or strength to us. Before we get into them, though, let us give you a word of caution: they might seem simplistic, weak, and hackneyed. You probably won't find a counseling book or self-help seminar about them. You might be tempted to look on them with disdain and regard them as ineffective or unimpressive. So let us encourage you to ask the Spirit to open your eyes to your temptation to negate them. Ask him to help you see how he will make use of these means, even though they aren't new, flashy, or exciting. Let's try to avoid the Athenian hunger to continually hear "something new" (Acts 17:21) and instead rest in these ancient but powerful measures.

THE MEANS OF GRACE

1) *In the Word Preached*

Like us, the Corinthians couldn't see Jesus Christ with their physical eyes. Of course, he had been visible on earth to crowds who heard him preach and saw him heal and to his disciples after his resurrection. But the Corinthian Christians didn't get to witness the glory of his physical life, death, resurrection, or ascension. They couldn't gaze into heaven to glimpse God's glory either. Even so, they were transformed by it through the gospel message Paul preached.

The Word of God, in particular, the gospel message, which is the integrating center of the whole Word of God, is the means that the Spirit uses to transform the hearts and minds of the elect. When we refer to "the gospel message," we mean far more than what might be preached at a so-called evangelistic service. We are referring to the message we hear as we gather for worship each Sunday when our pastor rehearses what Jesus accomplished for us through his life, death, and resurrection. Although the pastor may rightly start

41

out giving us the law, telling us of our obligations, if he uses the law to draw us to Christ and to make us grateful for his perfect life and substitutionary death, then our hearts will be filled with love for God, with the desire to obey, and with the faith to believe that we actually can progress by the power of Christ's Spirit.

By the work of the Holy Spirit, the gospel preached is the seed that brings us to life (1 Pet. 1:23–25), the power of God for salvation (Rom. 1:16). It strengthens us (Rom. 16:25); it makes us stable and steadfast (Col. 1:23). It is the gospel preached and received that initiates our salvation by the Spirit's power and continues to save us, and it is the ground upon which we stand (1 Cor. 15:1–2). It cleanses us (John 15:3) and washes our conscience (Heb. 10:22). The Word preached reminds us that we are loved by God and therefore ought to love one another (John 3:16; 1 John 4:10–11). The Spirit uses the gospel message to create the faith we need to call on the Lord and be saved (Rom. 10:13, 17).

I assume that you are already aware of how powerful the word of the gospel is, but I wonder if any of us realize how desperately we need to hear it repeated. We so often think that once we have believed the message we don't really need to hear it again. But we couldn't be more wrong. It is the glorious message of God's love for us in Christ that engenders the faith and perseverance that will enable us to grow in godliness. It is in the gospel message that we see the glory of God; it shows us the face of Jesus Christ and transforms us.

The gospel message—that God has made us his own in spite of our sin—is what we need to hear over and over again. By the Spirit's work we will see the face of Jesus Christ in the Word preached to us, even though it might be presented by weak and unimpressive men. The power to transform hearts belongs to God, not to men, but God has promised to transform us through the message that the world calls "folly" and through men that the world despises as fools.

Because of this, some of the first questions we should ask are: How are you doing with church attendance? Does your pastor preach the gospel to you every Sunday, and when he does, do you listen intently? How long has it been since you gave your soul a delicious draught of the glorious gospel message by listening attentively, expectantly, and prayerfully as it is preached from the pulpit?

Of course, personal study of the Word in daily reading and meditation is also necessary for growth in godliness. Although God plainly promises the Spirit's work in conjunction with gospel preaching (see Rom. 10:14–17; 1 Pet. 1:25),[2] there is also a great feast to be had in daily consumption of the Word. Whether you read through the Bible in a year to gain an appreciation of the broad sweep of the history of redemption or narrow down your study to a deeper perusal of shorter passages, the primary means of God's grace to you will be found in his Word.

True transformation is rarely experienced where there is a lack of interaction with his powerful Word. We see the gospel most clearly in all the Word, not merely in the Gospels (Matthew, Mark, Luke, and John); we see it throughout the Bible as we see God's glory: his holiness, love, mercy, and justice, and his determination to save a people at great cost to himself and for his own pleasure.

We know how easy it would be right now for you to think, *But I read my Bible and go to church! I need more help than this!* Please believe us when we say that we understand your concern, and we will give you more specific direction in the chapters to follow. What we want to do now, however, is remind you that God will use these means as a way to illumine your heart and give you the strength you need to continue in the war. Don't despise them. They may seem weak and ordinary, but so did your Lord when he hung on the cross. Yet look at all he accomplished for you (2 Cor. 13:4). Have faith that he is as powerful as he says he is.

2) In Baptism

When God banned visible images of himself in the second commandment (Ex. 20:4–6), he was not ignoring the fact that he created us with five senses—sight, touch, taste, smell, and hearing. Rather, he was protecting us from the proclivity of our sinful hearts to envision God in ways of our own choosing. At the same time, he provided an abundance of visible signs to confirm our trust in his audible words. Think of the rainbow that Noah saw after the flood, the pillar of cloud and fire that led Israel through the desert, and the sacrifices in tabernacle and temple. Jesus' and his apostles' miracles, too, were signs that confirmed and illustrated their God-given message.

For us, Jesus instituted two ongoing signs to confirm our confidence in the gospel of his grace, the first of which is baptism. Though simpler and less obviously supernatural than the ten plagues on Egypt or bodily resurrection from the dead, baptism is a strong tool of the Spirit to refashion us in the image of the Son.

Baptism was given by Jesus to display and assure believers of the washing away of our sin, our union with Christ in his death, and our new resurrection life. The feel of the water on our skin and the observance of others being washed in this way remind and assure us that Christ's sacrifice on the cross was for us *personally*. In it we are promised that "as surely as water washes away dirt from the body, so certainly his blood and his Spirit wash away my soul's impurity, in other words, all my sins."[3] Through baptism we are assured that we are washed with Christ's blood and, therefore, by grace, he has forgiven all our sins (Zech. 13:1; Eph. 1:7–8).

We can't overemphasize the importance of knowing that all our sins are forgiven, once for all time, when we strive to become more like him. Love is the only motive that can impel true heart transformation, and love will be present only when we see, demonstrated before our eyes, how we've been loved. Guilt over former sins never propels obedience; it only breeds doubt, fear, and bitterness. As eighteenth-century pastor William Romaine wrote, when "guilt comes in, love goes out."[4]

So, in baptism we see God's great love for us in Christ, and we are assured—not only by our baptism, but also when we see others being baptized—that we are completely free: forgiven, welcomed, and loved. This, and only this, can give us the zealous faith we need to pursue growth in godliness. Because we are completely forgiven, we can approach God with confidence that we will receive his grace to war against sin (Heb. 4:16), knowing that he is not angry, brooding, or disappointed with us.

In addition, baptism is a sign of our death to sin by the Spirit's cleansing work. It demonstrates our new life as we join with Christ's resurrection and guarantees our ultimate renewal. "To be washed with Christ's Spirit means that the Holy Spirit has renewed me and set me apart to be a member of Christ so that more and more I become dead to sin and increasingly live a holy and blameless life"[5] (see Rom. 6:3–4). Baptism corrects the thought that what we need is self-reformation and powerfully demonstrates that the only answers to our problem with sin are death and resurrection.

Baptism is a sign that he is dwelling within us (Ezek. 36:25–27), and because of that we can be assured that our hearts will be more and more inclined toward obedience. Through Christ's resurrection, the power of sin has been broken in our lives. Baptism reminds and assures us of this. Because our union with Christ the Son in his death and resurrection is now being applied to us by his indwelling Spirit, we can be certain that we will continue to die to sin and live to righteousness in our new lives (Rom. 6:4; Titus 3:5).

3) In the Lord's Supper

The Lord's Supper, or Communion, is another means of grace God uses to remind and assure us. It is the second ongoing sign given to confirm our confidence in the gospel. In it we see the gospel portrayed. As we see the bread broken before our eyes, we are to remember Jesus' body crushed by the Father out of love for us (Isa. 53:10; John 3:16; 1 John 4:9–10). As we taste the wine, we are to remember not only that his blood was poured out for the forgiveness of sins but also that, because of it, we are completely welcomed, loved, and cleansed. We are seated with him, dining at his table, eating the meal that he paid so dearly to purchase.

The Supper is meant to warm our affections toward our Savior.

We are tasting his hospitality, seeing the table spread before us. In it, the Spirit feeds our souls, using the bread and wine that we see, touch, taste, and smell. We actually feel his goodness toward us when we savor the elements. Just as a good father nourishes his family by lovingly providing for them, by the Spirit our Savior spreads his bounty before us and says, "Take, eat; this is my body . . . which is given for you" (Matt. 26:26; Luke 22:19).

When we taste and feel the wine in our mouth, we hear him saying, "Drink of it, all of you, for this is my blood of the covenant, which is poured out for many for the forgiveness of sins" (Matt. 26:27–28). Because Jesus himself has chosen this as a means of grace whereby he reminds and assures us of his love, we are to remind ourselves that

> As surely as I see with my eyes the bread of the Lord broken for me and the cup given to me, so surely his body was offered and broken for me and his blood poured out for me on the cross . . . as surely as I receive from the hand of the one who serves, and taste with my mouth the bread and cup of the Lord, given me as sure signs of Christ's body and blood, so surely he nourishes and refreshes my soul for eternal life with his crucified body and poured-out blood.[6]

In this meal that he generously prepared for us, he also demonstrated our dual union with him and with one another. Through his Supper, we remember that we are one with him, flesh of his flesh and bone of his bone, by the Spirit, even though he is in heaven and we are on earth (1 Cor. 10:16–17).

The Supper also helps us love others because we see that he also feeds them (1 Cor. 11:28–29). It tells us that we are one with each other. It transmits grace to us by the Spirit so that we will have the strength we need to love as he loved and to resist sin. "Remember me" are the words that should ring in our hearts when we taste the bread and drink the wine.

Can you see how important the sacraments are to growth in godliness? If we want to change, to become more like him, then we need to attend soberly and intentionally to these means of grace—even though they might seem weak or devoid of any real transforming power. Let us not assume that we know better than God what means he will use to transform us, for he says, "My thoughts are not your thoughts, neither are your ways my ways, declares the LORD. For as the heavens are higher than the earth, so are my ways higher than your ways and my thoughts than your thoughts" (Isa. 55:8–9).

4) In Fellowship with Other Believers

Even though the primary means of grace are those in which God speaks good news to us through his messengers (the Word, baptism, and the Supper), the Bible also mentions another conduit through which the Father pours his mercy and power into the hearts of his children: deep, meaningful fellowship with our brothers and sisters in the church.

Many Christians believe that church is something they *do* on any given Sunday morning. They believe that it is a weekly obligation that they fulfill by attending one or two services on the Lord's Day, even though they have little or no true biblical fellowship with others during the rest of the week. In contrast to this perspective, the New Testament paints a picture of life in the body of Christ that is significantly different. Fellowship includes accountability, encouragement, and counsel.

Peter calls all believers to earnest love for and cheerful hospitality toward one another, summoning us to use our gifts, whether they involve speaking or serving, "as good stewards of God's varied grace" (1 Pet. 4:8–11). Likewise, Paul affirms, "Grace was given to each one of us according to the measure of Christ's gift," and he goes on to portray members of the body as *joints* through which life flows from Christ, the head, to other members, so that the body grows in love "when each part is working properly" (Eph. 4:7, 15–16).

It is very difficult to see ourselves as we really are; we need the help of others who will both encourage us with the evidences of God's grace and confront us with the areas of sin that they see. This kind of encouragement and confrontation is meant to occur within ongoing relationships with other believers.

As we have said before, it is common to believe that we need some special or unique answers in order to change. We often jump to the conclusion that we need specialized help from counselors or psychologists. Could it be that we are looking for help in this way because we have ignored the ordinary means of grace that God has given us?

Please don't misunderstand! We are not saying that there is no place for men and women who have been specifically called and trained in the Word to counsel others. Nor are we claiming that medical expertise never has a role in addressing certain personal problems. What we are saying is this: the ministry that furthers growth in Christlike desires, emotions, and behaviors belongs in the church and is a function of the church. It is only within the context of the church that ongoing spiritual care, encouragement, and accountability can occur. It is only as we use the powerful word of the gospel in each other's lives that we can change.

Another problem with much counseling outside of a local church context is the lack of ongoing accountability. People seem to want to get help anonymously, thereby avoiding the struggle with sin in front of the very people God has placed in their lives to help them. This flies right in the face of passages like James 5:16, "Therefore, confess your sins to one another and pray for one another," and Galatians 6:1–2, "Brothers, if anyone is caught in any transgression, you who are spiritual should restore him in a spirit of gentleness. . . . Bear one another's burdens, and so fulfill the law of Christ." Within the local church there should be ongoing confession of sin, personal prayer, and bearing of one another's burdens.[7]

The writers of the New Testament believed that there was, within the local congregation, all the wisdom and knowledge needed for true transformation: "I myself am satisfied about you, my brothers, that you yourselves are full of goodness, filled with all knowledge and able to instruct one another" (Rom. 15:14). Of course, not everyone is called to a specific ministry of counseling, but we are all called to be known and cared for by one another. How can we love one another or seek to "outdo" one another in showing honor to each other (Rom. 12:10) if we never see each other or have a deeper conversation than "Hi, how are you?" and "Fine, thanks. How are you?"

The gospel of Jesus Christ—that we are all more sinful and flawed than we ever dared believe but more loved and welcomed than we ever dared hope[8]—is meant to be lived out in relationship: each of us assuring, reminding, confronting, counseling, and listening to one another, praying for one another, and bearing one another's burdens. It's here, within gospel-centered relationships, that the Spirit will reveal the Son to us.

FROM ONE DEGREE OF GLORY TO ANOTHER

How are we transformed? "We all, with unveiled face, beholding the glory of the Lord, are being transformed into the same image from one degree of glory to another" (2 Cor. 3:18). We are transformed from glory to glory, not instantaneously, but gradually. The powerful means of grace he has provided are not magical elixirs that instantaneously transform us into the person we wish we were. But they are his appointed means to strengthen and feed our souls. Do they seem too ordinary, too weak? Isn't it just like the Lord to use the weak things of this world to confound the wise?

But we have the treasure of the life-giving, life-changing gospel in jars of clay, "to show that the surpassing power belongs to God and not to us" (2 Cor. 4:7). We still struggle with sin, but we don't lose heart because we know that even though our outer person is wasting away, our inner person is being renewed day by day by the work of the Spirit as we partake of these means of grace. Indeed, seeing him through the Word, the sacraments, and the church will impel and motivate our transformation:

See what kind of love the Father has given to us, that we should be called children of God; and so we are. . . . Beloved, we are God's children now, and what we will be has not yet appeared; but we know that when he appears we shall be like him, because we shall see him as he is. And everyone who thus hopes in him purifies himself as he is pure. (1 John 3:1–3)

Because we've got the wonderful promise of adoption and the hope of transformation, we don't lose heart. "Just as we have borne the image of the man of dust, we *shall* also bear the image of the man of heaven" (1 Cor. 15:49); he "will transform our lowly body to be like his glorious body" (Phil. 3:21). As we see him, we'll experience fullness of joy and pleasures (Ps. 16:11) that will wean our hearts away from the paltry baubles of the world. Even though with your eyes "you have not seen him, [yet] you love him. Though you do not now see him, you believe in him and rejoice with joy that is inexpressible and filled with glory" (1 Pet. 1:7–8). There will come a day when we will see his face, and his name will be on our foreheads (Rev. 22:4), and we will be completely and eternally transformed. But until that day, we must attend to every portrait he has given us of himself in the Word, in the sacraments, and in the compassion and correction of our siblings in the family of God.

MOSES BEHELD THE GLORY OF THE LORD

As we close, think back to Moses' second journey up Mount Sinai. You will remember that he had shattered the tablets of the law, symbolizing the Israelites' rebellion. But later he headed up the mountain again, and this time his heart was filled with anticipation. Not only was he to receive a second copy of the law, but also he was to be granted a privileged vision that would transform him. He had implored God, "Please show me your glory," and the Lord had granted his request with this one restriction: "You cannot see my face, for man shall not see me and live" (Ex. 33:18, 20). In an amazing demonstration of condescension and grace, God made a way for Moses to see him:

Behold, there is a place by me where you shall stand on the rock, and while my glory passes by I will put you in a cleft of the rock, and I will cover you with my hand until I have passed by. Then I will take away my hand, and you shall see my back, but my face shall not be seen. (Ex. 33:21–23)

Let's not let our familiarity with this story rob it of its magnificence. Imagine, for a moment, the God of heaven humbling himself to appear before his creation, as if he had to perform for anyone! Imagine the gentle compassion that hid Moses there in the cleft of the rock, taking care to shelter him and keep him from the judgment that was due him. Consider how the Lord's heart longed for Moses to share in the happiness of his personal glory. What a demonstration of divine mercy and grace! It's no wonder that when Moses returned from the mountain his face actually glowed.

Indeed, Moses had been transformed by what he had seen: God's glory in gracious splendor. But as great as his experience was, Moses remained a mere mortal who had been touched by God's glory but not yet eternally transformed. The glory would fade. So Moses placed a veil over his face so that people would not see the dimming of what was passing away.

In Paul's second letter to the church at Corinth, he employs this narrative to demonstrate the superiority of the new covenant over the old. The old covenant of law had glory, but its glory was diminishing, even while it was still being employed. The new covenant, based on the gospel, has permanent glory that will never fade or dim. It will never be replaced or superseded by any superior scheme or plan. It is the ultimate and final word on God's disposition toward us and our approach to him. The work and glory of Jesus Christ is now and will always be the preeminent demonstration of God's will: he has hidden the church in his Son, who was cleft for us, and now we are enjoined to behold his glory and be transformed.

Do we ever stop to consider the great honor and privilege that is ours? We have been invited, even commanded, to look on, to contemplate, the glory of God. We don't need to cover our faces before the Lord (as the angels must), nor do we need to be protected from God's glory by God's hand (as Moses was) because we are in union with his Son; Jesus Christ is the Rock in whom we are hidden.

The wrath that was Moses' (and our) due was poured out in full upon the Rock that was cleft for us. The perfect law keeping necessary for unhindered, face-to-face fellowship with Almighty God has been credited to us. And now, because of this, we are enjoined to look upon his glory as if we had a right to be there, gazing at him, as if we were good enough to be near him. And seeing him will transform us, just as it transformed Moses, but our transformation won't fade away; it will grow brighter and brighter until we are finally, perfectly transformed by his presence in heaven. Look on his faith, believe in his power, and be changed!

PURSUING COUNSEL FROM THE CROSS

1) Read John 1:14, 18; 6:46; and 14:9. Each of these passages has something to say about our ability to see God and to behold his glory. What do they tell you?

2) In Exodus 34:6–7 the Lord proclaims his glory to Moses. What does he say about himself? How can study of his character transform us?

3) Have you been baptized? If not, please make arrangements to do so right away. If you have, what does your baptism say about you? Do you regularly receive the Lord's Supper? If not, why? (Don't let guilt over sin stop you: the Supper is the very thing you need to fight against sin!) What does the Supper mean to you?

4) Do you regularly attend a gospel-preaching church? Are you in regular fellowship with others who know and love you well?

5) Summarize in four or five sentences what you have learned from this chapter.

CHAPTER THREE

God's Immeasurable Love

*For the love of Christ controls us, because we have con-
cluded this: that one has died for all, therefore all have died;
and he died for all, that those who live might no longer live
for themselves but for him who for their sake died and was
raised.*

2 CORINTHIANS 5:14–15

IN THE LAST CHAPTER we spent time looking at some of the
ordinary means of grace that God has provided for Christians: the
Word, the sacraments, and biblical fellowship in the local church.
In this chapter we are fulfilling the promise we made to point you
to specific passages that will help you see the gospel and engender
true heart transformation. But before we get to this task, we want to
remind you why it's so important for you to remember these truths.

OUR LOVE PROBLEM

In a profound sense, we have been given only two commands: to
love God with our whole heart, soul, mind, and strength and to
love our neighbor as ourselves (Matt. 22:37–38). Jesus affirms
that all other directives in Scripture depend on these two and
provide commentary on what it means to love God supremely
and to love others as we love ourselves. Just these two simple
commands, and, yet, every sin we commit finds its genesis in
a failure to obey one or the other or both. Think of it: every

false god we serve—whether gods of power, pride, respect, lust, romance, security, vanity, greed, or any of a thousand other idols—has the power to entice and entrap only because our love for the Lord is weak. We sin against God because we don't love him as we should.

Every sin against our neighbor flows out of insipid love too. How can we love our neighbor, who has been created in the image of God (1 John 3:17; 4:20–21), when our love for God himself is so apathetic? When love does not motivate and undergird all our relationships, we will find that, instead of protecting and rejoicing with others, it is easy to gossip about them and to judge and envy them. When we don't love others, we will fear them too (1 John 4:18). We will fear what they might think of us, say about us, or do to us. Our fear will enslave us; we will be tied to their opinions, wants, and demands. Without fervent love driving and informing all our relationships, we will constantly swing back and forth between slavish, joyless servitude (motivated by guilt and self-love) and self-sufficiency and anger (motivated by pride and self-love.)[1] Love is the key to every sin problem in our lives both vertically, between ourselves and the Lord, and horizontally, between ourselves and others.

Our inability to progress in godliness isn't really very difficult to diagnose. We just don't love God or our neighbor as we should. And yet, what can we do? Telling ourselves over and over that we really ought to love better doesn't seem to be working, does it? Knowing that we should love won't make us love; it only makes us feel condemned or angry or both, and neither self-condemnation nor anger stimulates love.

When I (Elyse) tell myself that I really ought to do a better job loving my husband, Phil, this self-lecture won't ever result in my being a more loving wife. It will only mire me in self-condemnation, and then I'll find myself trying to justify my actions. Thoughts such as "Yeah, maybe I don't love him like I should, but look at what he does" will be the inevitable result of such self-condemnation. The law, that I should love my neighbor as myself, won't cause me to love him.

Of course, I might be able to make a nice meal for Phil or acquiesce to his desire to spend the afternoon on the golf course, but I could do so selfishly—I want to obligate him or feel good about myself, or I am simply too apathetic to fight, or I want an afternoon alone. Can you see how, even though it appears that I'm acting in a loving manner, my actions are actually evidences of self-love?[2]

In those rare moments, when we are being brutally honest with ourselves about the poverty of our love, isn't it painful to realize that we are, by nature, so sinful and flawed? We don't love as we should, we feel guilty, and we hide from the Lord because we think he is like us: selfish, loveless, disappointed, and angry (although we would never say so openly). We assume that he is displeased with us, so we determine again to be more loving to try to get in his good graces. We inevitably fail again. Try as we might, while our attention is focused on ourselves, we just don't change. Failure drives us away from our Savior; we are blind to his eternal smile. We see the law, we see how we sin, we struggle to believe that he continues to love us with such great love, and we condemn our lack of zeal. What will ignite a white-hot passion in our hearts? Only trusting in God's love for us. Only the gospel annihilates self-condemnation. Only love stimulates love.

So now we are going to remember God's love for us in Christ for this one reason: our love for God and for others is *responsive* in nature. The apostle John has made it perfectly clear: we love God in response to his love for us. We love others in response to God's love for us and for them. Indeed, as John wrote, "We love *because* he first loved us" (1 John 4:19–20). If we are unsure or doubtful about God's disposition toward us, if we think that he is unloving, displeased, or angry, then we will never be able to mortify our sin. Love is the first cause of all the graces we desire; it "warms the heart, and sweetly and powerfully influences our affections to delight in, and to walk in love with such an exceedingly gracious and merciful God."[3]

THE LORD'S STEADFAST LOVE

The topic of God's love for us is so rich in Scripture and the references to it so numerous that we could not fully cover it, even if it were the only topic of this entire book. In fact, just one facet of God's love, his *hesed*, or "steadfast love," is spoken of 123 times in the Psalms alone! His *hesed* was a prominent feature of his self-disclosure when he graciously revealed himself to Moses:

> "The LORD, the LORD, a God merciful and gracious, slow to anger, and abounding in *steadfast love* and faithfulness, keeping *steadfast love* for thousands, forgiving iniquity and transgression and sin, but who will by no means clear the guilty." (Ex. 34:6–7)

We're sure you are familiar with that passage, but let us encourage you to go back and reread it once again. In fact, read it in the context of Exodus 32–34 and notice the situation in which the Lord so strongly emphasized his *steadfast love*. While Moses had been on Mount Sinai receiving God's law of life for his newly liberated people Israel, they were committing spiritual adultery with the golden calf. On the honeymoon, while Israel's Divine Bridegroom was laying the foundation for their married life together, Israel the bride had already taken another lover. Surely the Lord had grounds to pursue a speedy divorce from this fickle wife. Yet he did not; his love was steadfast.

Although Israel deserved destruction, the Lord responded graciously to Moses' intercession for this unworthy people. He spared them from his wrath, promised his continuing presence with them, and even granted Moses' plea, "Please show me your glory." Then, as Moses stood hidden in a crevasse on the rocky mountain face, having experienced God's astonishing patience and faithful mercy toward his wayward people, he heard the Lord's momentous self-description seen in the words above.

Look at the way your God speaks of himself. Drink deeply of his condescension. Is he holy? Does he hate sin? Yes and yes. But what are the first qualities he wants you to see? He wants you to see that although he is the Lord God, he is a God of mercy, graciousness, and patience. He wants you to rest in his abounding steadfast love and faithfulness. Again, is he holy? Yes, and we can be oh-so thankful for that, for it is because he is so holy that he consistently keeps steadfast love for thousands and forgives iniquity, transgression, and sin. His holiness binds him unchangeably to his covenantal promise to continue to steadfastly love us in spite of our sin.

He knows us so well. He is intimately acquainted with our frailty and fears; he remembers that we are nothing more than "dust" (Ps. 103:14), so he pours profuse words of love upon us. He knows our unbelief; he understands the terrors of our hearts and our enemies' accusations. He wants nothing more than for us to believe that he is, in fact, as completely loving as he promises. Like a father who shows great pity and compassion for his weak and faltering children, he tells us over and over again that he is "merciful and gracious, slow to anger, and abounding in steadfast love."[4]

One obvious echo of the Lord's words in Exodus 34:6 is found in Psalm 103:8: "The LORD is merciful and gracious, slow to anger and abounding in steadfast love." Then the psalmist, speaking under the inspiration of God's Holy Spirit, employs two profound portraits to help us see how wonderful God's steadfast love is: how far the heavens are above the earth (v. 11) and how far the east is from the west (v. 12). To what do these portraits refer? The first refers to the greatness of God's steadfast love for us. Can we measure the distance between the heavens and the earth? No? Then neither can we measure the grandeur of God's love for us. The latter refers to the distance he has made between us and our transgressions. Can we measure the distance between east and west? No. Neither can we measure the distance he has removed our transgressions from us.

What does he want us to learn, believe, and rest in? He wants us to be assured that his love is steadfast, abounding, and unending. He wants us to believe that, because his love has no limits, our sin has been completely, unalterably, perfectly removed from us. Remember the heavens above the earth, the east from the west: his unsearchable love, and his boundless forgiveness.

Put this book down for a moment and, if you are able, go outside and stare up into the sky. See the immensity of the heavens. Think *this is how colossal God's steadfast love is for me.* Now look from east to west. See what he is saying. Get the picture? Do you believe his words? He has removed your sin from you; it is removed farther from you than you can see. His love towers above you and engulfs you; your sins are gone!

GOD'S SURE LOVE

In the Old Testament, that rich word *hesed,* which the ESV translates "steadfast love," carries a connotation not only of love but also of strength and steadfastness. Our love can become sentimental, a sweet but fleeting thought on a Valentine or butterflies in the stomach. God's love is different. It is strong and steadfast. It is utterly determined. He has contracted to place himself in covenant relationship with us and to make us his own.

Yes, his love for us is a contractual agreement, but it is so much more than cold, lifeless obligation. He has generously determined to satiate our souls with happiness. He has chosen to betroth us to himself: "I will betroth you to me in righteousness and in justice, in steadfast love and in mercy. I will betroth you to me in faithfulness" (Hos. 2:19–20).

God's love is simply this: a passionate, unwavering, joyous determination to do us good and to bestow upon our souls eternal happiness, no matter what the cost. Here's how the prophet Zephaniah described it: "The LORD your God is in your midst, a mighty one who will save; he will rejoice over you with gladness; he will quiet you by his love; he will exult over you with loud singing" (Zeph. 3:17). God's love for us isn't some duty-driven obligation; no, he "takes pleasure in those who fear him" and "hope in his steadfast love" (Ps. 147:11). He "delights" in his steadfast love (Jer. 9:23–24; Mic. 7:18). His love isn't a detached commitment to bless you, nor is it a grudging compliance with old vows after all affection has waned. No, it's his *delight*.

Maybe you think it is possible to deplete his love for you. He replies that the "earth is full" of it (Ps. 33:5). We can know that our sins won't overwhelm his love because he loves to "adorn" the humble with salvation (Ps. 149:4). When we think our sins are just too great, we need to remember that Jesus' promise of salvation is only for lost sinners, not for the "righteous" (Mark 2:17). How can we know that we can trust him to follow through and never give up on us? We look at Bethlehem, we see Calvary. At great cost to himself, he removes every impediment that would separate us from him. He places all of our transgressions upon his Son, he pours out our punishment upon him, he transfers his perfect record to us, and then he does the most indescribably loving thing ever—he gives us himself in the personal presence of his Holy Spirit. "God's love has been poured into our hearts through the Holy Spirit who has been given to us" (Rom. 5:5).

Here are a few more Old Testament verses for you to soak your soul in. Don't be concerned that you will spend too much time thinking of his love and forget about your obligation to obey. In fact, you will find that as you think about his love, the opposite will begin to happen: you will find within your heart a passion to love him and others.

The psalmists reminded themselves of God's steadfast love over and over again. It helped them know that they could enter his house boldly (Ps. 5:7) and that they could rejoice in salvation and sing because he had "dealt bountifully" with them (Ps. 13:5–6). When David was crushed by the memory of his sins, he prayed, "Remember your mercy, O Lord, and your steadfast love, for they have been from of old. Remember not the sins of my youth or my transgressions; *according to your steadfast love remember me*, for the sake of your goodness, O Lord!" (Ps. 25:6–7).

David relied on God's *hesed* in times of great trial too. He encouraged his heart by remembering God's intimacy, condescension, and protection:

I will rejoice and be glad in your steadfast love,
  because you have seen my affliction;
  you have known the distress of my soul,
and you have not delivered me into the hand of the enemy;
  you have set my feet in a broad place. . . .

Blessed be the LORD,
  for he has wondrously shown his steadfast love to me
  when I was in a besieged city.
  (Ps. 31:7–8, 21; see also Ps. 94:18–19)

Do you think God wants you to learn to stand on your own, self-sufficiently "maturing" past your need to remember his love? Never! He wants you to know how "precious" his love is; he invites you to "take refuge in the shadow" of his wings, to rest in his bosom (Pss. 36:7; 59:16–17; Isa. 40:11). Have you sinned grievously? Have you murdered, committed adultery? You can plead with him for mercy, as David did, "according to [his] steadfast love" (Ps. 51:1) and know that he still loves you (see also Ps. 86:5, 13, 15).

LOVE NEVER ENDS

How many times have you heard the "love passage" from 1 Corinthians 13 read at weddings or rehearsed in a sermon and thought, *That's so beautiful. I wish I could love like that!* Have you ever studied those verses and determined to be more patient or kind or self-sacrificing, only and all too quickly to find yourself impatiently yelling at your children, speaking sharply to an irritating coworker, or wondering why it's always your job to sacrifice (and never anyone else's)?

Even though we assume you are very familiar with 1 Corinthians 13, we recommend a different, perhaps novel, approach to this wonderful passage: rather than looking at it as a series of commands, consider looking at it first as a sneak preview of what we'll see when we finally gaze upon him "face to face" (1 Cor. 13:12).[5] Rather than automatically asking, "What does this passage tell *me* to do?" let's ask, "What do these verses tell me about God's love for me through Christ?" We have taken the liberty to paraphrase the passage with that emphasis to help you see what we mean:

As the author of language and as God's Living Word, Jesus can speak in the tongues of men and angels, and yet he condescends to speak simple words that nourish, soothe, and delight our souls. He knows the past and the future, understands all mysteries and knowledge; has all faith and reigns as Ruler over all;[6] and yet, his love caused him to humble himself and remove our mountain of sin. Because of his love, we who are nothing have become "beloved." He gave away what was rightfully his, humbled himself, and delivered up his body to be burned in the scorching furnace of the wrath of his Father.

Jesus is patient and kind; he doesn't envy or boast. When faced with Satan's temptation to prove his Godhood in the wilderness and on the cross, he never showed off his power. He was utterly humble. He wasn't arrogant or rude, railing on the disciples, deserting them because of their selfish ambition. He isn't arrogant or rude with us either. When standing before his accusers he didn't insist that they treat him with respect, nor did he proudly demand their accolades. He was silent, like a lamb before her shearers. The humble King of heaven wore a crown of thorns and a purple cloak. He is never irritable or resentful, picking away at every little foible he sees. In love, his blood covers our multitudinous sins.

He doesn't gleefully rejoice when you sin, glad to finally have an opportunity to give you your comeuppance. He rejoices when you believe the truth, not simply the truth about you—that you are sinful and flawed—but also the truth about him—that he loves and welcomes you. Out of love for you, he bears all things. He has unflinching faith and hope in your transformation because he knows the power of his love. He knows that one day he will bring you to be with himself. He has endured and continues to endure *all things* out of love for you. His love *never* ends. Never.

Ten zillion years from now, when he has had time to *really* see what sort of person you are, his love won't have worn out. In fact, he knows you through and through right now and loves you all the same. Your shameful secrets cannot shock or repel him. His love *never* ends. One day we will see him face-to-face and then we will fully understand, for the first time, what real love looks like.

God has declared his love for us. His love makes him patient with us even though we refuse to believe that he is as good as he says he is; he is "slow to anger" (Ps. 86:15). Love causes him to be kind to "the ungrateful" (Luke 6:35)—to us who once were his enemies and still don't completely trust his Word. His love declares his goodness and makes him want us for himself, but he isn't puffed up, arrogant, or demanding (Isa. 42:1–3). Instead, he comes to us, seated on the lowliest of animals, a donkey's colt (Zech. 9:9). He continues to love us even when we foolishly insist that our way is best or are irritable or resentful toward him (1 Pet. 2:22–24). He never repays us in kind but always blesses us with what we don't deserve (Matt. 5:44–45).

Sometimes people wonder what will occupy our attention for the countless millennia we'll spend in the new heavens and earth. Although we don't know everything about occupations in the consummation of the new creation, we do know this: the New Jerusalem will be filled with jubilant worship: "His servants will worship him. They will see his face, and his name will be on their foreheads. And night will be no more. They will need no light of lamp or sun, for the Lord God will be their light, and they will reign forever and ever" (Rev. 22:3–5). We will spend our days looking at him and exclaiming, "Look at that! I never noticed that facet of his love before! Look at those scars! His love is so powerful it has made even the ugliness of our sin look beautiful!"

BEHOLD WHAT MANNER OF LOVE!

In his apostolic letters, John the beloved was simply beside himself as he described God's great love for his people in Christ. He testified that "the Father has sent his Son to be the Savior of the world. . . . So we have come *to know* and *to believe* the love that God has for us" (1 John 4:14, 16). What do we need to know? What do we need to believe? Simply this: we need to know and believe that he loves us. We are assured of his love every time we look at the cross; he has sent his Son to be our Savior so that we might "live through him" (1 John 4:9).

We know his love when we hear the Son's cry, "My God, my God, why have you forsaken me?" (Matt. 27:46). Jesus Christ was the propitiation for our sin. Propitiation is simply the amazing truth that God's righteous wrath, which we richly deserve, has been deflected from us and focused instead on his innocent Son (Rom. 3:23–25). He bore the Father's wrath; he assumed our guilt as God poured out upon him every drop of punishment we so justly deserve. Do you wonder if God really loves you? Look at the cross! Do you think he might still be angry with you? You're not seeing Calvary!

So much of what passes for Christianity doesn't have anything to do with this simple premise: God set his love upon undeserving sinners by turning his back on his deserving Son—all because he loves. How is it possible that we will stand confidently before him on the day of judgment? Because his love "casts out fear" (1 John 4:18). How can we war against our selfishness and learn to love God and our neighbors? Because "he first loved us" (1 John 4:19).

Drink deeply of his love, the kind of love he has given us—justifying, propitiating, adopting love. Because of his love we are the "children of God" (1 John 3:1–3). Don't let familiarity with this truth anesthetize your soul to its power: his beloved Son left his heavenly home, traversed down into our world, lived sinlessly, died shamefully, was forsaken by his Father, and was buried in a cold tomb. The Father gave his Son in exchange for us so that he might claim us as his sons. And then he raised him from the dead to assure us again that we are now and forever his. Jesus Christ, the God-Man, has taken our flesh into the throne room of heaven, and therefore nothing—not our weakness, not our sin, "neither death nor life, nor angels nor rulers, nor things present nor things to come, nor powers, nor height nor depth, nor *anything else in all creation*, will be able to separate us from the love of God in Christ Jesus our Lord" (Rom. 8:38–39).

Think on his love. You can't do it enough. Be enraptured by it; let it overwhelm you. Don't worry that it will make you apathetic; just the opposite is true. Hoping in his transforming love causes us to strive after purity, to be pure, "as he is pure" (1 John 3:3).

Your enemy wants to blind you to God's love, to make you think that God isn't as good as he says he is. He sneers with wicked glee when you gloss over verses about the Lord's love for you and seek to know only your obligation. He will flatter you and tell you that, now that you are mature, you don't need to think on his love. But if you believe Satan's lies, you will cut yourself off from the very engine that will empower true obedience. He will continually try to distract you from thinking on God's love for you in Christ, and he will do it either by pointing out your sin or impressing you with your achievements (and others' failures) or by enticing you with some worthless trinket. He will do anything he can to keep you from basking in God's steadfast love for you and pursuing purity in loving dependence. He doesn't care if he keeps you down by pointing out your sin or pointing you to sin. He seeks to damn both the religious and irreligious. What do we need to remember? "God is love" (1 John 4:8, 16).

DOUG'S SECRET

If you ask Doug about his childhood, he will tell you that he was raised in a "good Christian home." His mother stayed home most of his childhood, and his dad was a faithful provider. The family was very involved in the church, with both mom and dad working on different committees and making their faith a priority. Doug came to faith early in his childhood, and he truly believed that Jesus had died for his sin.

But now that Doug is nearing his twenty-first birthday, he has a terrible secret. It actually began when he was twelve. He had heard some of his older brother's friends talking about looking at "girlie" pictures and masturbating. At first he was disgusted by it and threatened to tell their mom, but soon the desire for what he'd overheard grew within him, and he found himself thinking about it all the time.

Sometimes he would wake up in the middle of the night, and it was all he could think of until he gave in. He knew what he was doing was wrong; and even though he privately prayed for help, it seemed that help never came. For the first time in his life he felt alienated from God, sinful. He was sure that God had stopped loving him. He stopped taking Communion, fearing that God would punish him if he dared eat of it while he was so unworthy. He knew his parents would be disappointed if he told them of his struggle.

So he kept silent and soon he began to think that Christianity might work for other "good" people, like his mom and dad, but it certainly wasn't working for him. He thought he was too sinful, too defiled. The promises of God's love surely weren't meant for him. Year after year he continued to attend church, keeping his secret to himself, making sure that there wasn't anything for which his parents, teachers, employers, or pastor could criticize him. His desire for pornography grew. Soon he had his own laptop and his own special sites. It was all he could do to control himself, to pretend to be interested in anything else.

Now he is utterly ensnared. Whenever a thought of God's love for him in Christ flashes through his mind, his enemy tempts him by reminding him of all the times he has tried to quit but been unable to do so. Satan slanders God's character and tells Doug that if God really did love him, he would have delivered him from this sin. Then Doug remembers a particularly alluring woman in the very pose that most entraps him, and he gives up in shame, discouragement, and humiliation again. He hates his slavery and yet loves every minute of it.

How will Doug get free? What does he need? First, Doug needs grace. Faithful brothers need to remind him of both gospel *declarations* and gospel *obligations* like the ones found here:

> For the love of Christ controls us, because we have concluded this: that one has died for all, therefore all have died; and he died for all, that those who live might no longer live for themselves but for him who for their sake died and was raised. (2 Cor. 5:14–15)

Doug has tried to overcome his sin by condemning himself, but he is sure that God must hate him, and the mere fact that he never seems to have the power to say no simply affirms his unbelief. Every time he reads a passage like the one above, all he can see is the command not to live for himself. He never hears God speaking to him through it of his love and sacrifice. He never sees that Jesus Christ bore his sin—yes, even *that* sin—"in his body on the tree" so that he might be free to die to it and live to righteousness. Rather than the "love of Christ" controlling him, he is tormented in the grip of guilt, obligation, lust, and shame. Doug needs to hear the gospel again and again until his heart begins to be enraptured by something other than his lust.

Doug needs the means of grace: gospel preaching from a pastor and a counselor, both of whom are willing to admit the sin that still entangles them. He needs to know that he is not alone in this struggle and that, although they might not struggle in exactly the same ways he does, they do continue to struggle with sin. He needs to understand that God hasn't promised to love the righteous but, rather, lost sinners (Luke 19:10). In humility, he needs to confess his sin, weakness, and poverty of soul. Much of the power and allure of his sin lies in the mere fact that it is secret (Prov. 9:17). Bringing his desires, habits, and deceptions out into the light will begin the process of liberating him from bondage.

Doug also needs to take practical steps to protect his heart from all that lures him away from the Lord who loves him. He needs to seek out God's grace to fight his sin by availing himself of the biblical fellowship within his local church. Faithful, loving brothers need to hold him accountable and ask him personal, pointed questions in a setting made safe for transparent honesty by a deep awareness of Christ's mercy for sinners. His brothers need to assist him in putting an anti-pornography program on his computer, and he needs to promise to stay away from other computers or report to his brothers if he uses one.[7] When he is tempted to sin again (as he surely will be), he can remind himself:

> It's true that I'm facing this temptation now, but what's even truer is that my old, selfish life of slavery is actually dead. I died with Christ, and I am not going to live for myself anymore. I am dead

to this sin and alive now to God. Self-gratification is a cheap imitation of the deep love that my heart hungers for, which I can find in only one place: Calvary. Christ's sacrificial, indescribable love for me, as he hung on that cross, being humiliated and forsaken for this sin, is the only source of power that will enable me to say no to it, and so I'll flood my heart and mind with gospel-centered preaching and music. Not only did my Savior die for my sake, but he was also raised for my justification (Rom. 4:25). Although I am a sinner, I have the perfect record of Jesus Christ, a man who never gave in to sinful temptation. And now, he reigns in heaven as my King, who will give me grace to love him today. He knows me, he was a man like me, and he understands and loves me.

Doug needs to replace the soul-impoverishing pictures in his mind with soul-nourishing ones. He needs to see the water of baptism that signifies cleansing from sin and remember that he needed cleansing and *has been* cleansed by Christ's blood. His baptism is to remind him that he, too, can walk in newness of life (Rom. 6:4). He needs to see the broken bread and remember that the body of his Savior was broken for him, not only for his really "bad" secret sin but also for failing to believe that God would continue to love and help him even though he sinned. He needs to look at the wine, drink it, let it sit for a moment in his mouth, taste it, and then remember that it signifies that he has been cleansed from former sins, just as surely as if he had borne the penalty for them himself. His mind and senses need to be filled with these means of grace as often as his church observes them.

As he grows in his recognition of God's unbounded love for him, he will be able to love his neighbor better too. In particular, he should be encouraged to see women as sisters to cherish and protect. The deception that his pornography habit has been fueled by too deep a love for women must be replaced with the truth—he is a misogynist. His actions demonstrate that he has hated women, has used and exploited them, hasn't cared about their welfare, and hasn't wanted to protect them. Every penny that he has invested in this detestable industry has been fueled by his self-love and unconcern for women's souls. He has viewed women as chattel, pieces of meat created solely for his perverse pleasures.

As he grows in love for God and others, his brothers should help him find ways to serve the sisters in his congregation. They should teach him how a godly man lays down his life for others, particularly women, and how men are to protect, provide for, honor, and seek to free women from the world's twisted perspectives.

A passage from Galatians will then begin to take on personal meaning for Doug. He can use it as a prayer, as a confession of faith, and as a cry for help when he's tempted:

> I have been crucified with Christ. It is no longer I who live, but Christ who lives in me. And the life I now live in the flesh I live by faith in the Son of God, who *loved me and gave himself for me.* (Gal. 2:20–21)

GOD'S LOVE FOR YOU

Do you feel yourself to be too great a sinner for his promises of love to be true for you? You must remember that Christ did not die for the righteous but for sinners (Matt. 9:13). His love rests on those who know they don't deserve it. Answer your conscience and your adversary who would accuse you, as Martin Luther did:

> Because you say I am a sinner, I will be righteous and saved. . . . I fly to Christ who has given himself for my sins. Therefore, Satan, you will not prevail against me when you try to terrify me by telling me how great my sins are. . . . On the contrary, when you say I am a sinner, you give me armor and a weapon against yourself . . . *for Christ died for sinners.* . . . You do not terrify me but comfort me immeasurably.[8]

Rest, rejoice, imbibe, and delight in his love for you now. "May the Lord direct your hearts to the love of God and to the steadfastness of Christ" (2 Thess. 3:5).

PURSUING COUNSEL FROM THE CROSS

1) Here is a flood of Scriptures about the love of God for you. Bask in this blessedness, feed your soul with this heavenly food, and put on these weapons so that you can war against sin:

- Jesus spoke to his Father, ". . . so that the world may know that you sent me and loved them even as you loved me." (John 17:23)

- But God shows his love for us in that while we were still sinners, Christ died for us. (Rom. 5:8)

- Who shall separate us from the love of Christ? . . . We are more than conquerors through him who loved us. (Rom. 8:35, 37)

- In love he predestined us for adoption as sons through Jesus Christ, according to the purpose of his will, to the praise of his glorious grace, with which he has blessed us in the Beloved. (Eph. 1:4–6)

- But God, being rich in mercy, because of the great love with which he loved us, even when we were dead in our trespasses, made us alive together with Christ. (Eph. 2:4–5)

- As beloved children . . . walk in love, as Christ loved us and gave himself up for us, a fragrant offering and sacrifice to God. (Eph. 5:1–2)

- Christ loved the church and gave himself up for her. (Eph. 5:25)

- By this we know love, that he laid down his life for us. (1 John 3:16)

2) Now, make Paul's prayer your own: "Lord, please cause me to be 'rooted and grounded in love,' grant that I 'may have strength to comprehend with all the saints what is the breadth and length and height and depth,' and that I might 'know the love of Christ that surpasses knowledge,' and 'be filled with all the fullness of God'" (see Eph. 3:17–19).

3) Summarize in four or five sentences what you have learned from this chapter.

CHAPTER FOUR

God's Love and Our Hearts

IN THE LAST CHAPTER we pointed you toward God's love for you in Christ. We did that for two simple reasons: we want you to believe in his love for you and then let that love impel you to love and obey him. We know that there might be any number of responses to a discussion of God's love. Here are three of them:

- I know God loves me; why wouldn't he?
- I can't believe that God loves me like that; why would he?
- I'm amazed and enthralled every day as I consider his love for me!

Let's take a few moments now to discuss how our responses to God's declaration of love reveal our hearts' disposition toward the gospel and our resultant obedience. The first two responses—those of the Happy Moralist and the Sad Moralist—are typical of Christians who have let the gospel slip from the center of their faith and for whom the love of God is beginning to lose its power to transform.

THE HAPPY MORALIST

The Happy Moralist says, "I know God loves me; why wouldn't he?" There have always been people who think that a kindly disposed, easily satisfied God is a given.[1] These folks recognize there is a God who has rules of some sort, but they assume they are doing a pretty good job at keeping them. They know that they need a little bit of help from "the man upstairs" from time to time, but aside from that they figure God is pretty lucky to have them on his team. In recent times, this belief has grown exponentially, especially in Western evangelicalism.[2]

Assuming that God should love us just because we are, well, *us*, will result in a bleak existence mired in happy moralism. Of course, the Happy Moralist will give a nod to the fact that God has made certain demands on our lives but will reduce them to two or three outward duties and assume that God is pleased if we just fulfill those obligations and avoid the flagrant sins that "bad" people commit. When we don't see the depth of our depravity, it's easy to look down on and judge other people who don't conform to our practices and to give ourselves the proverbial pat on the back.

Jesus' harshest criticisms were aimed at Happy Moralists. He relentlessly contrasted their outward show of religion with the "weightier matters of the law: justice and mercy and faithfulness" (Matt. 23:23). He wasn't terribly concerned about protecting their self-esteem when he called them "hypocrites," "blind guides," and children of their "father, the devil" (Matt. 23:13, 16; John 8:44).

Why would he speak to them in such a way? For this one reason: he wanted to tear apart their self-reliance and self-confidence. He understood that they would never embrace the childlike humility that is essential for salvation as long as they trusted in their own goodness. In addition, the great gift of God's love would never thrill or delight them while they assumed their own worthiness.

One night when the Happy Moralist Nicodemus surreptitiously sought out Jesus, the Lord annihilated him with five simple words: "You must be born again" (John 3:7). When another Happy Moralist asked him, "Good Teacher, what must I do to inherit eternal life?" (Luke 18:18), Jesus purposely crushed his proud heart with the words, "Sell all that you have" (Luke 18:22). Jesus deliberately told them both to do something beyond their ability because he wanted them to recognize the full extent of their helplessness.

Paul too was continually fighting against Happy Moralists, men who wanted to add obedience to the law as a prerequisite to attaining righteousness before God. They also had too much confidence in their abilities and too little confidence in God's goodness and generosity. They recognized Jesus as Messiah, but they balked at the idea that his law keeping had to replace their own if they were ever to know God's favor. They mistakenly thought that if God loved obedience, then he would really approve of them if they were overly scrupulous and added works of the law to their faith. Their superficial law keeping was merely another way to avoid the humiliation intrinsic in entrusting their standing before God to a crucified Messiah and standing beside unwashed Gentiles as helpless dependents on sheer grace. It enabled them to keep some semblance of self-respect.

Although that sounds nice, it was actually an insult to the honor of God's Son and denuded the gospel of all its power. And so Paul spoke some of his harshest words to those who were trying to ruin the Galatians' simple faith: "I wish those who unsettle you would emasculate themselves!" he thundered (Gal. 5:12). To his dear Galatian children he wrote:

- Are you so foolish? Having begun by the Spirit, are you now being perfected by the flesh? (Gal. 3:3)
- But now that you have come to know God, or rather to be known by God, how can you turn back again to the weak and worthless elementary principles of the world, whose slaves you want to be once more? (Gal. 4:9)
- Look: I, Paul, say to you that if you accept circumcision, Christ will be of *no advantage* to you. (Gal. 5:2)

If, when you read the last chapter on love, the prevailing thought in your mind was, "Of course God loves me! Why wouldn't he? What's all the fuss about?" we want to encourage you to ask yourself the following questions.

Why would a perfectly holy God love me? If you answer, "Because I'm not such a bad sort," or "Because I tithe," or "Because

I try to serve him the best I can," you must see those as the wrong answers. You are missing the humiliation that comes with having to accept the truth about your own "goodness." God's Word says, "Cursed be everyone who does not abide by *all things* written in the Book of the Law, and do them" (Gal. 3:10, citing Deut. 27:26). "All things"—does that strike you as an unreasonably high standard for achieving God's approval? Why not 70 percent for a passing grade, or even 90 percent? Then again, remember that every command in Scripture uncovers what it means to love God supremely, and every violation exposes a heart that is not focused on that supreme demand. There are no innocent missteps. Every violation of God's laws, large or small, reveals a heart prone to wander from our divine Husband and to flirt with other lovers.

Two days after my wife and I (Dennis) welcomed our first-born into the world, he was diagnosed with neonatal meningitis. Physicians immediately began a course of antibiotics to combat the bacterium that had infected his spinal fluid. For the next month they took a spinal tap every few days to determine the effectiveness of the treatment, and we were grateful to hear that the bacterial numbers were steadily declining. But the pediatric team would not consider the infection defeated and release him from the neonatal intensive care nursery until two successive spinal taps showed *no evidence whatsoever* of bacterium. Any reading above zero signaled that the infection was still present.

So also any sin—of thought, word, or deed—reveals that the infection of our hearts has not been utterly eradicated. A record of merely above-average obedience, in comparison to others, falls short of the standard of *thorough and absolute purity*—inside and out—that is required as the basis for the holy God's declaration that anyone stands righteous in his sight. Only Jesus has met that standard, and our only hope is that, when we trust in him, his flawless record of infection-free innocence is credited to us. If you think God should love you because you have obeyed enough, you have underestimated the depth of God's law. Even more seriously, you have missed the gospel.

What makes me acceptable to him? "Oh, I get it; yes, well, then, Jesus makes me acceptable to him." Do you really believe that? When you are facing a difficult trial, do you get mad at God or think that he isn't holding up his side of the bargain? Do you rehearse all the good things you have done for him or all the temptations you have resisted? Are you trying to avoid the truth that all you can bring to him is debt that must be paid by another? You are missing the love of God in Christ.

Do I find that others irritate me? Is it easy to judge them? Do people who break the law (or your own rules and expectations) annoy you? When you are standing in the "ten items or less" line at the grocery store, are you irritated at that woman in front of you who has thirteen items? Do you fume at other drivers who don't signal before changing lanes, or tailgate, or talk on cell phones? Do you find it easy to look down upon those who are unsaved or other Christians who are not as theologically sound as you are? If so, you are missing the gospel; you are more sinful and flawed than you ever dared believe, but God graciously chose you when there wasn't one drop of grace in your soul and nothing to recommend you to him. Are you beginning to see how amazing his grace is?

Do I find it difficult to receive criticism? Are you transparent and vulnerable before your friends or defensive and self-protective? In your mind do you rehearse your accomplishments or others' faults when someone corrects you? Do you think that criticism is always a bad thing? If you find it difficult to take criticism, it's because you haven't believed what the cross says about you. The cross is the most blatant statement of criticism ever displayed. It says that you deserve to die. You deserve to be stripped naked and humiliated and then to receive the righteous wrath of a just God for all eternity. That's what we all deserve. But we have been given grace, forgiveness, and relationship with him. You would need to defend yourself from criticism only if you didn't have a Savior who loved sinners. If you are defensive, you are missing the gospel.[3]

Each of us has something—some more, others less—of the Happy Moralist in him or her. We all lower God's standards to something we are able to accomplish. For the Galatians it was circumcision; for others it might be avoiding R-rated movies or music that wasn't written before the 1800s. The problem, of course, is that God is the law giver (James 4:12), not we, and his law is utterly impossible for fallen, flawed people like us to obey perfectly. His law is easy to remember but impossible to do. Here it is again:

> You shall love the Lord your God with all your heart and with all your soul and with all your mind. This is the great and first commandment. And a second is like it: You shall love your neighbor as yourself. On these two commandments depend all the Law and the Prophets. (Matt. 22:37–40)

There hasn't been one minute of one day in our entire lives that we have ever really obeyed this command. Because it's so hard to do, we replace it with other easier rules so that we can stay happy and complacent, our self-esteem intact. The problem, of course, is that we are never made deeply joyful by the gospel because we have never been deeply crushed by it. We haven't known death, so we can't know life. We are still trying to assure our hearts that we really are quite competent and, "doggone it, people like us."

If the love of God bores you, you are a Happy Moralist. Take yourself to Calvary and see what your sin has wrought. But don't stand there thinking you are an innocent bystander. Instead, let Luther's words pierce your soul:

> You must get this thought through your head and not doubt that you are the one who is torturing Christ thus, for your sins have surely wrought this. . . . Therefore when you see the nails piercing Christ's hands, you can be certain it is your work. When you behold his crown of thorns, you may rest assured that these are your evil thoughts.[4]

Are you beginning to despair of being worthy of his love?

Yes? Good. Now, let the love of Christ richly soothe your troubled conscience and humbly admit, along with the hymn writer, Augustus Toplady, "nothing in my hands I bring, simply to thy cross I cling." How does the love of God look to you now? Is it still boring?

THE SAD MORALIST

In contrast to the Happy Moralist, the Sad Moralist really does see the law and says in response, "I can't believe that God loves me like that; why would he?" He knows that God is transcendent, not to be trifled with. The Sad Moralist is a "serious" Christian. When he reads the commands in Matthew 22:37 and following, he doesn't think for one moment that he has fulfilled them. He knows his sin. But, just like the Happy Moralist, he has a pride problem. He believes that he *ought* to be able to do better, so he is harsh with himself, and he thrashes himself with condemnation, hoping that by so doing he will be able to obey and finally find rest.

He is trying to justify himself by his repentance. He is scrupulously religious and frequently outpaces other Christians around him. But sadly that is never enough to calm his conscience. He thinks that if he could just see his sin as it really is and be sorry enough for it, God would be pleased with him. When he reads about God's love for us in Christ, he isn't comforted or enthralled. He is terrified and condemned. He doesn't know the peace that Christ promises or the joy that should infect his heart.

He, too, is trying to avoid the realities of the gospel but from a different perspective: he is trying to prove that he is worthy, thereby removing the "stumbling block" of the cross (1 Cor. 1:23). He is not alone. Here are two testimonies of godly men who were Sad Moralists before they really grasped the ramifications of grace. The eighteenth-century preacher George Whitefield admonished his listeners:

> Our best duties are as so many splendid sins. Before you can speak peace to your heart you must not only be sick of your original and

actual sin, but you must be made sick of your righteousness, of all your duties and performances. There must be a deep conviction before you can be brought out of *your self-righteousness; it is the last idol taken out of our heart.* The pride of the heart will not let us submit to the righteousness of Jesus Christ.[5]

David Brainerd, an early missionary to the American Indian, wrote:

When I had been fasting, praying, obeying, I thought I was aiming at the glory of God, but I was doing it all for my own glory—to feel I was worthy. As long as I was doing all this to earn my salvation, I was doing nothing for God, all for me! I realized that all my struggling to become worthy was an exercise in self-worship. I was not worshipping him, but using him. . . . Though I often confessed to God that I, of course, deserved nothing, yet still I harbored a secret hope of recommending myself to God by all these duties and all this morality. In other words, I healed myself with my duties.[6]

Aside from an insensitivity to the sweetness of God's love, the Sad Moralist is forced to rely on his own righteousness and, because he is aware of the requirements of the law, he knows that he never makes the grade. In his desire to prove his love for God, he will be tempted to resent God for being so demanding. When he is overwhelmed and exhausted from these wrestlings of soul, he will give up in apathy and give in to self-indulgence. Then, of course, the whole cycle begins again with renewed efforts at self-reformation. Following are a few questions to ask yourself if you suspect that you might be a Sad Moralist.

Why would a perfectly holy God love me? If you answer, "I suppose he might love me because he promises to, but then those promises are for people who love him with all their heart and prove their love by their actions. So I guess I don't know why he would love me or, actually, even if he does," can you see how you are hoping to earn his love by being worthy of his love and thereby negating the grace that is the essence of the gospel?

What makes me acceptable to him? "Well, I suppose that Jesus' righteousness makes me acceptable to him, but I just can't help but think that I must be pretty much of a disappointment to him." Do you picture God as a forbearing parent who puts up with defective and delinquent children—not disowning you, but also not wanting you too near? Can you see how the gospel is good news only because it isn't about you or your record at all? You have been completely justified simply by believing! Believe Paul's words, "For we hold that one is justified by faith *apart* from works of the law" (Rom. 3:28). Take all your, "yes, but . . ." responses and humbly sing these lovely verses:

Cast your deadly "doing" down—
Down at Jesus' feet;
Stand in Him, in Him alone,
Gloriously complete.
"It is finished!" yes, indeed,
Finished, ev'ry jot;
Sinner, this is all you need,
Tell me, is it not?[7]

James Proctor, the author of this hymn, prefaced it with these lines:

Since I first discovered Jesus to be the *end* of the law for righteousness to every one that believeth, I have more than once met with a poor sinner seeking peace at the *foot of Sinai* [the law] instead of *Calvary*, and I have heard him again and again in bitter disappointment and fear groaning out, "What must I do?" I have said to him, "Do, do? What can you do?"[8]

If you think similarly to that poor sinner, you have forgotten your union with Christ. You are *in* him. Is the Father disappointed with his Son? Of course not! Then he cannot be disappointed with you.

Am I critical of others who seem to be enjoying God's blessings especially because I know they don't work as hard as I do? Are you censorious, envious, or hateful of Christians who have weak theology or who seem overly emotional? If so, you are missing the gospel. Like the elder brother in the parable of the welcoming father (Luke

15:29), you are trying to earn a reward, or you imagine that you have already earned it and resent the fact that it hasn't yet been paid.

Although it might seem counterintuitive, you don't need to be assured that you have a better record. You need to embrace your utter helplessness. Then, as you begin to believe that the only way you can be justified is through Christ's righteousness, you will be able to be welcoming and gracious toward other Christians, even those with whom you do not agree, because they are only his by grace too. Remembering that we have all been saved by grace alone makes us love others and be more patient with them.

Do I find it difficult to receive criticism? For the Sad Moralist, who is always so self-critical, criticism from others can feel devastating. But criticism has the power to devastate only because the Sad Moralist is hanging onto shards of self-respect. He is still hoping to be good. Embrace your helplessness; it's the only qualification you have that enables you to be saved.

THE GOSPEL-CENTERED CHRISTIAN

The gospel-centered Christian says, "I'm amazed and enthralled every day as I consider his love for me!" Although we are going to discuss what a gospel-centered life might look like, we want to make something very clear right up front: none of us lives every day in the light of the gospel as we should. Even the most gospel-loving believer you know *never* lives consistently in the light of these truths. We are reminding you of this because we want you to avoid the temptation to judge yourself or compare yourself to others and then become mired down in self-condemnation or unbelief.

Our Relationship with the Law

To begin with, the gospel-centered Christian has a proper relationship with the law. Many Christians are confused about the place of God's law in their lives. Some ignore it entirely and think that Christianity is something akin to a spiritual social event. Some vaguely know that the law has been abrogated in some way; they know that they didn't get saved by obeying it and believe that the Ten Commandments (and the rest of the Old Testament) were probably fine for their time but are now passé. Both of these approaches militate against the law and may indicate a belief that seeking to live an obedient life is legalism.

Of course, there are other Christians who are overly attentive to the law. These would-be serious Christians believe that their justification is only by grace but forget that sanctification (our slow change into Christlikeness) is a "work of God's *free grace*,"[9] even as justification is a legal "act of God's free grace."[10]

Our response to the love of God for us in Christ will be, in part, determined by whether we understand the role of God's law in our lives. Since we want you to rejoice in God's love and respond in grateful obedience, we offer here a simple way to think of it: the law, Paul writes, is "holy and righteous and good" (Rom. 7:12), but it is an instrument of condemnation to us all because we are not able to obey it perfectly (Rom. 3:9ff).

For the gospel-centered Christian, the function of the law is to drive us to Christ and to make us continually more and more thankful for his perfect keeping of it in our place. It is to make us more and more dependent upon his righteousness, not our own. When we sin, as we do every day, then we are to respond to the Lord in light of our failures in humble contrition. We are to:

1) Confess our sins to God (openly and freely), while praying to God for the grace of the Holy Spirit to strive against them.[11]
2) Thank God for our ongoing struggle with sin because, when rightly viewed, it makes us love and appreciate Jesus Christ more.
3) Strive to put off our sin and obey all the moral law in the light of God's ongoing forgiveness, love, and grace.

Most Christians practice points 1 and 3. They confess and strive to obey. But they miss point 2. They miss the truth that God is sovereign even over our sin and that, even though he hates sin, he uses it to bring praise to his Son. At any point that it pleased him, he could put an end to sin, but he doesn't. We must then assume that he uses it for his glory, as he uses everything else (Rom. 11:36).

We are not saying that our sin pleases God in itself. God is not tempted by sin, nor does he tempt us to sin (James 1:13); he doesn't rejoice in sin. What we are saying, though, is this: *God is sovereign even over sin* (Gen. 20:6; 50:20; Ex. 4:21; Acts 2:23; 3:18). He allows it and uses it for his own glory. Of course, this *never* means that we should assume it is God's will for us to sin when we face temptation. God hates sin. He has revealed his will to us, declaring that we must always strive to avoid sin and put on righteousness. Obedience is God's *revealed* will for our lives. And his *revealed* will, disclosed in the Bible, is the only (and completely sufficient) guide that we need for our decisions and actions. But God also has a *secret* will (Deut. 29:29). We never know his secret will before it happens.

So every morning we should pray, "Father, let your will be done by me today," knowing that it is his revealed will that we obey his instructions in the Scriptures. Then, every night when we look back at the day and see the ways in which we failed to obey, we humble ourselves before his secret will and say,

> Father, please forgive my sin and cause me to walk in holiness. Thank you that my sin reminds me again how desperately I need the cross and how thankful I am for your grace. Thank you that you love me despite my sin today and that you will use even this for your glory. Lord Jesus, thank you that you bore those sins in your body on the tree. Thank you for your love and grant me grace to obey because of it.

The gospel-centered Christian sees God's law for what it is: a perfect reflection of God's character. He loves the moral law, longs to obey every part of it with his whole heart, and recognizes that the law is good. But he doesn't allow the law's demands to strengthen or diminish his confidence in his justification in any way. As Martin Luther wrote in his study on Galatians, "God does not slack his promises because of our sins . . . or hasten them because of our righteousness. He pays no attention to either."[12]

As far as God is concerned, our obedience to the law has been utterly satisfied in the Son. We are perfectly justified. It's in light of this justification then, and only in light of it, that we obey. Any other relationship to the law will result in either a lessening of the commands (so we can breathe) or an oppressive guilt and a joyless thirst after self-achieved divine approval.

Our Relationship with the Trinity

The gospel-centered Christian recognizes that his relationship is with the Trinity—Father, Son, and Holy Spirit. He sees his relationship with the Father as one of joyful love and acceptance. Rather than viewing the Father as cold, merely transcendent, or angry, he knows that it's because of the Father's choice that he has been loved and welcomed. It is the Father who forgives (Mark 11:25), to whom we are invited to address our prayer (Matt. 6:39), who keeps us for himself (John 17:11), and who loves us as he loves his Son (John 17:23). The Father has lovingly chosen and adopted us (Eph. 1:4–5). We need to soak our souls in this truth: the Father so loved the world that he sent his beloved Son (John 3:16).

Our relationship with the Son is that of a younger brother to a strong elder brother or that of a wife to her husband. The Son, out of love for both his Father and us, gave up what was rightfully his and came to earth to redeem a people for his pleasure and glory. Like a compassionate high priest, the Son is able to sympathize with our weaknesses and in every respect has been tempted as we are, yet without sin (Heb. 4:15–16). At the cost of his life and the Father's smile of approval, he powerfully crushed all our enemies and removed every impediment that separated us from his Father. He bore every drop of God's holy wrath in our place. He now lives, enthroned at his Father's right hand, ruling sovereignly over all things and protecting and providing for his bride, the church. The Son is our brother, our bridegroom, our king.

The Holy Spirit has been sent into our lives by both the Father and the Son. It is the Spirit who brings us to new life, who reveals the Son to us, who makes us know all that the Father has bestowed upon us. The Spirit empowers us to strive against sin and counsels and comforts us when we fail.

As children who are sinful and flawed yet loved and welcomed, we can rejoice in the Trinity. We can relate to our triune God as he is: our heavenly Father, our kinsman-redeemer, our counselor and guide. We don't need to cringe in fear from the Father or think that the Son continues to suffer in our place. Redemption has been accomplished. The Spirit has been given to all believers and dwells within them, conforming them to Christ's image by making him beautiful in their eyes. Through the work of the Trinity, all things are ours and "we are Christ's and Christ is God's" (1 Cor. 3:21–23).

Our Relationship with Others

Because our fellowship with the "Father and with his Son Jesus Christ" (1 John 1:3) has been cemented by God himself, the gospel-centered Christian is free to have true fellowship with others. He can love others, be transparent before them, eagerly desire correction, and look for opportunities to encourage and serve them. He can live freely in this way because he no longer has to impress them. He can walk in the light with them, as John wrote:

> But if we walk in the light, as he is in the light, we have fellowship with one another, and the blood of Jesus his Son cleanses us from all sin. If we say we have no sin, we deceive ourselves, and the truth is not in us. If we confess our sins, he is faithful and just to forgive us our sins and to cleanse us from all unrighteousness. (1 John 1:7–9)

When our relationships are built around the truths of the gospel—the truth that we are walking in light even though we are still sinners in need of cleansing by his blood—we can be free from feelings of inferiority and the demanding spirit that is born of pride. We can pursue relationships without fear of being discovered as the sinners we are. This kind of open relationship rests solely on the realities of the gospel. We are more sinful and flawed than we ever dared believe, and so is everyone we know. Because of this, we won't be surprised by other's sins. They won't expect us to be sinless either, so we don't have to give in to self-condemnation and fear when they see us as we really are. We don't have to hide or pretend anymore.

The gospel also tells us that we are loved and welcomed without any merit on our part, so we can love and welcome others whose merits we can't see. We can remember the circumstances under which we have been forgiven, and we can forgive in the same way. We don't deserve relationship with the Trinity, but it has been given to us. We can seek out relationships with others because we know that we have been sought out by him and that he is carrying us all on his shoulders. (Yes, he is that strong!)

I JUST DON'T FIT IN

Jeannie's conversion was radical and joyous. Before coming to the Lord, she'd been involved in every sort of base sin. She'd had numerous abortions and two children from different fathers. She'd been on welfare, and her life had degenerated into a revolving door of relationships with men, women, drugs, and despair. Then, through a new neighbor, she heard about Jesus, the man who loved sinful men and women, and she was truly born again. Her desire for illicit relationships and partying began to change. She felt clean, new, and alive. For the first time in her life she had hope. Then a new trouble arose.

Her new problem isn't one of wanting her old life back as much as it is of wishing to be like all the other women in her church. Although they are welcoming, she never feels like she fits in. "How many of them have tattoos?" she cries. "I've had abortions, lesbian relationships, done drugs. If they knew what my life used to be like they would be horrified!"

Although she believes that she has been forgiven by God, she isn't sure that the "straight" women in her church will forgive her, and loneliness is starting to take its toll. She wants friends but is afraid she will be ostracized. The old life is starting to look good again. She is beginning to wonder if she has really been saved after all.

How can we help Jeannie? What does she need? She needs 1 John 1:7–9. She needs to know that everyone in her local congregation is in the same position. They are, all of them, more sinful and flawed than they ever dared believe. Some of them are Happy Moralists, never taking the law to heart and assuming that they are loved just because they are alive. Others are Sad Moralists, trying to prove their worth, beating themselves up, struggling with hating themselves just as she does. Perhaps their sins aren't quite as destructive as Jeannie's were, but they are heinous nevertheless. Maybe they don't have actual tattoos, but "sinner saved by grace" is written on every one of them.

Jeannie needs friends. She needs the accountability, transparency, encouragement, and fellowship of women in her local church. She needs to see that they struggle, just as she does, to believe they are saved by the work of Jesus Christ alone. She needs to hear them confess sins and to be encouraged by others. And then she needs to learn to be thankful for her sin since it is what keeps her constantly aware of her endless need for Jesus and his forgiving and transforming mercy. Although she has been buffeted by sin and Satan, she can know that her life isn't any different from that of other Christians. All the women in the church are just like her, tattoos or not.

First Corinthians 6:9 and following speaks directly to her. After listing those whose lifestyles would bar people from the kingdom of God, Paul writes, "And such were some of you. But you were washed, you were sanctified, you were justified in the name of the Lord Jesus Christ and by the Spirit of our God" (1 Cor. 6:11). Instead of feeling alienated from other women, Jeannie needs to understand that she is just like them. We *all* need to be washed, sanctified, and justified by Jesus Christ and the Spirit. None of us is loved because we are good people.

Jeannie then needs to seek to serve the other women in the church. She can offer to babysit or make a meal for a new mother. She can avail herself of women's Bible studies or ask for help on what books to read.

She can tear down walls of self-condemnation and judging by loving her sisters as she loves herself. Instead of keeping her eyes on herself, she needs to look to the needs of others. Instead of judging her sisters by assuming they won't accept her, she needs to excel in serving them. Then, whenever her eye happens to fall on one of her tattoos and she is tempted to be embarrassed and cover it up, she can thank God that she will never forget how great God's grace is.

Of course, the women in the church need to go out of their way to assure Jeannie of their love and acceptance, even if they have to do it over and over again.

THE FATHER HIMSELF LOVES YOU

At the beginning of this chapter we asked about your response to God's love for you. And now at the end of the chapter we are going to ask the same question again. Earlier when you read, "The Father himself loves you," what did you think? Are you beginning to believe that, although you don't now and never will deserve it, the Father himself loves you? Are you ready to admit your sin without fear of reprisals or despair? Are you growing in the awareness that you can face the harsh reality of your moral failures honestly because you are deeply assured that Jesus "bore the blame" wholly and completely on his cross? Do you believe that you are welcomed by the Father, wholly and completely, because of Jesus' perfect obedience?

We believe that it is your Father's desire to convince you of his love and that he yearns for you to believe it. Let him speak of his love through his Word, through the sacraments, and through other believers. Believe that he is that good. Believe that you are that loved.

PURSUING COUNSEL FROM THE CROSS

1) How do you respond to the thought of God's love for you in Christ? Do you see yourself primarily as a Happy Moralist or a Sad Moralist? Why?

2) How much of an inroad has the gospel made into your relationships with others? Are you afraid of their censure if they discover your sin? Do you judge others when you see their sin? Do you find yourself, like David Brainerd, trying to "heal yourself by your duties?" In other words, are you still trying to prove to God and others that you really aren't that bad? Let your heart rejoice in George Herbert's words:

> Love bade me welcome: yet my soul drew back,
>   Guilty of dust and sin.
> But quick-ey'd Love, observing me grow slack
>   From my first entrance in,
> Drew nearer to me, sweetly questioning,
>   If I lack'd anything.
>
> A guest, I answer'd, worthy to be here:
>   Love said, you shall be he.
> I the unkind, ungrateful? Ah my dear,
>   I cannot look on thee.
> Love took my hand, and smiling did reply,
>   Who made the eyes but I?
>
> Truth Lord, but I have marr'd them: let my shame
>   Go where it doth deserve.
> And know you not, says Love, who bore the blame?
>   My dear, then I will serve.
> You must sit down, says Love, and taste my meat:
>   So I did sit and eat.[13]

3) How do you respond when you sin? Do you see that aside from confession and prayer for change, you should also thank God because your sin reminds you of your Savior and drives you to trust only in him?

4) Psalm 78 is a history of Israel's refusal to respond to God's gracious love. [We've included it in Appendix 4 in case your Bible isn't handy.] Where do you see yourself in it? Do you hear his patience and love calling to his people to believe that he is as good as he says he is?

5) Summarize in four or five sentences what you have learned from this chapter.

CHAPTER FIVE

Gospel-centered Counseling

*You . . . were taught in him . . . to put off your old self,
which belongs to your former manner of life and is corrupt
through deceitful desires, and to be renewed in the spirit of
your minds, and to put on the new self, created after the likeness of God in true righteousness and holiness.*
EPHESIANS 4:20–24

DURING A RECENT CONVERSATION that I (Elyse) was
having with a group of pastors' wives, someone commented that
counseling is quite in vogue these days. "Twenty years ago," one of
the wives remarked, "people didn't want anyone to know they were
getting counseling. Now, it's almost a badge of honor."

"Yes," I replied, "we live in the Age of the Counselor. It's not
much of a question anymore whether people will get counseling at
some time or other. The question is what kind of counseling they'll
get. There are all sorts of counseling methods out there, some that
claim to be Christian, others that bear the label 'biblical.' Some
don't bother with those terms at all. But every one of them has
foundational beliefs about what is wrong with people and how they
can be helped."

In this chapter we will present a particular paradigm for counseling. Very briefly, gospel-centered counseling, as we are defining
it, is the process of one Christian coming alongside another with
words of truth to encourage, admonish, comfort, and help—words

drawn from Scripture, grounded in the gracious saving work of Jesus Christ, and presented in the context of relationship. The goal of this counseling is that the brother or sister in need of counsel would grow in his or her understanding of the gospel and how it applies to every area of life and then respond in grateful obedience in every circumstance, all to the building up of the church and for the glory of God.[1]

You will notice that this gospel-centered paradigm is derived from the Bible.[2] You will see that our answer to the questions above—What is wrong with people? How can they be helped?—will clearly differ from what one might hear from Dr. Phil or Oprah. It will also differ from what many other Christian counselors would say. We derive our paradigm from the Bible because we distrust merely human diagnoses of what's really wrong with us and because we recognize our utter powerlessness to effect deep change in anyone by our own efforts.

Only God's Word has the power to discern "the thoughts and intentions of the heart" (Heb. 4:12) and to illumine our darkened understanding (Ps. 36:9; John 8:12; 1 John 1:7). Only the Holy Spirit is powerful enough to convict us of sin (John 16:8), implant faith (2 Cor. 2:12, 14), teach us the truth (John 14:17), bring new life (1 Cor. 6:11), and transform us (1 Pet. 1:2, Eph. 1:17–18), enabling us to feel, want, and do the good we desire. Mere human counselors, including ourselves, as well-intentioned as we may be, simply aren't equal to this monumental task.

Gospel-centered counseling seeks to answer the questions, "What is wrong with us?" and "What can be done to help?" by intentionally applying Scripture in a balanced way, recognizing both what the gospel declares about us and what it demands of us. Counseling that neglects the *Scriptures* when seeking to answer these questions always eventuates in a bloated self-opinion and an enslaving and futile self-focus. Counseling that neglects what the *gospel* says about us will eventuate in works-righteousness and its ultimate and inescapable fruit, either pride or despair, or a vacillation between the two.[3] Counseling that neglects the *obligation* forced on us by the gospel always eventuates in complacent laziness, excuse-making, and loose living.[4]

So gospel-centered counseling is counseling based on Scripture that defines us as God does and then applies both gospel declarations and gospel obligations to every problem we encounter.

THE LAW AND THE GOSPEL

The Bible contains both gospel and law, indicatives and imperatives, declarations and obligations. When we use the words *gospel*, *indicatives*, and *declarations*, we are referring to those portions of Scripture that tell us what Christ has already done (or has promised to do) for us. On the other hand, when we use the terms *law*, *imperatives*, and *obligations*, we are referring to those verses that tell us what our response to this good news should be.

5.1: THE BIBLE CONTAINS

LAW	GOSPEL
Obligations	Declarations
Imperatives	Indicatives

By way of illustration, let's look at a very familiar passage from the New Testament, one that is rightly used in the practice of biblical counseling.

> Put off your old self, which belongs to your former manner of life and is corrupt through deceitful desires, and . . . be renewed in the spirit of your minds, and . . . put on the new self, created after the likeness of God in true righteousness and holiness. (Eph. 4:22–24)

As you read that passage, what impresses you most? Some of us would glance at the first few words, figure that it is simply a command to put off the old and put on the new, and then jump on down to see what the point is. Please let us encourage you to back up and reread the passage again. Is there something more there? Does this passage contain both law and gospel, both declarations and obligations? Let's dig a little deeper.

Our Old Identity

What are the *gospel declarations* in this passage? What does it tell us about our identity in Christ, what he has already done for us, and where our hope for change comes from?[5] To begin with, we are told we have an "old self" and a "former manner of life." Therefore, because of what Jesus Christ has *already* done, those of us who are in Christ are profoundly different from who we were before Jesus' grace entered our lives. We had one identity; now we have another. We *were* in bondage to sin, but now we are no longer slaves.

The fact that we have an old, former manner of life reminds us of a particular aspect of the gospel—death. The death of Jesus Christ is not a detached fact; instead, it applies to us personally because we have "died *with*" him (Rom. 6:8). When Jesus Christ suffered in indescribable anguish on the cross, receiving an eternity's worth of wrath in three short hours, he was doing so as our representative. When he died, he died in *our* place.

This passage reminds us of the depth of our depravity. We are far more sinful and flawed than we know. It should humble us to the dust to realize that the only way for us to become holy was for the beloved Son to suffer like this and to die in our place. We must abandon our futile pursuit of good self-esteem and see ourselves for what we are: the cause of the greatest suffering ever known, the suffering of the Lamb of God. We will never be truly free from self-condemnation and the desire for approval until we grasp this fact. We were so sinful we had to die. Personal reformation won't help. We need death.

In addition, we must see the substitutionary suffering of Jesus Christ when we struggle against those deeply rooted "corrupt, deceitful desires" that characterized our old manner of living. When the war heats up and we doubt that we will ever change, we must remember that our old person, filled with self-deceiving desires, no longer has power to rule over us. Our former self is dead.

When we wonder if we are truly forgiven, we have to remember the suffering and death of the Savior. When we doubt that we can ever change for the better, ever gain the upper hand over shameful desires and sinful behavior, we need to remember that our union with Jesus in his death not only cleared our record of sin's guilt but also freed our heart from sin's tyranny. Because of the gospel, we can continue to "consider" ourselves "dead to sin" (Rom. 6:11). Only the terrible suffering of the Son has the power to avert our gaze from ourselves and onto him. Only the awful beauty of a suffering Savior can draw our attention away from those desires that seem so beautiful and enticing. Only the gospel can motivate us to "put off" our old manner of life.

Now let's look at Ephesians 4:22–24 again to see what other gospel declarations we'll find there.

> Put off your old self, which belongs to your former manner of life and is corrupt through deceitful desires, and . . . be renewed in the spirit of your minds, and . . . put on the new self, created after the likeness of God in true righteousness and holiness.

For the moment, we are going to skip over the middle portion of the passage, "be renewed in the spirit of your minds," and proceed to the last portion, "put on the new self, created after the likeness of God in true righteousness and holiness." What do these words tell us about the gospel? What declarations do they make about who we are, what Christ has already done for us, and what our hopes should be?

Our New Identity

Simply put, we're new! As we bear the physical image of our earthly fathers, we bear the image or likeness of God now in our hearts, which is our true identity. We no longer bear the spiritually corrupt image of our original father, Adam; we have put on the image of the second Adam, Christ, the head of the new humanity. We have not only lost our old identity, but we have also been given a new one.

We have not only been completely forgiven for sin, but we have also been given new spiritual DNA. The image of God that was radically distorted and disfigured at the fall in the garden has been recreated in us. We have great hope for ultimate transformation because we have been remade in the "likeness of God."

You'll recall that in the Genesis account of creation, man was created in the image and likeness of God (Gen. 1:26). Since every creature was to reproduce "according to its kind" (Gen. 1:11, 12, 21, 25), we can safely assume that had Adam and Eve not sinned they would have borne children in the image and likeness of God, not only as creaturely persons whose attributes (thought, purpose, decision, etc.) reflected the personality of their Creator but also as those whose personal attributes responded in ethical obedience to him (truth-informed thought, holy purpose, righteous decision, etc.)

But, of course, they did sin, and so we find Adam giving birth to a son "in *his* own likeness, after *his* image" (Gen. 5:3). The likeness and image of God was shattered in the fall. Although in one respect the image of God remained in fallen human beings (so that the image of God after the fall remained the basis for the sanctity of human life [see Gen. 9:6; James 3:9]), the "true righteousness and holiness" that Paul refers to in Ephesians 4:24 were completely lost.

Now here is the wonderful gospel news of this passage: this image, this true righteousness and holiness, has been restored to us! How can that be? How is it that we who are such sinners can have God's true righteousness and holiness? We can by the work of the Son, of course. We have his righteous record. We share in his holiness.

But not only that—he has also filled us with his Holy Spirit and is working this true righteousness and holiness into our daily lives. He is replacing our corrupt, deceitful desires with holy ones; he is causing us to "will and to work for his good pleasure" (Phil. 2:13). We can purpose to put on a new, holy way of life because the Lord has *already* placed within us the desire to do so.

In light of these declarations of the gospel, we are to be "renewed in the spirit of [our] mind." Our old, unbelieving, corrupt way of thinking needs to be changed. The thought that we are extra-wicked sinners needs to be replaced with the thought that we have been recreated in the image and likeness of God. The thought that our "dysfunctional" upbringing makes holiness impossible must be replaced with this thought: "*It's true that I was sinned against as a child, but God has given me a completely new identity. Jesus Christ himself had to bear the penalty for my corrupt, deceitful desires and yet has given me new life. I've been recreated into someone who can walk in true righteousness and holiness. I've got his image, his grace. I can change.*"

5.2: GOSPEL DECLARATIONS IN EPHESIANS 4:22–24

- We bear the image of Christ
- We have been recreated in true righteousness and holiness
- We have Christ's righteous record
- The Holy Spirit is working this true righteousness and holiness into our hearts
- He's replacing our corrupt desires with holy ones

Now . . . Put Off and Put On

Now it's time to look at the gospel obligations in this passage. The biblical method of change is clearly demonstrated for us here. We are to seek diligently to "put off" the old sinful patterns that marked our lives before we came to Christ.[6] But that's not all. We are not simply to stop practicing sin; we are to start practicing righteousness. We are to replace our old way of living with new, godly ways of living.

5.3: GOSPEL OBLIGATIONS IN EPHESIANS 4:22–24

- Put off the old sinful patterns
- Put on the new Christlike patterns of godly living

In Ephesians 4:25, the verse that immediately follows our passage, we are reminded that having "put away falsehood," we are to "speak the truth" with our neighbor. It isn't enough to simply stop lying. We are also to see others as our neighbors and speak the truth to them.

The New Testament is filled with passages that employ this put off/put on dynamic. Again, it's not enough to cease some thought or activity. We not only cease the evil activity; we also replace it with obedience instead.

COMBINING DECLARATIONS AND OBLIGATIONS IN COUNSELING

At the beginning of this chapter we defined gospel-centered counseling as the process of one Christian coming alongside another with words of truth to encourage, admonish, comfort, and help—words drawn from Scripture, grounded in the gracious saving work of Jesus Christ, and presented in the context of relationship. The goal of this counseling is that the brother or sister in need of counsel would grow in his or her understanding of the gospel and how it applies to every area of life and then respond in grateful obedience in every circumstance, all to the building up of the church and for the glory of God.

We have chosen to call the model we are presenting in this book *gospel-centered counseling* rather than just *Christian* or even *biblical* counseling. Because many Christians are still trying to integrate the failed methods of humanistic psychology[7] with the Bible, we have tried to construct a system of counseling that avoids the futility of psychology's humanistic self-reformation while at the same time correcting the pitfalls of what may be, in some quarters, a gospel-less approach to biblical change. Other counselors share our belief that humanistic psychology leads into blind alleys, but their solution is to focus extensively on the Bible's imperatives and the counselee's self-discipline with little attention to the patterns of self-doubt and unbelief that enervate the counselee's motivation and hope in the painful process of change.

Following is one very simple example of how this model differs from an integrationist approach. Let's pretend that you have just discovered that you are out of salt and you have company coming in twenty-five minutes. You look at the clock and calculate how long it will take you to shoot up to the store, grab the salt, run back home, and get everything on the table in time for a delightful time of hospitality.

Into the car you jump and you race up to the store, grab the salt, and go to the express checkout line. There in front of you is a woman who has sixteen items in her cart. You check again to be sure that you are in the "ten items or less" line. Anger and stress build up while you try to control yourself.

How would "Christian psychology" tell you to respond? Since psychology is not a uniform discipline,[8] there are several possible answers to this question. If you believe that you are a victim (of any sort) and therefore need to stand up for your rights, you could be self-assertive and tell the woman to move. If you believe that you need to love yourself more, you could spend your time reminding yourself that you are really a good person and you shouldn't let this get you down. After all, you can't help it if others don't obey the rules. If you are a behaviorist, you could get your anti-stress rubber-band out of your purse, place it on your wrist, and snap it until you have released all your stress and anger.

If you think that reality is created by your thoughts, you could move your mental focus off this distressing situation and go to your "happy place." You could take a mini-vacation in your mind until the line moves forward. And finally, if you think that all your anger and stress are caused by disturbed brain chemicals, you could take an anti-anxiety pill and hope that you'll feel better soon.

Next, how would a person who wants to put off sin and put on holiness apart from gospel declarations respond? Once you realize that you are becoming sinfully angry, you could tell yourself that you need to be "slow to anger; for the anger of man does not produce the righteousness of God" (James 1:19–20).[9] You could remind yourself of your obligation to be a good witness before the world, regret having worn a T-shirt that proclaims your Christianity, and stretch your lips into a forced smile when that lady fumbles for her checkbook. You could determine to say nothing unkind or to "accidentally" bump her cart. You could choose to do her good by picking up something she dropped from her basket.

But almost immediately you will probably begin to feel condemned, remembering all the times you have gotten angry, and wonder when you will ever get your act together. At the same time, you will also feel angry that she doesn't obey the rules like you do and wonder why God put her in your path. Then, of course, you will probably feel guiltier because you are charging God with wrongdoing, and then you will be angry and stressed all over again.

Honestly, when I (Elyse) am in this kind of cycle, I usually end up blaming my husband, Phil, for not being available to pick up the salt for me or for encouraging me to have people over when I'm already too busy.

If, however, you are seeking to counsel yourself in light of the gospel, you will see this scenario in an entirely different way. First, you will humbly acknowledge that the woman in line in front of you is just like you. Yes, she's a lawbreaker,[10] but so are you (Rom. 3:9ff.). The gospel will tell you that your lawbreaking is so significant that there is no way for you to save yourself, so the Son of God had to become incarnate and die in your place. You will remember that his excruciating death on Calvary wasn't necessitated by our merely fudging a bit on man-made rules; no, he died there because we *never* perfectly obey God's law. He suffered not only for our obvious sins, but also for the self-righteousness that looks down on others who don't play by the rules like we do. "Oh, she's just like me," you'll think. "God is so patient with me [Rom. 2:4], so I can be patient with her."

In addition, you can see the depth of your sin in wanting to be (or at least appearing to be) a respected hostess who has (or seems to have) it all together for her guests. You can fully embrace your deep sinfulness without the despair that would crush you apart from the gospel.

Second, when you are tempted to slide down into a miry pit of self-condemnation, you can remember Jesus' sinless life and the perfect record that is now yours. Yes, it's true that you sin heinously and consistently, but you have a perfect record before God, the only one whose opinion matters (Rom. 3:24).

Next, you can remember the resurrection. The sinful self-ishness, pride, and self-righteousness that marked your former manner of life have been broken by the power of his risen life (Rom. 6:4). The power of those old enslaving, sinful habits has been crushed. You no longer have to live as a slave, grasping for respect or ease. You no longer have to prove that you've "got it all together." You can rest in the new life that he has given you as a son (Gal. 4:6–7).

Finally, you can rejoice in the ascension. Because Jesus Christ is ruling over your life from heaven (Rom. 8:34), still in human form, you can know that he sympathizes with your weaknesses (Heb. 4:15). He is praying for you as you fume in the express line, and he is quietly working by his Spirit to displace your frustration with grati-tude and patience. He knows what it's like to live in a sin-cursed world where people don't obey the rules. But he also rules over this world and has arranged this situation specifically for you because you needed to be reminded of his love (Dan. 4:34–35). Your sinful response to the lawbreaker in front of you can bring you sorrow mixed with joy as you remember what Christ has done for you and his great love for you in spite of your lawlessness.

In light of all the above, once your heart has been warmed by the great mercy and grace of God for you in Christ, you should remem-ber to be "slow to anger; for the anger of man does not produce the righteousness of God" (James 1:19–20). You will then remember to love your neighbor, not simply because you have been commanded to do so but because you have been loved (1 John 4:11). You can let the love of God, which has been poured into your heart by the Holy Spirit (Rom. 5:5), overflow to this woman, the checker, your guests, and your family. "Oh, I'm a great sinner," you might say to yourself, "but I've been loved by a great Savior, so I am free to love others."

In light of what Jesus has done for you, you can determine to do good to her. If she drops something, you can gladly pick it up for her. If the checker apologizes for this shopper's obvious infraction, you can remind her that we are all the same—sinners saved by grace alone. Moreover, remembering your sins and Christ's grace will also set your heart free from anxiety over what your dinner guests will think of you if the meal is served twenty minutes after you had planned. You could even use this circumstance—your sinful response and the Lord's grace in the midst of it—to remind your dinner guests of the Lord's ability to use our failures and sins to magnify his work in our hearts.

HIS COMMANDMENTS ARE NOT BURDENSOME

Here is a passage from 1 John that illustrates the necessity of grounding all our obedience and counsel in the gospel: "For this is the love of God, that we keep his commandments. And his commandments are not burdensome" (1 John 5:3). Although you might be familiar with this passage, have you ever stopped to really consider it? Have you ever wondered how John could write that God's commandments were "not burdensome"? During times of trial, when faced with a difficult obedience, "burdensome" could definitely be the adjective we choose to describe our struggle to obey.

Honestly, when it comes right down to it, doesn't it sometimes feel like obedience is too much to ask? The cost is too high, our love too weak. We don't love God as we should, so we see his commandments as a burden. Our problem with obedience is that we don't love as intensively as we should.

Even though that is our experience, the theme that love motivates joyous and obedient service is found frequently in Scripture. The story of Jacob and Rachel illustrates it well. You'll recall that Jacob indentured himself as a servant to his uncle, Laban, in order to obtain Rachel, Laban's daughter, for a wife. Why? Because Jacob loved her. And so he worked day in and day out for seven years to earn the right to have her as his wife. Lest we think that this service was easy, here's how he described it later: "By day the heat consumed me, and the cold by night, and my sleep fled from my eyes" (Gen. 31:40). And yet later Jacob remembered his service for her as years that "seemed to him but a few days because of the love he had for her" (Gen. 29:20). Think of that: seven hard years flew by like just a few days. Love is the reason. The years of work he endured were not burdensome. They were years of work, yes, but not burdensome work.

Conversely, Jesus told a story of people who had a very different perspective. In this story, a parable, a landowner hired day laborers for his vineyard at an agreed-upon wage. During the day he brought in others to work, and then, at the end of the day, he doled out their earnings. Those who labored all day and those who labored only for one hour all received an equal wage, the one they had contracted for. "These last worked only one hour," the angry workers complained, "and you have made them equal to us who have *borne the burden of the day and the scorching heat*" (Matt. 20:12).

Although these disgruntled workers received what was rightfully theirs, they were dissatisfied. They had no filial relationship to this landowner; they were day laborers, not sons. They had no concern for the other workers either. They were individuals, not family members. What was work like for them? They complained, "We've borne the burden . . . of the scorching heat." Did the hours fly by because they were glad to serve their master? No, absolutely not. Their labor was grinding; they struggled until that scorching sun finally set so they could get what they earned and get out of there. Their labor was burdensome.

In another familiar parable, we find the eldest son irate because his father had warmly welcomed home the younger brother. Notice how the older brother's obedience is described: "Look, these *many years* I have served[11] you" (Luke 15:29). Obedience was onerous to him because love was lacking. He saw his father as nothing more than a demanding taskmaster, so he was resentful of his father's generosity, mercy, and love. He meticulously tallied up his every hour and act of obedience. Life in this household was only a burden to be borne.

It's easy to see the difference between Jacob and those who were only working for their wages. Jacob's work flowed out of a heart of love. The other workers were in it only for themselves. They had obligations and life was hard; they were just trying to survive another day. There is ease and joy in love-driven obedience, a miserliness and drudgery in duty-driven obedience.

Our Savior's love-driven obedience was envisaged in Psalm 40:8: "I delight to do thy will, O my God" (KJV).[12] Like Jacob before him, Jesus' work to obtain his bride was a delight to him because of the great love he had for her. The One who created the sun languished under its scorching rays and struggled to keep warm when the cold penetrated his cloak at night. The One who multiplied loaves was hungry; he who sustained the universe by his word was tired. He perfectly completed the years of work his Father had given him to do, and his reward was given to others who joined in at the last moment. His inheritance was bestowed upon people, such as us, who had gleefully deserted him and spent their days in riotous living. The payment he earned was granted to proud, self-righteous ones like us, who had disdained him. But he called it all his delight because he loved. He gladly laid down his life for his bride.

We are sure that now, from the perspective of heaven, his days on earth seem but a moment to him because of his love for us. And these difficult years that we are apart from him will seem like nothing more than "one night spent in an inconvenient motel" when our eyes finally rest upon his face.

Do you find obedience a burden or a delight? Is loving your neighbor, whoever that may be, a source of joy or a grinding drudgery? Let us suggest that the obligations of the gospel become a burdensome duty simply because we don't spent enough time remembering what Jesus has already done for us. We have divided the love-inspiring declarations of the gospel from the obligations of the gospel so that obedience is simply a struggle, a discipline, a duty.

BRINGING GOOD NEWS TO ERNEST

Ernest is a conscientious breadwinner, a responsible husband and father, an ever-reliable volunteer in his church—and his family is on the brink of destruction. His wife, Jill, has always found so much to admire in her husband, but now she is at her wits' end as she sees their two adolescent sons, Bruce and Brian, withdrawing in hardened, embittered silence not only toward Ernest but also toward her. At Jill's gentle insistence, Ernest has finally agreed to meet with a counselor, but frankly he does not see what he could possibly have done to avert the increasing alienation and defiance that his ungrateful children are now displaying in their dyed black hair and dour Goth clothing.

After all, Ernest has always been committed to doing the right thing. That was what attracted Jill's admiration in college, almost twenty years ago: his academic and athletic achievements in combination with his leadership in student government and his selfless, strenuous commitment to service in a local church. After graduation Ernest was immediately and eagerly hired by an information technology firm, in which he worked long hours and was recognized through a succession of promotions to greater responsibilities, which also enabled him to provide well for Jill and the boys.

Of course, his intensive work schedule and his commitment to church responsibilities as a deacon, Sunday school teacher, and English as a Second Language tutor left him little time to deepen his relationship with Jill or to engage his sons. But Ernest prided himself on managing stress well and keeping control of his emotions, so he rarely exploded at his wife or sons. Rather, typically, he was able to explain calmly the ways that they had disappointed him—Jill's cooking, primarily, and the boys' indifference to schoolwork and sports—and how he expected them to strive for improvement. He had, after all, carved time out of his schedule to devote well-planned

Saturdays for maturity-building, outdoor activities with his sons, at least on a quarterly basis.

He is both mystified and distressed by their cold response, and annoyed—resentful, in fact—that their all-too-visible rebellion, broadcast in black, is tarnishing his reputation as a husband-technician-Christian father who does all things well. He is also puzzled and, well, angry, that Jill thinks *he* is the one who needs to be involved in this counseling; surely Bruce and Brian are the ones who need "fixing!"

How might a gospel-grounded counselor help Ernest? Although his emotional self-control and strong work ethic mask it, Ernest is, at heart, a Sad Moralist. Further probing may well reveal that Jill and their sons rarely hear anything from him but words that signal criticism and correction, and that the steady stream of discontent streaming from Ernest's mouth springs from a heart that is itself profoundly insecure, deathly fearful of failure in any area of life—or should we say, in any area of *performance*?

Early in life Ernest learned the lesson that self-discipline and hard work reap rewards in recognition and reassurance that he is an acceptable person, a respectable Christian, and a responsible student, employee, and family man. Now he needs a firm and loving counselor to break to him the unwelcome news that his strenuous, apparently successful pursuit of the approval he craves has put him on a collision course with God's preeminent commands. He doesn't love God with all that is in him, nor does he love his closest neighbors—his wife and his sons—as he loves himself. His tireless labors to provide materially for his family have not really been for their sake but for his own. His eager involvement in his church's ministries is likewise an expression of self-love, not an offering of love to a heavenly Father whose love he is reciprocating freely in astonished gratitude.

As Ernest is introduced to the uncomfortable truth that his proud heart falls far short of the love that God demands, we can introduce him to an even more ego-crushing reality: although "God opposes the proud," he also "gives grace to the humble" (James 4:6). Surrendering to grace will require Ernest to abandon his workaholism and his efforts to justify himself as a conscientious breadwinner, which are subtle forms of idolatry, violations of the first commandment, and attempts to compete with the living God, who declares that he alone can save (Isa. 45:22–24) and justify guilty people. Ernest will need to embrace at a depth that he has so far resisted the discovery that he can experience God's approval *only* as he rests wholly in *Jesus' accomplished work*—his flawless obedience and blameless sacrifice.

But if God's Spirit opens Ernest's heart to these truths and shatters his self-made strategies for silencing his uneasy conscience (we counselors cannot reach that deep place in Ernest's heart, but the Spirit can), a process of liberation will begin. Ernest will find the safety in the Father's welcome to set aside his reputation and embrace his sons, despite their sullen defiance. When he has heard Christ answer the Accuser on his behalf once for all, Ernest can begin to staunch the steady stream of critical speech that has been flowing from his mouth toward Jill and Bruce and Brian (and, no doubt, toward others).

He no longer needs to defend himself by finding fault with others to compensate for the faults in himself that he has desperately tried to hide. He can even ask their forgiveness, humbly and sincerely, acknowledging the pain he has inflicted on those he should have loved most. From this point, other changes will need to follow as well. Ernest should reconsider his hectic schedule—both his drivenness on the job and his frenetic volunteerism at church. Facing his finitude frankly, he may well withdraw from worthwhile activities for the sake of rebuilding (or building for the first time) his family on a foundation of God's grace.

Deep-seated patterns will not change overnight, and relapses may occur. But healing by grace will have begun in Ernest's heart, and from that grace-refreshed heart, grace will begin to flow out into his relationships.

OUR TRANSFORMED ATTITUDES

Spending time in the gospel before we spend time in the law will create within us a renewed attitude informed and motivated by love. If the message of the gospel does not inform every thought, word, and deed, our striving to put off and put on will disintegrate into another way to gain the approval of others, ourselves, and even the Lord. The only factor that can keep us from either grinding obedience spawned by self-love or habitual disobedience also spawned by self-love is a different sort of love—the love of Christ for us and our responsive love for him. Like Ernest, we need to have our attitudes transformed.

The gospel tells us that we are deeply sinful people but that we're also deeply loved people. This reality, therefore, is to be the ground upon which all of our subsequent obedience, all of our put-offs and put-ons, must be built. The fact that we are deeply sinful yet forgiven will cause us to love much, as Jesus taught Simon the Pharisee in Luke 7. And nothing teaches us these truths like the gospel.

Remember the gospel again; hear his humble plea in the garden, see his blood-stained brow, hear the whip crack as it tears his back, smell the scent of blood that fills the air as he is hoisted up upon the tree, hear him cry in agony as the wrath you deserve is poured out upon him, and he is forsaken. Then let his words sink deeply into your soul, "It is finished." All that he had come to do, all that you needed him to do, he has done for you. Feel the earth tremble, hear the curtain that separated you from the presence of God tear. Think about that kind of love and welcome, let your heart weep before him, and kiss him in worship as you humble yourself, loving him much. Now, let the love that's overflowing in your heart eventuate in true obedience, put off your old, dead, loveless ways of living, and let the love that has been poured into your heart by the Holy Spirit create true holiness of life.

PURSUING COUNSEL FROM THE CROSS

1) Explain the differences between psychological, biblical, and gospel-centered counseling.

2) Why is it important for people who already know the gospel to remind themselves and others of the gospel, especially when struggling against sin?

3) We seem to naturally militate against revisiting the gospel once we've been saved by it. Why do you think that is?

4) Jacob's service for Rachel seemed easy and light. The elder brother's service for his father was grinding slavery. What was the difference between the two? How are our attitudes transformed?

5) Summarize what you have learned in this chapter in four or five sentences.

CHAPTER SIX

The Gospel and Our Sanctification

And do not be grieved, for the joy of the Lord is your strength.
NEHEMIAH 8:10

WE LIVE AT A TIME in which there are more opportunities for fun and enjoyment than ever before. We have multitudinous options for entertainment and vacations, and many people live as though the whole purpose of life can be summed up in one thought: carefree retirement. Have you noticed that although there seems to be a lot of fun activity, there is very little true joy? We are amusing ourselves to death and coming up empty and joyless every time.

Further, in a strangely convoluted[1] desire to reach the unchurched, many churches have mimicked in their ministries the world's emphases on amusement. Skits, comic sermons, and featherweight vignettes masquerade as truth, while the souls of "seekers" thirst for a drink of living water and wonder if this is really all there is. Boredom is the great evil that must be avoided at all costs even though someone must have asked at least once, "How many 'Top Ten' jokes can one hear without having to stifle a yawn?" We think it would be safe to say that many people who attend this kind of church may be categorized as Happy Moralists.

On the other hand, there is also a vibrant though sober church that can be identified as serious and disdainful of the airier versions of church-lite. This church is truth-driven and assumes that there are serious realities, particularly about sin and obligation, that must be taken to heart and pondered by "the elect." These dear saints would have an unstated fear about too much joy or happiness and might suspect that too much smiling might lead to frivolousness. We think it would be safe to assume that we'd find the Sad Moralist here.

Where Happy Moralists need to grow in their understanding of the depths of God's demands and their utter failure to fulfill them, Sad Moralists are tempted to spend their days in mourning and self-condemnation. Even though each type is very different in religious orientation, the Happy Moralist and the Sad Moralist might be surprised to learn that they are alike in at least one way: *they both have something to learn from the gospel.*

The Happy Moralist needs to see the depths of sacrificial suffering that his cavalier self-righteous sin caused the Lamb. The Sad Moralist needs to see the depths of sacrificial suffering that his sober, self-righteous sin caused the Lamb. Both need to see themselves as sinful and flawed. The Happy Moralist needs to be humbled by a clear view of his laxity and self-love. The Sad Moralist needs to be humbled by the discovery that even his self-righteousness and self-loathing are symptoms of a heart too proud to abandon its self-reliance and surrender to the grace of Christ. And both also need to see themselves as loved and welcomed.

Perhaps the Happy Moralist won't struggle with God's love as the Sad Moralist will, but that is only because he's missed the "sinful-and-flawed" portion of the gospel. He needs to be awed by God's mercy. The Sad Moralist, on the other hand, must see that Christ's righteousness is sufficient and believe that faith is all that he has to offer (and even his faith is given to him). He is missing the "loved-and-welcomed" part of the gospel. He, too, needs to be awed by God's mercy.

There's another facet of the gospel that's missing from both their lives. Neither lives in the joy that is to be their strength. The true joy that is the core of their strength in the war against sin is missing, so the Happy Moralist won't have the impetus to put down the remote and follow hard after God. The Sad Moralist will feel burdened by his sin and estranged from the God who commands joy at his presence. *Rejoice? About what? Is this something else I need to feel guilty about?* he might wonder.

GOSPELIZED SANCTIFICATION

Before we tell you exactly what gospelized sanctification looks like, let's be sure that you understand what we mean when we use the term *sanctification*. Sanctification or being *set apart* is to be made holy or consecrated for God's use. It describes the transformation of the believer into the image of Christ. Wise pastors of a bygone time captured its biblical meaning well when they described it as "the work of God's free grace, whereby we are renewed in the whole man after the image of God, and are enabled more and more to die unto sin, and live unto righteousness."[2]

Sanctification may actually be spoken of in two ways. First, we might say that our sanctification is definitive, that is, already accomplished in time, as Paul does in 1 Corinthians 1:2, where he refers to the church at Corinth as "those sanctified in Christ Jesus, called to be saints" (see also Acts 20:32; 26:18). At the very moment that the Holy Spirit replaces our dead, stony hearts with living hearts of flesh so that we trust in Christ, the Spirit begins to apply to us the liberating effects of Jesus' death and resurrection. Paul therefore tells Christians that we have "died to sin" and that we have been raised in Christ to "walk in newness of life" (Rom. 6:1–4). In other words, when he drew us to trust Jesus, God's Spirit decisively, definitively separated us from sin's tyrannical grip and placed us securely in the Father's holy hands.[3] That's astounding, isn't it?

Second, we might say that sanctification is progressive. *Progressive sanctification* is the term used to define what occurs in us day by day as God transforms us by the work of the Holy Spirit. In progressive sanctification, we become in actuality what he has declared is already true of us. To use common parlance, we are *already* sanctified, but our sanctification is *not yet* perfectly evident in our daily lives. Both the *already* and the *not yet* are true of us.

Although we are still living in the *not yet*, if we are in Christ, we *are* progressing, we *are* changing.

Perhaps the change is as yet minuscule; maybe you don't see it in yourself at all, but you can be sure that if you are his, you *are* being changed. For some, sanctification is painfully slow; for others the process seems to be making a more speedy headway.[4] But however slow our progression seems, we can be sure that we are "being transformed into the same image from one degree of glory to another. For this comes from the Lord who is the Spirit" (2 Cor. 3:18). Although our progress may seem painfully slow (especially if we are Sad Moralists), it too is a guaranteed work of the Holy Spirit in us.

Here's how author and seminary president Bryan Chapell defined progressive sanctification:

> Sanctification is the work of God's grace in us that allows us to receive the benefits and power of Jesus, which in turn enable us to overcome the evil that can so burden our hearts.[5]

As you can see, sanctification is anchored in our union with Christ. It is possible only through the benefits of the gospel. We cannot and will not ever become genuinely godly men and women unless God's grace has enabled us to receive the "benefits and power of Jesus," the only truly holy person who ever lived. Only in union with him will we be able to progressively grow into holiness, "to overcome the evil" that's still part of our "not yet."

Up until this point, most Christians would agree with what we've said. They'd agree that sanctification is both definitive and progressive. That it's both the *already* and the *not yet*. They would agree that sanctification is only possible through our union with Christ and that it is accomplished by a work of God's grace as he transforms us into the image of the Son.

But the question that must arise now is one of method or mode. We are all agreed that we want to grow in godliness and that it's God's plan to grow us in this way, but exactly how does that happen? Are there certain perspectives that we should adopt that will enable us to more fully experience this grace? Are there other perspectives that will tend to make the going slower, more difficult? Here's where gospelized sanctification will change our perspective.

The gospel tells us that Jesus' life has been given for us and to us. His holy desires have been implanted in our hearts. We're one with him through the agency of the Holy Spirit. Meditating on these truths will energize our pursuit of godliness because our belief that we are in union with Christ "is the key to overcoming sin in our lives. . . . When any of us lose sight of our privileged position as a result of our union with Christ, we lose our ability to resist sin."[6]

Our union with Christ should refresh our hearts with joy and strengthen our faith to enable us to fight for holiness. Realizing that he has loved us so much that he has made us one with himself should engender fervent love in our hearts, resulting in fervent obedience.

The truth of the gospel—that we are "in" him—isn't meant only for those who are beginning the Christian life. It is meant for all of us *every day*, whether we've walked with him for a few weeks or many decades. In fact, it's such an important factor about who we are that it was one of Paul's favorite themes. Here are two references from Paul meant to encourage us as we pray that God makes us "worthy of his calling" and that we might fulfill "every resolve for good and every work of faith by his power" (2 Thess. 1:11). Please resist the urge to skim over these passages if you are already familiar with them. They are given here so you will believe that change really is possible.

> I give thanks to my God always for you because of the *grace of God that was given you in Christ Jesus*, that in every way you were *enriched in him* in all speech and all knowledge . . . as you wait for the revealing of our Lord Jesus Christ, who will *sustain you to the end, guiltless* in the day of our Lord Jesus Christ. God is faithful, by whom you were called *into the fellowship of his Son,* Jesus Christ our Lord. (1 Cor. 1:4–6, 8–9)

In him also you were circumcised with a circumcision made without hands, by *putting off the body of the flesh*, by the circumcision of Christ, having been buried with him in baptism, in which *you were also raised with him through faith in the powerful working of God*, who raised him from the dead. And you, who were dead in your trespasses and the uncircumcision of your flesh, *God made alive together with him*, having forgiven us all our trespasses, by canceling the record of debt that stood against us with its legal demands. (Col. 2:11–14)

As you reflect on those passages, can you see how important your union with Christ—with his life, death, resurrection, ascension, and ongoing incarnation—is? This is where what we are calling "gospelized sanctification" differs from other methods of change. Although all true Christians want to grow in godliness, many of us miss the truth that *the gospel is as necessary to our sanctification as it was to our initial justification.* Without the gospel, without drenching our souls in our union with Christ, the quest for moral improvement becomes just that: another quest for self-improvement doomed to futile failure or, worse, arrogant success. But in the light of the gospel, because of all that Jesus has already done, sanctification becomes another sweet evidence of his grace working in us, making us more and more delighted by his abiding presence and less and less enamored with the world's enticements. Only the extravagant love shown us in the gospel has the power to draw us away from other loves. The beauty of his grace makes everything else seem listless by comparison.

DO NOT GRIEVE

During the time of the Jews' exile from the Promised Land, while they were still in bondage under Persian rule, a group of Jews was permitted to return to Israel to rebuild the temple and the walls of the city. For nearly seventy years the nation had been in captivity, excluded from temple worship and the law. They had felt the judgment of God. God's displeasure wasn't some detached topic they studied in a textbook. They had personally experienced his anger at their sin. Many of their family members had been slaughtered. They had been uprooted from their homes, bound as slaves. They had lost their nation. Children had lived their entire lives in a foreign country, never having known their homeland or freedom. They knew what God's judgment tasted like. He had taught them to be sorry for sin. But now, by God's sovereign grace (Ezra 1:1), exiles were being allowed to return to their homeland and rebuild it.

In 515 BC, after quite a struggle the temple was finally rebuilt, and after that the walls around the city were completed. The Levites along with their leaders, Nehemiah and Ezra, gathered the people together to hear the law. When the people heard the law and understood how they had sinned against the Lord, they were grieved. Again, they were people who had been taught by experience how dreadful the consequences of sin are. They were afraid. But because the day was a holy day, a day of dedication to the Lord, the people were warned, "Do not be grieved, for the joy of the LORD is your strength. . . . Be quiet, for this day is holy; do not be grieved" (Neh. 8:10–11).

Although grieving over sin would seem apropos, this wasn't to be a day for sorrow. In fact, grieving on this day would have been sin itself because God is both immanent and holy, and in his presence is "fullness of joy," and at his right hand are "pleasures forevermore" (Ps. 16:11). Grieving at this point would have been an affront to his kindness. It would have impugned his goodness and slandered his love. He was with them; he had restored and forgiven them. Grieving would ignore what he had done and would focus all their attention on what they had done or failed to do. And it would also have drained from the people the very joy they would need if they were to grow in obedience.

MANAGE YOUR SORROW

God commanded his people to corporately mourn over sin only one day a year, on the Day of Atonement (which, in some ways, reminds us of Good Friday). On that day the people were commanded to fast both from food and from work. The high priest would appear before the Lord with the blood of animals and with two goats, one that would be slaughtered and the other to be led out into the wilderness. The people knew that blood was being shed to atone for their sin, and they knew that a goat would be abandoned to wilderness wandering and ultimate death for their iniquity. It was a solemn day of complete rest from labor, reflection on personal sin, sobriety at the necessity of the death of animals in their place, and celebration of God's merciful provision. But it was followed by the Feast of Tabernacles, a weeklong time of fellowship and rejoicing at God's providential supply (Lev. 23:26–43).

Does it surprise you that God commands affliction of soul on only one day annually? If you are a Sad Moralist, it might seem as though a life of self-affliction or mourning defines spirituality. In Matthew 5:4, our Lord promises blessedness—deep happiness—to those who mourn over sin, because the end of that mourning is comfort, not ongoing self-flagellation. Yes, we are to be deeply grieved by our sin, but we must manage our grief well lest it become another form of meritorious work.[7] Godly sorrow for sin is appropriate, but sad moralism and endless self-affliction will never motivate us to live godly lives. No, only joy will strengthen us for the war we must fight against sin.

Sanctification is never advanced by self-focused grief or guilt. It is energized by joy and driven by love.[8] This is the distinction that gospelized sanctification emphasizes. Only a remembrance of the gospel will free us from our habitual grief and guilt. Only the gospel can implant the joy and love in our hearts that will free, motivate, and inspire us.

REJOICE IN THE LORD

The exiles who had returned to rebuild the temple in Jerusalem were to see what that day of remembering the law and rejoicing in God's goodness meant about what kind of God they served. Rather than being swallowed up by our grief or ignoring God's law and living for temporal comforts or amusements, we, along with them, are to know the joy that is "founded on the feeling of communion with the Lord, on the consciousness that we have in the Lord, a God long-suffering and abundant in goodness and truth. . . . This joy is to be to them . . . a strong citadel or refuge, because the Almighty is their God."[9]

Our ongoing rehearsal of the weight of God's law, the depth of our sin, and the generosity of his mercy should produce within us a "feeling of communion" with him, a responsive joy that guards our hearts when either temptation to laxity or temptation to sad moralism calls. We can whisper to our souls: *He's here with me. He loves me. He knows my weakness and failure and yet he's in union with me. Who could imagine such love? It causes me to overflow with joy!*

The knowledge of such long-suffering or abundant goodness would crush us if we didn't know that it was *for us*, sinful and flawed as we are. The realization that his love is never ending is a balm to our souls, bringing the joy, comfort, and assurance that is our very lifeblood as we fight for holiness. When we face the uphill battle to grow in our sanctification, we must remember that we are sinful and flawed, but we are loved and welcomed. There is great joy in realizing that even though our sin is much deeper than we'll ever grasp, God sees every bit of it and yet loves us.

Nehemiah writes that joy functions as a strong citadel or refuge for us. When we are tempted to give in to despair, to give up to self-indulgence or apathy, we have a place of refuge that will protect us from the attacks of a battered conscience. When we read the Word or hear a strong sermon that convicts our hearts, our conscience is apt to begin its attack on our souls. "Who can stand before his indignation? Who can endure the heat of his anger?" (Nah. 1:6). We are convicted of sin, we mourn over and confess our sin, and yet conscience doesn't give up. It continues to beat us. "You're not properly sorry. You're such a disappointment. God is ashamed of you and angry."

How are we to fight against the accusations of our conscience? How can we silence conscience's condemning voice? We take refuge *from* God *in* God. We quiet our conscience by remembering, "The Lord is good, a stronghold in the day of trouble; he knows those who take refuge in him" (Nah. 1:7). We send the law (as means of obtaining God's favor) away, as Martin Luther wisely counsels us: "Send Moses away, with his law, to those who are complacent, proud and obstinate and in these terrors and this anguish lay hold upon Christ, who was crucified and died for our sins."[10]

We remember that the gospel tells us that we don't have any weapons of our own. We have no righteousness, no strength, and no faith to protect us from God's just indignation. We are sinful and flawed. And yet, we don't have to protect ourselves from a holy God because he knows our sin and yet has poured all of his indignation on his Son and has clothed us in his righteousness. He not only knows of our sin because he knows everything, but his perfect Son also knows our sin because "for our sake he made *him to be sin* who knew no sin, so that in him we might become the righteousness of God" (2 Cor. 5:21). Think of that! We've got the righteousness of God!

When our conscience won't quiet down as it should, when we've taken ourselves over and over to Calvary in repentance, we've got to declare to our self-condemning hearts, "My righteousness isn't made up of my repentance, my good record, or even my faith. No, I've got the righteousness of God. If that's not enough for you, you proud, demanding conscience, nothing will be! Now, silence yourself before the love of this great God. Rather than spend time thinking about your demands, I now choose to rejoice in all God's done for me."

Our enemy, Satan, wants to point out our sin so that we will curse God "to his face" (Job 1:11). He wants to strip our confidence from us and make us go through life mourning, sad, self-focused, and self-condemning. He wants to make God seem unjust, angry, demanding, and hateful in our eyes. The Devil hates joy. He has never tasted true happiness. Joy at what our Savior has done infuriates him, so he accuses us "day and night" (Rev. 12:10).

How can we respond to his accusations? We can respond by the "blood of the Lamb" and the "word of [our] testimony" (Rev. 12:11). When he viciously attacks, what shall we say? "Yes, it's true that I am a worthless sinner, but I've been given the righteousness of God by the blood of the Lamb. My only testimony is that I'm completely loved even though I don't deserve it. Therefore I will rejoice because you have been thrown down and have no right to remind me of something that God no longer remembers! My Savior is worth praising and I will praise him now. You have reminded me to do this!"

The joy that this good news brings will keep us safe. It is a strong fortress; it is meant to protect us as we rest securely as God "quiets us by his love" (Zeph. 3:17). Sorrow for sin is good, as far as it goes, but it will not protect us from our conscience or from our adversary's cruel attack. Hear these words from Nehemiah again: "Do not be grieved, for the joy of the LORD is your strength" (Neh. 8:10). Do not be afraid that freedom from grief will make you lax. We are in union with Jesus Christ; all that he has is ours. He will carefully watch over our souls, convicting us and comforting us as he deems best. We do not need to take on his work of making ourselves righteous but, rather, we can rejoice in what he has already done.

"A joyful heart is good medicine, but a crushed spirit dries up the bones" (Prov. 17:22). The gospel makes us strong and spiritually healthy. The Great Physician has diagnosed our problem as being worse than we would ever dare to imagine, but he has also supplied all the medicine we need. The gospel is "good" medicine for our souls. It makes us strong and joyful. We have been loved and welcomed. Our utter dependence on him and our joy in the realization of how needy we are cures us of our sinful pride and makes our souls healthy.

THE RIGHTEOUS SHALL LIVE BY FAITH

Many Christians know that the Reformation was born, at least in part, because the Holy Spirit had illumined Martin Luther's heart to understand the verse "The righteous shall live by faith" (Rom. 1:17; Gal. 3:11, both quoting Hab. 2:4). As a conscientious Augustinian monk, Luther, the quintessential Sad Moralist, was radically transformed by the realization that "no one is justified before God by the law" (Gal. 3:11), but rather that the righteousness that pleases God is the perfect obedience of Christ, received through faith alone as a free, unearned gift by those who live by faith in God's Son and God's promises. It's axiomatic that we begin our Christianity by faith in the righteousness that he supplies through Jesus Christ. What most of us miss is that we progress in our sanctification the same way.

What is the faith that we need to hang on to as we seek to grow in godliness? That Jesus Christ has fulfilled every point of the law, that he also suffered torment as a lawbreaker on Calvary, that his Father poured out every drop of his righteous wrath on him, and that the resurrection declares the Father's approval of Christ's complete righteousness—divine approval in which we now share by the gift of his grace. We must believe (and continue to "beat it into our heads daily," as Luther once said) that God is perfectly satisfied in Christ's sacrifice for us, that we have obtained full adoption, and that God is pleased with us and calls us his "beloved." These truths will stimulate joy and expand our faith.

> So then, there remains a Sabbath rest for the people of God, for whoever has entered God's rest has also rested from his works as God did from his. Let us therefore *strive to enter that rest.* (Heb. 4:9–11)

The striving that will command our energy is a striving to enter into rest, a striving to live "by faith in the Son of God, who loved . . . and gave himself" for us (Gal. 2:20). Most of us think that our efforts should be focused solely on godly living. While this is partly true, it's not the whole story. We've also got to focus our efforts on "striving" to *enter into the rest* he has provided for us. If our souls are not fully resting in his love and welcome we won't have the energy we need to fight for godliness. Christianity will be utterly exhausting. This rest of soul is found only in the gospel message: we are sinful and flawed, yet loved and welcomed.

THE ROLE OF THE LAW IN OUR SANCTIFICATION

If we live by faith in Jesus Christ rather than by faith in ourselves and our works, we'll know the joy that protects us from accusation and we'll live in the love that will constrain true obedience. Since we no longer view the law as the means to obtain righteousness, since it no longer has the power to either harm or threaten us, we may now use it as it's meant to be used. *We will be free to delight in the law because we are freed from the power of the law to curse us.*

All of the wonderful obligations of the law will then help us on our way toward godly living and sanctification. Since we cannot be made any more perfect in God's eyes than we already are, we are now free to make the law serve us. It will serve us by making us more thankful for Christ when we see how we fail to obey it, and it will serve us by showing us how to love God and our neighbor as we long to. Rather than viewing the law as our enemy, we'll learn to say along with our Savior, "I delight to do your will, O my God; your law is within my heart" (Ps. 40:8). From this position of security and rest in God, the psalmist wrote:

> The law of the LORD is perfect,
>   reviving the soul;
> the testimony of the LORD is sure,
>   making wise the simple;
> the precepts of the LORD are right,
>   rejoicing the heart;
> the commandment of the LORD is pure,
>   enlightening the eyes;
> the fear of the LORD is clean,
>   enduring forever;
> the rules of the LORD are true,
>   and righteous altogether.
> More to be desired are they than gold,
>   even much fine gold;

sweeter also than honey
and drippings of the honeycomb.
Moreover, by them is your servant warned;
in keeping them there is great reward. (Ps. 19:7–11)

When the law is kept where it belongs—as a means to draw us to Christ and to show us how to love—it is delightful and causes us to rejoice. When it goes beyond this and attacks our conscience, we must silence its threatenings by remembering the gospel and putting the law back in its place. The law is a light on our path, but it is not *the* path, and it cannot impel us toward holiness nor make us love God.

SAD PASTOR JACK

Although Jack wasn't raised in a believing home, he has loved God from his earliest teen years. A serious and bright student, Jack quickly came to realize that he was called to serve as a pastor. It was to this end that he went to college and seminary. Upon graduation and marriage, Jack landed in full-time ministry, but over time he grew discouraged; he understood deep truth but found himself unable to live out that truth, and that is still where Jack finds himself today.

He is frequently snappish and judgmental with his wife and people in the church office. He continually feels bad about his behavior and tries to control himself, but even when he is able to avoid outbursts, he still fumes inwardly. When he reads (or preaches on) passages about how we are to love one another, the law enslaves, crushes, and terrifies him. He feels guilty, and his guilt causes his anger and faultfinding to grow.

The guiltier he feels about his lack of love, the more unloving he becomes. He labors to become more loving and patient, to punctiliously fulfill the law, but still his anger and self-condemnation crowd out all his good intentions. If you ask Jack how he would characterize his faith, he could tell you all about justification by faith and progressive sanctification. He knows all the right answers, but he has forgotten the gospel.

Some time ago, during a particularly stressful situation, Jack was overcome by feelings of self-condemnation and worthlessness. He no longer had the ability to handle all the problems in the church while trying to suppress or answer his feelings of self-loathing. He didn't have the energy to get up and preach, and his hands shook continually. Observing this, the deacon board decided that Jack was depressed and in need of a leave of absence.

One thing led to another, and soon Jack found himself in a residential treatment center for the severely depressed. Once the therapists at the center had time to get to know him, they concluded that he wasn't deeply depressed, so they put him on medication and released him.

What does Jack need? Does he need medicine? Does he need someone to tell him that the church abused him? Does he need to learn to love himself so that he can love his neighbor? No, of course not. Okay then, but does he need to simply put off anger and put on kindness? Yes, he needs to do this, but not before he has soaked himself in the truth about *what Jesus Christ has already done on his behalf.* He needs to refocus his mind continually on the truth that God loved him and sent his Son to be the propitiation for his sin. Until he does that, until the joy of the Lord becomes his strength, the biblical mandate to love his neighbor will be just as out of reach as it always has been, and just as condemning to his already guilt-ridden conscience.

Jack's life is changing now because he has committed himself to constant fellowship with other pastors who are mentoring and counseling him to see himself in the light of the gospel. They are reminding him of his true identity. Jack is a sinner, but he is also loved immeasurably. Being with other brothers who both confess their sins and lovingly confront his anger and faultfinding is helping Jack to avoid his old habitual self-condemnation. He is learning to encourage himself with words of grace from the gospel. Because he is beginning to realize that he is irrevocably loved and welcomed, his slavery to the law has no more power to condemn or terrorize.

His friends are teaching him to see that the hours he spends in self-recrimination are not only wrong but also futile. Sadness won't impel obedience; only love and joy can do that. Like the Israelites who were commanded to afflict their souls only one day and then rejoice for a week, for every one day Jack spends looking at his sin and failures, he is to spend a week rejoicing in God's mercy and provision. Although the thoughts of God's love for him used to make him only more ashamed and guilty, now God's love for him serves to bolster his joy.

Jack is now battling on another front too: he is battling the self-condemnation that he feels because he doesn't have as much joy as he thinks he should have. When he starts down that well-worn path to despair, he will need to remind himself, "Of course I don't have joy. I'm sinful and flawed. But I won't get joy by looking at myself. Instead, I'll think about how I've been loved and welcomed in Christ. I'll direct my thoughts away from myself and onto my Savior. If it pleases him, he'll fill me with joy. If it doesn't, that's okay because my righteousness doesn't depend on me anyway. I'm going to praise him instead of thinking about myself."

As he is "renewed in the spirit" of his mind (Eph. 4:23), Jack is beginning to put off his old way of life. His hypercritical judgment of others and of himself is being replaced by a willingness to admit his sin and be patient with others. He sees more clearly that he and they are equally sinful and flawed, yet equally loved and welcomed. He is also seeing himself and his Savior in an entirely new light. He is drinking in great draughts of mercy and dispensing it to others and to himself. The joy of his salvation is gradually growing and shoving aside all his anger, self-condemnation, and self-righteousness, and he is becoming a joyful, merciful, free man.

LOOKING TO JESUS

In one sense, we are all just like Jack. We all long to approve of ourselves and want to use the law (either God's law or our own standards) as the way to do that. Then, when our inconsistencies become so glaring that we can no longer avoid them, we slip into some form of self-indulgence. Like Jack, we could fall into faultfinding, self-righteousness, and its eventual self-loathing, or we could just become apathetic and decide to spend more time pampering ourselves in some way.

We are all sinful and flawed. The only answer to our slavery both to sin and the law is our Savior. The writer of Hebrews encouraged his readers to lay aside their sin by "looking to Jesus, the founder and perfecter of our faith, who for the *joy* that was set before him endured the cross, despising the shame, and is seated at the right hand of the throne of God" (Heb. 12:2).

Although Jesus Christ was perfect and perfectly loved doing his Father's will, joy was a factor in his obedience. He was looking ahead—past the cross, past the shame, past the suffering—to the joy. What was his joy? Simply this: that he would be seated at the right hand of the throne of God, clothed in flesh, *presenting his bride* to his Father. He found his joy in his bride. *You are his joy.* He suffered so that he might bring you the joy of knowing his love and welcome, and he prayed that his joy might be in you and that your joy might be full (John 15:11).

We all want to grow in godliness. We all want to obey the law and know that our lives are glorifying to our Lord. We won't get there by looking solely at the law and then hoping that our sorrow will motivate us to change. No, Nehemiah's words are just as apropos for us today as they were when Jerusalem was rebuilt: "Do not be grieved, for the joy of the LORD is your strength" (Neh. 8:10).

PURSUING COUNSEL FROM THE CROSS

1) Luke 2:10–12 reads, "And the angel said to them, 'Fear not, for behold, I bring you good news of great joy that will be for all the people. For unto you is born this day in the city of David a Savior, who is Christ the Lord. And this will be a sign for you: you will find a baby wrapped in swaddling cloths and lying in a manger.'" Why is this Savior described as a "great joy"? How does the baby in the manger create joy in your heart? Why did the Spirit have Luke record the nativity scene in just this way?

2) What words would you use to describe your Christian walk? Would *joy* be among them? Why or why not?

3) John 17:13 (part of Jesus' prayer) reads, "But now I am coming to you, and these things I speak in the world, that they may have my joy fulfilled in themselves." Why did Jesus pray about your joy?

4) When you recognize sin in your life, how do you motivate yourself to change? After reading this chapter, how do you think you should motivate yourself?

5) Would you say that you are a Happy Moralist or a Sad Moralist? What does a Happy Moralist need to see? What does a Sad Moralist need? How are they alike or different?

6) Summarize what you have learned in this chapter in four or five sentences.

CHAPTER SEVEN

The Gospel and Our Emotions

Consider him who endured from sinners such hostility against
himself, so that you may not grow weary or fainthearted.
HEBREWS 12:3

PURITAN RICHARD BAXTER ONCE WROTE, "If God would not give me a heart to love him, I would I never had a heart."[1] Obviously, Baxter was not hoping for a new physical heart, he was hoping that his appraisal of God would enliven his emotions to such an extent that his desires, thoughts, choices, words, and actions would reflect what he knew to be true about God. He believed that life without this Godward passion would not be worth living. He also believed that his feelings were to be used in service of his Lord.

In this chapter, we are going to take a look at what has become one of the most controversial areas of counseling, that of our emotions.[2] Our emotions are a good gift from God for us. They enliven and color our daily lives and empower us to accomplish great good. Even uncomfortable emotions such as sorrow, anger, or fear can be of great value to us as we use the pain they cause to effect change in our lives.

ALL THAT MATTERS IS MATTER

Although counselors have always been concerned with emotions, disagreements about the *source* of our uncomfortable feelings have recently become more marked. Over the past few decades, Western science and medicine have been captivated by the theory that all emotions, both pleasant and painful, are caused by the levels of certain chemicals in the brain, most notably serotonin. The theory is that when serotonin levels are out of balance, uncomfortable feelings such as depression, anger, and anxiety result.

This belief is based on a very specific theory of human nature. The theory is this: there is nothing immaterial about human beings. All that matters is "matter," the stuff we are made up of. There is nothing invisible or unverifiable about us. This theory is called *materialistic determinism.* Just as the name sounds, this theory states that what we are, every decision we make, and how we live our lives have been predetermined by the material part of us, most notably the levels of certain chemicals in our brains. These chemicals then determine the choices we make, how we feel, what we'll become. There is no inner person to bother with; we are simply a complex bag of chemical reactions. The materialistic determinist doesn't believe in what the Bible calls our heart, soul, mind, or will.

Belief in this theory has consequences, not the least of which is the removal of personal responsibility for the choices that we make. After all, if who we are (and will be) is predetermined by our brain chemistry, then we aren't responsible for our actions, whether good or bad.[3]

Another consequence of materialistic determinism is the belief that altering the levels of certain chemicals in the brain is the proper way to create emotional health. And so, whereas in the past, a person who was sad or anxious might have tried to discover the source of his emotional pain, might have gotten in touch with his "inner child," might have sought some sort of therapy, he now takes a pill. After all, if our emotions are only a by-product of the chemicals in our brains, then why not adjust the chemicals? Again, the theory that all we are is what can be seen, scientifically tested and verified, has eventuated in a generation of people who believe that the answer to their troubling emotions will be found in medicine.[4]

YOU ARE A BODY *AND* A SOUL

On the other hand, the Bible presents us as responsible beings comprised of both an outer person, which includes the brain, and an inner person, which includes the heart, soul, mind, or will. We have both a brain (part of the outer body) and a mind, will, heart, or soul (part of the inner person). The Christian believes that although his outer person is important, his inner person is where the real action is. The Bible teaches that it is in his inner, hidden person that he:

- *Thinks and reasons.* "Now some of the scribes were sitting there, questioning in their hearts" (Mark 2:5–6); "When Jesus perceived their thoughts, he answered them, 'Why do you question in your hearts?'" (Luke 5:22); "Now set your mind and heart to seek the LORD your God" (1 Chron. 22:19); "The inward mind and heart of a man are deep!" (Ps. 64:6).

- *Emotes.* "Be not quick in your spirit to become angry, for anger lodges in the bosom of fools" (Eccl. 7:9); "Though an army encamp against me, my heart shall not fear" (Ps. 27:3); "You shall love the LORD your God with all your heart and with all your soul and with all your might" (Deut. 6:5); "Say to those who have an anxious heart, 'Be strong; fear not'" (Isa. 35:4).

- *Chooses or wills.* "I have chosen the way of faithfulness. . . . I will run in the way of your commandments when you enlarge my heart!" (Ps. 119:30, 32); "Who is the man who fears the LORD? Him will he instruct in the way that he should choose" (Ps. 25:12); "If they repent with all their mind and with all their heart . . ." (2 Chron. 6:38).

7.1: INNER AND OUTER MAN

INNER MAN	OUTER MAN
The heart, soul, or mind	The body, including the brain,
• thinks	responds to and mediates the
• reasons	thoughts, intentions, and emotions
• emotes	of the inner person.

WHAT ARE OUR EMOTIONS?

As we stated above, we think, emote, and choose in our inner person, in the immaterial or invisible part of us. These thoughts, emotions, and determinations are then mediated and interpreted by the brain and experienced in our physical body. What we experience as feelings or moods are a *physiological response to the thoughts, emotions, and judgments of our inner person* (mind and heart).

If our mind, our inner person, is musing on something pleasant, we'll experience pleasant feelings. For instance, if we are pondering God's great love for us in Christ, our brain will respond to these thoughts, emotions, and judgments through specific neural pathways and will release certain chemicals, which are measurable, that will eventuate instantaneously in our having a sense of well-being or happiness. If, on the other hand, the thoughts of our mind are anxious and fearful, our brain will also respond to them through specific neural pathways and with certain chemicals. We then experience fear in our body that shows as sweaty palms, rapid heartbeat, and increased energy.

The brain does not create these feelings. It simply mediates and interprets the thoughts and intentions of the heart, the inner man, to the rest of the body, the outer man. This is why we are told to think in a specific way—so that our feelings will be changed: "Consider him who endured from sinners such hostility against himself, so that you may not grow weary or fainthearted" (Heb. 12:3).

The writer of Hebrews enjoins us to "consider" or contemplate the life and death of Jesus Christ. We are told to meditate on him so that we will experience the zeal and emotional and physical strength we need to persevere, so that we don't grow "weary" or "fainthearted." In this passage we learn not only that our thoughts should linger on the gospel, but also that doing so will change our attitude and mood. Both our outer and inner person are transformed by what we meditate on or contemplate, as Paul taught: "We all, with unveiled face, beholding the glory of the Lord, are being transformed" (2 Cor. 3:18).

Along the same line, in Romans 12:1–2 we are told to consider the "mercies of God," so that we will have the desire and strength to offer our bodies as living sacrifices to him. Contemplating God's mercy will renew our minds and subsequently transform our lives. We are "transformed by the renewal of [our] mind." The outward transformation of our feelings and actions is accomplished through the inner transformation of our mind.

7.2: MIND-BRAIN-BODY CONNECTION

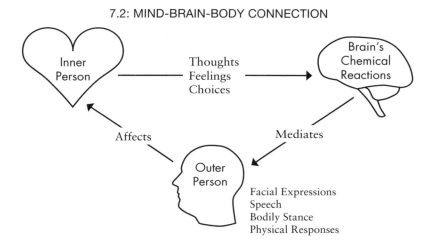

WE ARE BODY AND SOUL

Sometimes our feelings are a result of a combination of physical problems (or our interpretation of them) and our inner person. For instance, certain medications for the heart can cause us to feel down or depressed. This is because these medicines make our bodies feel as they do when we are depressed. We feel listless and slow, and we don't have energy. We feel like our brains are stuffed with cotton. We begin to wonder if something isn't really wrong with us, and then we determine that we must be depressed. The mind sends these signals to the brain, and the body responds, making us feel even more down. That isn't to say that the original feelings of listlessness and apathy aren't real—they are. But there is another factor at work here: our interpretation of our physiological state. This interpretation will intensify our feeling of depression. It is extremely difficult for our inner man to fight against the perception that feeling depressed must mean that we are, in fact, depressed.

If, on the other hand, we have been experiencing a rapid heartbeat, we are probably going to be filled with some anxiety about what this might mean. And then, of course, our anxious thoughts will be interpreted by the brain to mean that we are facing danger of some sort, and it will respond by ordering the release of certain chemicals and hormones (most notably adrenaline), which will make us feel even more anxious and will further increase our heart rate. It's easy to see how our interpretation of our body's condition exacerbates our already uncomfortable feelings and physiological abnormalities.

Our outer man also influences the thoughts of the inner man when we are ill or don't care for our bodies as we should. If we are in constant pain, or if we don't sleep or eat well, then it will be very difficult for our inner person to respond faithfully. Our inner person is very obviously influenced by lack of sleep or starvation.

In addition, the hormonal fluctuations that women experience every month and at pregnancy and menopause cause physiological changes such as bloating, cramping, nervousness, and hot flashes, which make them feel uncomfortable. These very uncomfortable physical symptoms may be interpreted by the inner person as mysterious, unfair, or endless, and the brain will respond by releasing chemicals that will exacerbate the situation.

Certain chemicals such as caffeine, sugar, and alcohol can effect a change in our bodies. Almost everyone is happier after they have drunk a caramel macchiato or a glass of merlot. The inner person interprets these feelings of energy or well-being, speaks to the brain to remember how they happened, and perpetuates the experience through its interpretation of it. Of course, a person who is addicted to caffeine and sugar will experience other (negative) physical symptoms and resultant emotional feelings when these chemicals are withheld.

In *very rare* instances, such as in the case of hyperthyroidism[5] and Cushing's syndrome, the body can cause the brain to malfunction, leading to feelings and perceptions that don't correspond to thoughts, circumstances, or physiological factors. When a person experiences moods that don't correspond to their circumstance, it is always a good idea to have a physician test for these diseases and others like them.

As you can see, the body, including the brain, and the inner person (or the mind) communicate instantaneously and seamlessly. How we feel physically does influence how we think and vice versa. We are an integrated whole with both an inner and outer person that instantaneously responds to and interprets data from each area, even though we are not usually aware that we are doing it.[6]

In fact, even though we know that we have an inner and outer man, we are never fully conscious of the activity of our inner person, as the Bible tells us in Jeremiah 17:9: "The heart is deceitful above all things, and desperately sick; who can understand it?" One of the psalmists vividly expresses bewilderment over his own inner distress: "Why are you cast down, O my soul, and why are you in turmoil within me?" (Pss. 42:5, 11; 43:5). Of course, we can know something about what our inner person is doing when we examine our emotional life, which leads us to our next discussion.

WHAT DO OUR FEELINGS SAY?

Generally speaking, our feelings tell us what's going on in the hidden person of the heart. It is for this reason that listening to them instead of silencing them is usually very important. Since the heart is unknowable by us and yet so important in our relationship with God, our feelings help us discover what it is that we love, what we long for, and what we are meditating on.

We can remember times as children when we played war games and had to spy out what our enemy was doing. Of course, we could have just stuck our heads around the corner to see where our enemy was hiding, but doing so made us liable to a blast from a Nerf dart or a paint ball. So, as kids we devised primitive periscopes—elongated boxes with mirrors attached so that we could peer around corners safely. In the same way, we have to get to the activity of our hearts by using the mirrors God has given us.

Our feelings are one of the mirrors of our hearts.[7] They reveal to us our hidden inner person. For instance, when we find ourselves feeling anxious, that feeling tells us that something we treasure is being threatened. Our Savior pinpointed our problem with anxiety:

> Do not lay up for yourselves treasures on earth, where moth and rust destroy and where thieves break in and steal, but lay up for yourselves treasures in heaven, where neither moth nor rust destroys and where thieves do not break in and steal. For where your treasure is, there your heart will be also. . . . Therefore I tell you, do not be anxious about your life, what you will eat or what you will drink. (Matt. 6:19–21, 25)

When we feel anxious, we can ask ourselves questions such as, "What am I afraid of losing?" or "What am I afraid I'll never get?" Jesus, the Heart-Knower, tells us that our inner person is wed to our treasure: "Where your treasure is, there your heart will be also." If our treasure is something that can be lost either through "natural" disasters (moths), the wearing of time (rust), or the actions of others (thieves), we'll worry and be anxious. Our anxiety will be a mirror to our heart. We are worrying because we have treasure that is vulnerable and open to loss, and the discomfort of our anxiety tells us that.

At such times our anxiety, although uncomfortable, is a gift. It's a signpost telling us that something is amiss with our hearts. We are not loving the Lord as we should—which is to say, we have lost sight of his supreme loveliness and forgotten that in his presence *only* is fullness of joy (Ps. 16:11). We have other gods. Perhaps we treasure respect or a good reputation. Perhaps we fear that we won't be successful or loved as we want to be. There can be as many treasures in our hearts as there are desires. When left unchallenged, these treasures will breed anxieties that weigh our hearts down and lead to self-indulgence (Luke 21:34). The discomfort of our anxiety is a good. It helps us peek around a corner and get a glimpse into the inner recesses of our heart.

Our Savior, the one who loves and welcomes us, tells us where our treasure should be: with his kingdom and his righteousness (Matt. 6:33). If our treasure is in living our lives for him and in leaving our success and security to his providential care, and if our treasure is his righteousness, not ours, then we will be able to appreciate all the good things he bestows without succumbing to worry. On the other hand, when we find ourselves plagued by anxieties, we have to conclude that his kingdom and his righteousness are not the chief delight of our heart.

When we feel anxious, we are to remind ourselves of the gospel. Because of the ongoing incarnation, we can rest assured that the One who bore and continues to bear our flesh is providentially watching over us. Because of his sinless life, we can stop worrying about our reputation or trying to make ourselves look good in the eyes of others. We are sinful and flawed but loved and welcomed. We have been counted righteous.

Because of the crucifixion, every debt that we owe to God's justice for our failure to honor, love, and obey him and the people he has put in our lives has been paid in full. We are absolutely forgiven from top to bottom. Because of the resurrection we can rejoice that his new life is flowing in us. We don't have to try to establish our own identity. Christ is our life. And because he has ascended, we can trust that our heavenly Father looks on us with favor.

Whatever comes into our lives comes through his loving hands to us because we are his children, not illegitimate interlopers. Considering Jesus Christ and the gospel answers all our anxiety and produces feelings of peace and well-being. Our experience of anxiety is a good gift when it forces our eyes away from our false treasures and onto our true treasure, Jesus Christ.

DEPRESSION: AN OPPORTUNITY IN DISGUISE

In like manner, if we find ourselves habitually feeling depressed, and we have ruled out any of the mitigating circumstances we mentioned above, we can use our depression as a mirror to investigate the hidden corners of our hearts. Because Scripture tells us that "hope deferred makes the heart sick" (Prov. 13:12), we can begin by asking ourselves, what hope has been so crushed that we have become hopeless?

We all know what it's like to want something and then to have that desire unmet. Depression sets in when this has happened so often, or when our desire for it is so strong and its satisfaction seems impossible, that we simply give up hoping that we'll ever obtain it. When we determine that our goal is completely unreachable no matter what we do, our hope is crushed and we become depressed. That's why it is hard for people who have been habitually depressed to even remember what it was like to have hope. They have sunk so far into the dungeon of despair that if you ask them what they think they want or wanted, they won't be able to tell you. They have shut down because they believe it's no longer any use trying. And they have shut down for so long that they can't remember what trying even feels like, and they are afraid to allow themselves to try again.

Although depression is very painful, it too is a mirror of our inner person. It's a painful opportunity that tells us what we value, what we think would make us happy. As with the rest of us, the depressed person needs the gospel. Like Pastor Jack in our last chapter, the depressed person needs to see himself as he really is. Pastor Jack was locked in the grip of both the desire to approve of himself and the desire that others would approve of him. When circumstances in his church escalated to the point that he was unable to keep everything in control while suppressing his feelings of self-loathing and worthlessness, he fell into depression, confusion, and hopelessness.[8] Jack thought his depression was telling him that he was a loser, when actually it was telling him he had set his heart on a faulty treasure. It was also telling him that he had forgotten the gospel. Jack needed the good news again.

PRECIOUS MIRRORS

Please don't misunderstand what we are saying here. We are not cavalierly saying that painful emotions are pleasant. We know (by experience) that they aren't. But just as chemotherapy makes us feel terrible for a time, while it destroys the cancer that will destroy us if left untreated, our painful emotions are a necessary remedy for our souls. They function as an incessant reminder that we have heart trouble. No one enjoys a round of chemotherapy. Initially no one likes feeling depressed, anxious, angry, or fearful.[9] But God has given these emotions to us to help us.

Because our hearts are so desperately wicked and because we are so easily hardened by sin's deceitfulness (Heb. 3:13), we need to learn to see our emotions as precious mirrors into our hearts. Without the prodding of our pain to force us to ask difficult questions, we would blithely skip through life without a second thought about the things we treasure and live for. Without our feelings shining the light on our hidden inner person, we wouldn't know that we have treasures that are in competition with God's place in our lives.

Take anger, for example. Although we profess to believe that God is good, wise, and powerful, our anger frequently tells us that we believe something else. When a rude driver cuts us off on the freeway and we become angry, the true beliefs of our inner person are made evident. Do we really believe that a good God means for us to be stuck behind this smoke-spewing truck? Why should this inconsiderate driver be blessed with an open road? Do we believe that a wise God has decreed that we arrive a few moments late to our destination? What would be wise about that? Although we confess that we believe in God's sovereignty, do we humbly acknowledge that God's will for us at this moment is to be trapped behind this inconsiderate driver?

If we get angry at such things, our feelings of anger are a billboard on the side of the road that reads, "You say you believe, but right now you don't! Look at your heart! You are envying the prosperity of others! You're forgetting the Savior who trudged up Calvary's road for you!"

We are not the only ones who have ever struggled this way. Consider this paraphrased testimony of the psalmist: "I almost

COUNSEL FROM THE CROSS

stumbled when I envied the prosperity of the wicked . . . but when I entered your sanctuary I discovered their coming destruction" (Ps. 73:2–3); and (better yet!), "I am continually with you; you hold my right hand. . . . There is nothing on earth that I desire besides you. My flesh and my heart may fail, but God is the strength of my heart and my portion forever" (Ps. 73:23–26).

CHANGING OUR FEELINGS BY RENEWING OUR MINDS

Since our feelings are a by-product of our inner person, we won't be able to change them directly. There is just no sense in telling ourselves to be happy when we feel sad, or to love when all we feel is disgust. The only way that we can change our feelings is by changing our core beliefs and the thoughts that occupy our minds. As we learned earlier, we need to be "transformed by the renewal of our mind" (Rom. 12:2).

We need to learn and then continually remind ourselves of the truth about God himself, what he says about who he is. As we stated before, he declares that he is:

> The LORD, the LORD, a God merciful and gracious, slow to anger, and abounding in steadfast love and faithfulness, keeping steadfast love for thousands, forgiving iniquity and transgression and sin, but who will by no means clear the guilty, visiting the iniquity of the fathers on the children and the children's children, to the third and the fourth generation. (Ex. 34:6–7)

When we are stuck behind a smoke-generating heap and we feel our blood begin to boil, we can remind ourselves about who God is. He is merciful and gracious, slow to anger. We must think: he has been merciful and gracious with us personally. Thankfully, he has also been slow to anger with us. He is not sitting in heaven fuming because we are so slow to believe or change. He abounds in steadfast, unchanging love for us, and he is completely faithful to his promise to continue to love and forgive, no matter how quickly we cut him off, no matter how blind we are to our sin. Our anger does help us know that we need to repent, but we never repent fully of all our sin, because we don't know the deep secrets of our own hearts. Yet still he loves us, pardoning our transgressions and sins. He doesn't do this because he thinks that sin is no big deal. No, he punishes all sin. We can be thankful that the punishment for our sin has already been poured out on his Son.

When we choose to think these thoughts, to renew our minds with the truth, then we will usually experience a change in our mood. Of course, there are times when we have to wrestle with our hearts and continue to pound away at our unbelief before our feelings change, but our feelings will eventually respond. When David had fallen into the hands of the Philistines, he fought fear by repeatedly speaking words of truth to himself:

> When I am afraid,
>> I put my trust in you.
> In God, whose word I praise,
>> in God I trust; I shall not be afraid.
>> What can flesh do to me?
>
> . . . .
>
> In God, whose word I praise,
>> in the LORD, whose word I praise,
> in God I trust; I shall not be afraid.
>> What can man do to me? (Ps. 56:3–4, 10–11)

David was in a difficult circumstance, and his feelings weren't helping. He was facing trouble and knew that he had to encourage his inner man so that he could stand in the face of his adversity. Look at the way he spoke to himself: "When I am afraid, I put my trust in you." On this occasion he didn't allow his feelings to overcome his faith, but his heart did tremble. He was afraid, so he told himself to trust. Trusting in God's character was the answer to his fear. He reminded himself of all that God had done for him and declared, "This I know, that God is for me" (Ps. 56:9).[10]

David did well on that occasion, but he didn't always respond to his feelings with words of faith.[11] Only one Person has ever done that, our blessed Savior who prayed in the garden in unimaginable grief and torment, "Nevertheless, not my will, but yours, be done" (Luke 22:42).

RENEWING OUR MIND WITH TRUTH
ABOUT OURSELVES

Paul's prescription for fear and anxiety begins with a repeated command to rejoice *in the Lord* (Phil. 4:4–6). Rejoicing in the Lord is a very specific command that we are to find our grounding, our joy, in a recollection of Christ and his grace. Paul's remedy for anxiety is the offering of prayer *with thanksgiving*, and he promises the protection of God's peace surrounding our hearts like a military garrison (as the Greek verb rendered "guard" implies).

When we experience overwhelming emotions, we've also got to remember what God says about us. As we renew our minds with the truth, our feelings will be changed. Ephesians 1:3–9 is one of the most beautiful descriptions of God's disposition toward us. Please take a moment to read it in its entirety and to consider how these words can impact your feelings:

> Blessed be the God and Father of our Lord Jesus Christ, who has blessed us in Christ with every spiritual blessing in the heavenly places, even as he chose us in him before the foundation of the world, that we should be holy and blameless before him. In love he predestined us for adoption as sons through Jesus Christ, according to the purpose of his will, to the praise of his glorious grace, with which he has blessed us in the Beloved. In him we have redemption through his blood, the forgiveness of our trespasses, according to the riches of his grace, which he lavished upon us, in all wisdom and insight making known to us the mystery of his will.

Look again at the words the Holy Spirit uses to describe God's disposition and activity toward us: he has blessed us in Christ with every spiritual blessing; he chose us before the worlds were fashioned; he has declared that our lives will be holy and blameless.

It is his will to love us and predestine us for adoption so that our hearts will overflow with the praise of his glorious grace. We have been redeemed, bought with the most precious commodity in the universe—the blood of God. He has richly forgiven us all of our trespasses, lavishing his grace upon us. He has even brought us into his inner circle, making us privy to mysteries hidden for eons from the wise and powerful. Talk about good news!

These words were meant by the Spirit to bolster our faith, inform our hearts, and enliven our emotions and then to burst out of our inner person in joyous words, feelings, and actions because of his glorious grace. It is in this way that our painful feelings can be used to show us our inner person and to tear down hidden residual unbelief and force us to build our faith. Painful as they may be, our feelings really are a good gift.

CHAD AND SALLY'S DISAPPOINTING MARRIAGE

When Sally married seven years ago, she thought that her dreams had all come true. Her husband, Chad, seemed to be a spiritual man; he loved God and wanted to serve him together with his wife. But now, all that Sally can see are three young children under the age of five, a mortgage, and a growing coldness in their home. Sally consistently feels depressed, desperate, anxious, and hopeless. There seems to be no end to the washing, whether it's dishes, diapers, or floors. Her children's continual needs overwhelm her. She loves nursing her youngest but his demands do drain her physically. She believes that she should be able to handle it all, but it's obvious that she can't. She feels resentful that other women don't have to struggle with organizing and running their homes the way she does.

When her children finally go to bed, Sally can't wait to join them, and she frequently does, letting the youngest child sleep with her. Sally finds comfort in his little body and also in the solitude that his presence brings, for when the baby is in the bed, Chad sleeps in the guest room. Sally hates the loneliness she feels but doesn't think that Chad is the answer to it. She feels trapped and alone. She can't remember the last time she smiled.

Although Chad says that he doesn't really like his job, he is spending more and more time at work. He feels frustrated that Sally is so unhappy, but he just doesn't know what to do to satisfy her. He is beginning to think that he made a mistake, and that she is not the right one for him. He wants to make her happy but feels completely baffled about how to do it. In an effort to respond to her increasingly infrequent interest in communication and closeness with him, he has arranged for babysitting and "date nights," but these tortuous evenings always end in arguments about time spent at work or money spent on the kids' clothing, and his hopes for physical intimacy are usually dashed. He says that he'll never understand Sally and that she is just too demanding, sullen, and immature. Because the house is chaotic and Sally is so demanding, he has taken to turning on the television as soon as he walks through the door so that he can lose himself in mind-numbing entertainment. Sundays have turned into frustrating drudgery as he waits for Sally to get the kids ready, and then they fight all the way to church because they are late. He feels trapped and alone also.

To say that both Chad and Sally feel bad would be an understatement. Sally characterizes her emotional state as empty, depressed, hopeless, and weary. Chad says that he feels angry, ripped off, stressed, and unappreciated. The question is not one of whether they need help; that they do is obvious. The question is what kind of help will actually help them.

If either Chad or Sally goes to the doctor and complains, the doctor will most likely want to prescribe antidepressants. If Sally were to decide to take antidepressants, she would be forced to give up nursing the baby. On the one hand, she enjoys nursing and wouldn't want to give it up, but on the other hand being free from nursing would seem inviting. She would feel guilty about wanting to stop nursing, and she would look at the offer of antidepressants and her supposed genetic problem as a good way out of the drain of nursing as well as a way out of feeling guilty for wanting to stop. Because their doctor tacitly embraces materialistic determinism, he would think that their genetics are to blame for their painful feelings, so he would try to help them out by changing the chemistry of their brain. He would be seeking to alleviate pain in the best way he knows how.

Let's say that Sally decides to go ahead with a course of antidepressants and begins to feel better after a few days.[12] Perhaps she'll use her renewed emotional vigor to begin to address the problems in her marriage. If she does, that may eventuate in positive changes in their relationship. On the other hand, she could feel so good that she assumes that, as the doctor said, the problems in her marriage were simply because of her genetics. So, since the pain seems to be fading, she continues on with inner heart treasures, and glorious truths about the Lord remain undiscovered.

Suppose, on the other hand, that instead of resorting first to a medical remedy, Sally and Chad seek counseling and accountability in their local church, the process and outcome may be quite different. Rather than teaching them that their painful feelings originate outside of themselves (in their genetic legacy from previous generations), their counselor tells them that they are responsible for their problems, at least in part.[13]

Their counselor advises them both to get a thorough physical exam to be sure that there are no underlying causes for their feelings. Because Sally has had three children in such a short time, questions about anemia and also about hormone imbalances should be asked. If at some point either Sally or Chad decides to take these medicines before or while they work on their problems, their counselor shouldn't object or make taking or avoiding these medicines the primary (or even a secondary) issue in counseling. The decision to take the medicine while they work on their marriage is not sinful in itself.

CHAD AND SALLY CONSIDER JESUS

What do Chad and Sally need to hear? They need the gospel. Their minds need to be renewed so that their lives can be transformed.

They need to see the areas in their inner person where they have believed and embraced a lie and to consider Jesus so that they aren't weary and fainthearted when dealing with their own sin or the sin of the other.

To begin with, they need to hear that they are both sinful and flawed. Because the propensity of each has been to blame the other for their problems, they need to begin by asking the Lord to help them see their own sin. They have both expected something from the other that only the Lord could grant them. They thought that marriage was primarily for enjoyment rather than for sanctification and mutual labor for the kingdom. They were also seeking to establish their own righteousness by refusing to admit their great need and by blaming one another.

Sally has falsely expected that she should be able to handle all the daily demands on her time without feeling overwhelmed. She needs to humble herself and ask women in her congregation to help her with her children. In the past, she has refused help when it was offered and then resented the fact that Chad wasn't around when she needed him. She has also envied other women whose husbands seemed more involved in their families and whose lives seemed more organized.

Now, in the light of the cross, she needs to admit to herself, to her husband, and to others that she is in need. Her pride and determination to make it on her own are at the heart of her painful feelings and their marital conflict. Because of the gospel she can now freely admit her sin. This freedom will also be extended to Chad, who is a sinner just as she is.

Chad has falsely expected that Sally should understand and respond to his efforts to serve her. He has given up trying to lead because he can't figure out how to make it work. He has been impatient with Sally when she hasn't responded as he wanted her to and when she has been resentful. He thinks that working hard at his job is his part, and the home is hers. He doesn't see that his primary calling is to love his wife as Jesus Christ has loved him. He needs to see that he is sinful and flawed and that, like his Savior, washing feet is also part of his calling.

Like Sally, Chad needs the help of other believers who will hold him accountable to be home at a certain time so that Sally is free to make dinner without having to manage the kids simultaneously. Considering Jesus will enable Chad to work hard all day and then pray on the way home for grace and strength to serve Sally and the family as he should. Chad needs to lead the way in patient confession of sin and asking for prayer. They both need to confess their anger, pride, and selfish demands.

Both Chad and Sally also need to drink deeply of God's mercy. They are more loved and welcomed than they ever dared hope. Rather than seeking to justify themselves before each other and other believers, they need to admit that they are sinful and yet so marvelously loved. For every one look that they take at their sin, they need to take ten looks at God's love for them in Christ.

Chad can lead in this, reminding Sally how the Lord loves her even though she is not perfect. He can continually remind her how much he loves her but that his love isn't the answer to all her desires. He can remind her that they are both in great need of the comfort of God's love. Sally can respond by humbly asking for help when she needs it and then being aware that it is God's love for her that has led her to this circumstance. The births of their three children in quick succession and the resulting marital and emotional problems have been good gifts because they have revealed their false treasures and can result in praise for God's glorious grace.

Accountability with their counselor and with their local church will help them grow in their understanding of the gospel and in their service to each other. The women in Sally's life can gently confront her when she is tempted to give in to self-pity, resentment, and isolation. They can encourage her by reminding her of her great salvation and by offering practical help with the kids. The men in Chad's life can also confront him when he focuses on his desire for a stress-free home life, a contented and compliant wife, and children who are seen and not heard. Chad and Sally are now free to grow together in transparent service to each other and their church.

CONSIDERING JESUS AGAIN

Just like Chad and Sally, we all need to consider Jesus again and again. We need to consider how the hostile actions and emotions of sinful people caused him to suffer, and we need to know that it was simply because of love, his never-ending love, that he persevered to the cross.

Jesus experienced all the damage that our sinful emotions could do, as rebellious people like us focused their rage and hostility on him. Yet, he loves us and calls us to himself. This is the primary thought that we must keep before our eyes as we press through our feelings to love and serve him.

Because we began this chapter with a quote from Puritan writer Richard Baxter, we will close with another of his insights. When discussing how to overcome our sin Baxter gives us this counsel:

> Consider well of the office, the bloodshed, and the holy life of Christ—His office is to expiate sin, and to destroy it. His blood was shed for it: his life condemned it. Love Christ, and thou wilt hate that which caused his death. Love him, and thou will be made more like him.[14]

PURSUING COUNSEL FROM THE CROSS

1) What have you learned from this chapter about your feelings? What do you agree or disagree with? Why?

2) Why did God create us with emotions?

3) How can our feelings, even painful ones, function as a blessing in our lives?

4) Are you or someone you know feeling overwhelmed, fainthearted, or wearied by your emotions? What do these feelings tell you about your heart and your perspective on your circumstances?

5) Summarize what you have learned in this chapter in four or five sentences.

CHAPTER EIGHT

The Gospel and Our Relationships

Beloved, if God so loved us, we also ought to love one another.
1 JOHN 4:11

RELATIONSHIPS DEFINE US. Who we love and who we think loves us in a very large part make us what we are. What we think of ourselves is greatly influenced by what others think of us. If we grew up in a very troubled home or if we are in troubled relationships now, anxiety, doubt, and fear may color every area of our lives. Yes, our relationships are very important, and many of us spend enormous amounts of effort, time, and money looking for the key to making our relationships stronger, more satisfying. This desire for relationship, although broken and self-focused, originates with God.

We were created to be social beings. God himself, in whose image we have been created, is social. He is not alone; he is three-in-one, a trinity. He is Father, Son, and Holy Spirit, in relationship. We see that he is social not only by the fact that he is three-in-one, but also by the fact that he delights in having society with his creation— the angels first and then humans who were created to be like him.

He could have kept to himself and never created other beings, or he could have created us but never chosen to reveal himself. But he hasn't done either. Instead, he created us, communicated with us, and opened the door for us to have relationship with him. God is the fountainhead from which all interpersonal relationship flows, and relationships are a good because God has established them and enjoys them himself.

Because he has made us in his image, we too are social. Being utterly alone, shipwrecked on a desert island, is terrible because God has declared that it is not good to be alone (Gen. 2:18). We need relationships from the very moment of our birth until our death. We need to be fed and cared for. We need our parents to teach us how to live and relate to others. As we grow and mature, we desire to care for others and be in strong lifelong relationships. Even at the end of our lives we never outgrow our need for others. We need them to feed us, care for us, and finally to carry our body to the grave. From our first days until our last, God has so fashioned us and the world in which we live that it is not good to be alone at any time. We are not to be independent. He has made us dependent, frail, and in need of the help of others.

WE ARE HIS CHILDREN

Of course, our most important relationship is with our heavenly Father. This one relationship is so significant that it supersedes and impacts every other relationship we have. From the gospel we learn who we are and how God sees us. Is he pleased with us? Does he love us? Has he welcomed us? Is he waiting for us to obey before he declares his love and commitment to us? The gospel answers these questions deeply and beautifully. We are sinful and flawed yet loved and welcomed. These simple truths change everything about the way we see ourselves and others. They teach us who we are and also how we are to respond in every conceivable relationship.

The good news tells us that we were rebellious children who "were once foolish, disobedient, led astray, slaves to various passions and pleasures, passing our days in malice and envy, hated by others and hating one another" (Titus 3:3–4). We were "children of wrath" (Eph. 2:3). God didn't save us because we made our beds and covered our mouths when we coughed; in fact, just the opposite is true. He saved us despite the fact that we hated him, even though we were created to be his children. We were weak (Rom. 5:6), helpless (Matt. 9:36), hopelessly sick (Luke 5:31-32), and lost (Luke 19:10).

God saved his enemies (Luke 6:35; Rom. 5:10). The enormity of his love for us is most clearly seen in the light of our great transgression. He doesn't love us because of any prior goodness on our part. He loves us because he chooses to love us, and the depth of our defection from him should produce in us great humility, gratitude, and patience with others' failures.

The good news also tells us that although we were rebels, he made us his own (Phil. 3:12). He loves us. We are not outcasts, houseguests, foster children, slaves, or strangers. Like an attentive Father, he has yearned over us (Jer. 31:20) and chosen us before the foundation of the world, and he has brought us into his family as his beloved, adopted children (Eph. 1:4). We've been born "not of blood nor of the will of the flesh nor of the will of man, but of God" (John 1:13).

If you are in the family today, you didn't sneak in by the skin of your teeth. You were brought in by the divine foreknowledge and sovereign power of God. "When the fullness of time had come, God sent forth his Son, born of woman, born under the law, to redeem those who were under the law, so that we might receive adoption as sons. And because you are sons, God has sent the Spirit of his Son into our hearts, crying, 'Abba! Father!' So you are no longer a slave, but a son, and if a son, then an heir through God" (Gal. 4:4–7).

Because of his great love for you, you are invited to speak to him in the most intimate way. Call him "Abba," a term of endearment, an appellation forbidden to slaves or outsiders. Because he loves fellowship with you, he has made you part of his family. Go ahead—use this term with confidence. Yes, he is transcendent; he is the holy God who rules sovereignly over all. But he is also immanent. He is close to you; he carries you in his bosom as a beloved child. He tenderly cherishes you. "As a father shows compassion to his children, so the LORD shows compassion to those who fear him. For he knows our frame; he remembers that we are dust" (Ps. 103:13–14).

He has mercy and compassion for us. He knows what we are made of—we are dust. He knows better than we the great gulf that would exist between us were it not for his intervention. He knows our nature, our fallenness, our unbelief, our frailty. And yet he invites us to draw near "with confidence . . . to the throne of grace, that we may receive mercy and find grace to help in time of need" (Heb. 4:16). We must never let our need for help separate us from him or influence our perception of what he thinks of us. We are beloved children who have been invited to call him Abba. Our Abba welcomes us as his beloved children. He calls us his "holy and beloved" (1 John 3:1–2; Eph. 5:1; Heb. 3:1). He has flung the door open to welcome the family—his family. Come in, stretch out on the couch, take your shoes off, bring your laundry, raid the refrigerator. Act like a member of the family. You are not a stranger or a houseguest (John 8:35). You are his son, and he doesn't want you to keep your distance.

WE ARE HIS BRIDE

Not only are we Abba's children, but we are also espoused to his Son. We are going to wed his Beloved. Jesus speaks words of tenderness and compassion to woo his bride to himself (Matt. 11:28; John 7:37). Jesus visibly demonstrates his commitment to make her his. He becomes like her, a human; he lives the life she should have lived and dies the death she deserves (Phil. 2:5–9). By God's power he is raised, and he brings her with him into newness of life. And now he is watching over her, interceding for her, and joyously anticipating the day when she will fully experience what he has already declared about her. He is the sinless spouse we are all longing for.

Yes, Jesus Christ is the perfect bridegroom. When Paul taught husbands how to treat their wives, the example he used was our Savior. Jesus "loved the church and gave himself up for her, that he might sanctify her, having cleansed her by the washing of water with the word, so that he might present the church to himself in splendor, without spot or wrinkle or any such thing, that she might be holy and without blemish" (Eph. 5:25–28).

Our Lord desired a beautiful bride, and he was willing to pay the price for her. He brings her to himself, beautiful and holy, and he enjoys his relationship with her. But this woman didn't come cheap. No, she cost him everything, but he was willing to pay it. He "gave himself for our sins to deliver us from the present evil age" (Gal. 1:4); he "loved us" individually and corporately and "gave himself for" us (Gal. 2:20); he surrendered what was rightfully his and "loved us and gave himself up for us" (Eph. 5:2).

In order to free us from our slavery to sin he "ransomed" us, and the price he paid was not "perishable things such as silver or gold," although he had all riches at his disposal, but was rather his "precious blood" (1 Pet. 1:18–19). And even though he is preeminent (Col. 1:18), and reigns as the ruler of kings on the earth, he is also the "firstborn of the dead." Why would this "faithful witness," this ruler of all kings, know anything about death? Because he "loves us and has freed us from our sins by his blood" (Rev. 1:5–6).

Yes, Jesus Christ is our perfect example of loving leadership. But he is so much more than our example. He is our husband. No one has ever loved like this. No godly husband could ever love his wife as Jesus Christ has loved us. He has done what none of us can do, and his perfect record of sacrificial love is ours! Is there really any question whether relationships are important to him?

BECAUSE WE ARE HIS, WE LOVE

Because he loves and welcomes us as he does, we are transformed in our relationships with others. Because we have been loved as a child or a bride is loved, we are now free to love and welcome others generously, warmly, and joyously. His love for us is to have a powerful effect on our love for others, and it is the only thing that will motivate us to love as we have been called to.

We know that it's fairly easy to surmise that we are doing a good job loving God. In fact, I (Elyse) hadn't been saved for more than six months when I figured out that Christianity would be a breeze if it were just me and Jesus. But the problem was that there were other people in the picture. People I had to interact with and relate to made my newfound faith more difficult. I was surprised to learn that, rather than pursuing a hermit's existence away from troubling people and their troubling sins (while being reasonably comfortable with my own sins), I am commanded to love them and live in close relationship with them. I have to be patient and forgiving. I have to serve others when they don't appreciate me. And, even more shockingly, I discovered that my love for the Lord can be measured by my love for others! This issue of loving others is so important that we are told that we can discern whether we have true love for Jesus by our love for others:

> By this it is evident who are the children of God, and who are the children of the devil: whoever does not practice righteousness is not of God, nor is the one who does not love his brother. (1 John 3:10)

As you can see, this issue of our relationships with others is no small trifle. It is one of the litmus tests for true faith. God loves loving relationships, and if we love him, so will we.[1]

In addition, our love for others is a primary witness to an unbelieving world. Jesus said, "By this all people will know that you are my disciples, if you have love for one another" (John 13:35). Loving relationships are exceedingly important in our witness. How we treat others, how we serve them, is paramount for fruit bearing in an unbelieving world. Nothing shocks our world or makes non-Christians stop and wonder more than a person who continues to love even when treated despicably or when facing great persecution.

All of the Law and the Prophets are summed up in two commands. Yes, you guessed it: they are commands to love (Matt. 22:36–40; Rom. 13:9–10). We are to love God consistently and passionately, and we are to love our neighbors—whether spouse, child, or enemy—the way we already love ourselves. Real love—not just as a warm impulse washing over our minds but as a solid determination to lay down our lives and serve others though it may cost blood, sweat, or our very lives—is the royal command (James 2:8) to children of the God who "is love" (1 John 4:8, 16).

THE GOSPEL AND OUR FAMILIES

Over the past thirty years or so, the church has produced much material on proper relationships in the family. Hundreds of books on family life have been written, and proper roles for husband, wife, parents, and children have been defined. Because God has established the family and told us how to love each other, many of these books are useful. We do need to know what God's perspectives and desires on our relationships are, and we should seek to embrace them.

The problem with a large majority of these books, however, is that they have pointed out the obligations of the gospel without first rehearsing the declarations of the gospel.[2] Like most of us, these authors have made the mistake of assuming that we have heard enough about the gospel so that we don't need it any longer. Focusing on the obligations of Scripture without mentioning the declarations of the gospel has resulted in a works-oriented perspective in family relationships and idolatry of the family, and in despairing or self-righteous husbands and wives and children who wonder why it's so hard to obey.[3] When we forget that Jesus is our Savior, seeing him merely as our example, the motivation to love as he does eludes us.

So even though the relationships we have within our families and at our schools and workplaces are paramount in importance, most of us haven't been taught to think very deeply about how the primary relationship in our lives—that with God through Jesus Christ—impacts and influences us.

FORGETTING THE GOSPEL

Let's connect the dots now between the beautiful truth of our adoption and our espousal, on the one hand, and how to love our closest neighbors, spouse, and children, on the other. If we forget that we are sinful and flawed but loved and welcomed, our marriages and families will reflect that. We won't love, because we will have forgotten how we have been loved.

Forgetting That We Are Sinful and Flawed

If we forget that we are sinful and flawed, it will be easy to become self-righteous and harsh with our spouses. When we think we have it all together and we survey the landscape of our obedience (and others' failures), we will find it next to impossible to be loving or patient.

A husband who has forgotten this part of the gospel is often callous and demanding. He is tempted to rule his home as a dictator and is quick to point out that his wife and children *must* submit to him because, after all, God has made him the undisputed king of his home. He views every one of their failures as a direct attack on his leadership, and he insists on perfect obedience, whether in the way his wife cooks or in how his children make their beds.

Because he has forgotten this part of the gospel, he also forgets the servant leadership of his Savior, who washed the feet of those who were about to desert and deny him. If he doesn't remember how utterly destitute of personal goodness he is, he will think that all his problems are the fault of his family, and if they would just do what they are supposed to do, he wouldn't be tempted to be so impatient.

A wife who has forgotten that she is sinful and flawed can be harsh and judgmental. She finds it easy to point out her husband's failures, and she thinks that her growth in maturity is hindered because her husband isn't leading as he should. When her husband prays, she criticizes his prayer in her heart. When he watches television, she remembers all the hours she has spent in Bible study, comparing herself to him.

Because she has forgotten the gospel, she forgets that she already has a sinless Husband. But this sinless Husband married a polluted wife with no beauty in her, either before she was saved or after. He loved her out of his pure, unmerited grace. This wife has also forgotten that her growth in maturity isn't contingent upon her earthly husband's leadership. Rather, it was purchased by the precious blood of her Savior, who bought her sanctification at the cost of his life.

Parents who forget that they are law breakers expect their children to keep the law and to make them look good. They expect children who exhibit exemplary respect and self-discipline. Such parents are self-righteous and proud, and all too often they put confidence in themselves, their ability to obey God, and their methodology for extracting obedience from their children. They forget that the Lord didn't save or bless them because they were law keepers but, rather, because they weren't.

Although they may know they have failed to keep the law—loving God with heart, soul, mind, and strength and their neighbor as themselves—they give their children the law (or house rules) and expect perfect compliance the first time and every time, with a happy heart. Such parents are harsh and impatient and tempted to anger when their children fail. Although they might know the law doesn't change the heart (and is, in fact, a ministry of death [2 Cor. 3:7]), they expect the law to change the hearts of their children. They forget that they have been adopted and brought into the family, not only as those who misunderstood or slipped up from time to time, but as defiant rebels. Have parents consistently obeyed God the first time and every time, with a happy heart? Children need what parents need—the gospel. Certainly children need to learn God's law and to have house rules to follow, but gospel-oriented parents give the law to show children their need for a Savior, not to make them obedient.

Even children can forget the gospel. If they forget that they are sinful and flawed, they are quick to judge their parents' inconsistencies and failures. They take note that Dad tells them to do one thing and then hypocritically turns around and does the exact opposite. They watch how their parents discipline their siblings, and they are tempted to think that the parents play favorites or are easier on their brothers and sisters than they are on them. Children might wonder if their parents are even Christians. They need to remember that their parents are just like them—sinful and flawed.

Children can forget that even though they are young, they have already sinned enough to earn an eternity of punishment. Or they might think that Christianity might "work" for other good people, but it just doesn't work for them because they don't seem to be changing much. They might be tempted to think that, though their parents' religion is good for their parents, it doesn't work for them because they cannot keep its standards.

Here is where the gospel message is so important—even for children! First, Jesus Christ suffered as a child, having to obey sinful parents just as our children do. Jesus' parents were hypocritical, and no doubt there were times when they were also unfair toward him. Once, they accused him of being uncaring when they found him in the temple talking with religious leaders (Luke 2:48). Later on, even after he was grown, his mother apparently agreed with his brothers when they accused him of being crazy (Mark 3:21, 31). Jesus knows what it is like to have brothers and sisters and parents who don't do what they are supposed to do and who accuse others unfairly.

He also knows that every child struggles with sin. He doesn't love just good children. He isn't like Santa, making a list of who is naughty or nice. He loves all his children because he has decided to do so. Jesus knows what it's like for every child, and although he never sinned, he knows the struggle of trying to resist temptation. Children, like their fathers and mothers, need to remember the gospel.

Forgetting That We Are Loved and Welcomed

Let's take time now to see how forgetting that we are loved and welcomed might impact a home.

Husbands and wives who forget how they have been freely loved and welcomed by God will be tempted to cover up their failures and put on a good show. They will be slow to admit their guilt, and they will wear themselves out trying to prove that they are worthy of love. A husband might become overly committed at work, proving to his wife what a good provider he is and that he is worthy of her love and appreciation. A wife might try to become Super Mom, making sure that every little thing is done perfectly around the home so that no one can criticize her. She might point out the work she did. She might also forbid herself to rest, relax, or enjoy time off. Both husband and wife will be touchy when criticized and tempted to bouts of self-pity, depression, and unbelief.

When spouses crave love and acceptance from one another, they will never be satisfied, because they are lusting after something God hasn't commanded them to desire. A husband who is looking to satisfy his thirst for love through his wife will never be fully assured that she loves him as much as he loves her. If she doesn't have his dinner ready, he will think that means she doesn't love him. If she doesn't seem to want to have sex as much as he does, he will begin to fantasize about having a woman who *really* desires and loves him.

A wife who is craving love from her husband will feel as though she never has enough. If he brings her a card, it is not good enough because it is not the right kind of card. If he buys her a ring, it isn't good enough because other women have bigger diamonds. She will assume that he doesn't really love her as other husbands love their wives. She still believes all of the stories she heard as a little girl about the knight in shining armor, but she hasn't made the connection as to who that Knight really is.

A husband and wife who have forgotten how loved and welcomed they are will never be satisfied with each other. *They weren't meant to be.* They have been freely, lavishly, generously, passionately loved by their heavenly Father and their heavenly Husband, and that love is meant to satisfy them. When spouses begin to grasp the depth of God's love for them in Christ, the need[4] for romance, respect, and attention will rapidly diminish. Rather than seeing themselves as needy sponges, trying to soak up every drop of earthly, human love, they will see themselves as wells supplied by a divine Spring, overflowing with living water that is meant to satisfy, cheer, and serve those around them. They can delight themselves in the streams of water and the true bread that their Savior feeds them.

Come, everyone who thirsts,
  come to the waters;
and he who has no money,
  come, buy and eat!
Come, buy wine and milk
  without money and without price.
Why do you spend your money for that which is not bread,
  and your labor for that which does not satisfy?
Listen diligently to me, and eat what is good,
  and delight yourselves in rich food. (Isa. 55:1–2)

Parents and children who forget how they have been loved and welcomed will also always be on the prowl for signs of love. Parents who think they need their child's love will be afraid to correct them. They won't speak truth to them because they will fear what might happen if their child gets mad at them. Because they wrongly think that the best love a child can have is self-love, they will never correct him or tell him that he isn't perfect. They will be weak parents, supposing that the best that they can do is to tell their little darlings that they are absolutely wonderful, never telling them the truth about the depth of their depravity.

The result of such self-focused love is that sensitive children (who know that they are not good) will simply think that their parents are dishonest, and they won't trust anything they say. They will torment themselves with their failures and live as slaves to their own self-condemning consciences. Other children whose hearts are bent in a more proud direction will see themselves as wonderful and will resent anyone who tells them otherwise. They will be rebellious and strong-willed because they believe their parents' press releases: "Our Johnny is wonderful! He's such a good boy!"

In addition, parents who haven't satiated their souls in the love of the Father and the Son will seek to gain the love and approval of their peers through their children's successes. Such parents enroll their children in every sport, musical activity, theater arts program, and Christian discipleship club, exhausting their little bodies and minds in order to fulfill Mom and Dad's desire to prove that they are parents deserving of love and appreciation. Such parents need and demand straight A's from their progeny, because their children's failure would be a direct attack on their insecurities.

REMEMBERING THE GOSPEL: EFFUSIVE AFFECTION, GENTLE CORRECTIONS

Like our children, we need to hear the gospel. The Lord has so structured Scripture that he is effusive with his declarations of love. Our spouses, children, friends, coworkers, teachers, and pastors ought to hear from us the same expressions of affection and appreciation that God gives us. He showers us with grace, mercy, encouragement, and generous words of love. Because we are more loved and welcomed than we ever dared hope, we can become effusively loving and welcoming.

We are sinful and flawed, errant children who have been welcomed by a patient, long-suffering, kind Father. God loves us and draws us to himself. He speaks words of love to us continuously because we are so slow to believe. He is patient, kind, gentle, and faithful, and he always uses every opportunity to reveal himself to us. He lives in ineffable light, unconfined and completely free. He is an uncreated, eternal, omniscient, almighty Spirit. He doesn't see things from a wrong or partial perspective; he is not fooled by outward appearances. Yet he continues to be patient with us.

We are not like him. Like pots on wheels, we are made of mud—yes, fashioned by his hand but confined, finite, and tied to earth. We are "jars of clay" (2 Cor. 4:7). He sees what we are, and it causes him to have compassion on us. He remembers that we are dust. Think again of the gulf between our existence and his. Yet he treats us with great pity, gentleness, and compassion. He could demand without making a way, but he's chosen to make a way and to place all the demands on himself.

GOSPEL-CENTERED PARENTING

Because this chapter has been very practical in nature, we are going to conclude it by looking a little more deeply at parenting founded in the gospel.

What does gospel-centered parenting look like? Here is how Paul put it:

"Fathers, do not provoke your children to anger, but bring them up in the discipline and instruction of the Lord" (Eph. 6:4); and "Fathers, do not provoke your children, lest they become discouraged" (Col. 3:21).

Isn't it easy to see how Paul's counsel to parents is based on God's gracious pattern with us? We are not to be harsh or demanding with our children. We are not to provoke them to anger or discourage them. Of course, the obvious question we have to consider is what will provoke them or discourage them, and, by contrast, what does it look like to discipline and instruct "in the Lord"?

Although there are many ways we can provoke our kids in disciplining them, we learn from Paul's expositions of grace in these epistles that we provoke and discourage our children when we forget the gospel and demand, as a condition of our approval and affection, that they obey the law that "neither our fathers nor we have been able to bear" (Acts 15:10). By itself, God's law, although it is "holy and righteous and good" (Rom. 7:12), will serve only to aggravate or discourage them. The law will stir up within them the desire to sin because they are not able to obey it. It won't furnish them with the power or motivation to obey us or the Lord. The law has its uses with our children, but making them good isn't one of them. Only the gospel and God's grace can change hearts.

The proper place and function of the law is something that we might recognize in our own lives but fail to believe when it comes to raising our children. We know that we don't change and mature by making a list of things we need to do and then scrutinizing our failures when we don't do them. But, amazingly, we think that's how our children will change. But when they cry that they can't obey, we should agree with them, although it is true that we are to acquaint them with the law's demands.

Rather than telling them that they can *and will* obey, we must tell them—frankly, gently, sadly—that they cannot obey. They need help.

They need Jesus. Making a list and giving stickers and time-outs when they succeed or fail won't change their hearts. It may make them little Pharisees, knowing how to look obedient so that they can get approval, but it won't change their hearts. We are to use their disobedience as a gospel opportunity to remind them that they are sinful and flawed, but if they flee to Jesus he will love and welcome them. We must remind them that they "do not have a high priest who is unable to sympathize with [their] weaknesses, but one who in every respect has been tempted as [they] are, yet without sin. Let [them] then with confidence draw near to the throne of grace, that [they] may receive mercy and find grace to help in time of need" (Heb. 4:15–16).

Jesus understands their weaknesses. He knows about temptations. When we—and our children—struggle with obedience, we can draw near to the throne of grace where we won't receive judgment and punishment, but mercy and grace to help. That is the portrait of the Savior that our children need to see. This is the image that will transform their hearts and teach them to run to him, rather than away from him, when they sin.

Yes, we must discipline them when they defiantly disobey, but we do so as he disciplines us: gently, unselfishly, patiently, and for our ultimate good. The Lord is not capricious in his discipline, changing his mind from one day to the next. No, he is consistent and never pains us more than is absolutely necessary to teach us not to trust in ourselves and our ability but to trust in him. Our parenting is "in the Lord"; Jesus Christ is preeminent. It's all about him. The gospel is the environment of our parenting.

BEING TRANSPARENT ABOUT OUR SIN

It's easy to see how the gospel radically impacts the way we discipline and train our children. We shouldn't be surprised by their sin. After all, they're the children of sinners. We shouldn't withhold love from them when they sin either, because God hasn't withheld love from us. Because we're *his* children, because he's adopted us and called us beloved, we're to put on "compassionate hearts, kindness, humility, meekness, and patience, bearing with one another and, if one has a complaint against another, forgiving each other; as the Lord has forgiven you, so you also must forgive" (Col. 3:12–14).

When you as parents learn to openly confess your sin to your children,[5] you will help them know that you don't think you are perfect and that you struggle with sin just as they do. It will give them hope that there isn't something uniquely wrong with them that isn't wrong with you, too. They will see that although you sin, you are loved by God, which will inspire them to share in that truth.

BECAUSE HE HAS LOVED US

The gospel changes everything about us. Most particularly, it changes how we love and treat others. Soaking ourselves in the astounding love of God for us, weak and sinful as we are, will cause us to become people who love. The pure, undefiled Prince of heaven, Jesus Christ, was called a friend of "tax collectors and sinners" (Matt. 11:19). It should be obvious that he loves sinners, because he has loved us.

Living in the light of this truth will enable us to love. It will remove all our self-righteousness and craving for respect, it will free us to lay down our lives and not keep a running tally of who sins most (or who serves most!), and it will make us patient and gentle. The gospel is the environment for all our relationships. The gospel teaches us to love.

> In this the love of God was made manifest among us, that God sent his only Son into the world, so that we might live through him. In this is love, not that we have loved God but that he loved us and sent his Son to be the propitiation for our sins. *Beloved, if God so loved us, we also ought to love one another.* (1 John 4:9–11)

PURSUING COUNSEL FROM THE CROSS

1) What phrase most accurately describes you in terms of your relationships with others:

    a) Sin Detective: Do you find it easy to point out others' sins and failures?

    b) Grace Detective: Do you love to point out evidences of God's grace in others' lives, even when they fail?

2) Are your relationships based primarily on law or gospel? Do you love only those who obey as you do and treat you according to the rules you set out? Or are you filled with long-suffering and kindness, remembering how you don't obey the law yourself but have been loved nevertheless?

3) Paul wrote, "For through the Spirit, by faith, we ourselves eagerly wait for the hope of righteousness. For in Christ Jesus neither circumcision nor uncircumcision counts for anything, but only faith working through love" (Gal. 5:5–6). Do you have the "hope of righteousness" for yourself because of the Father's great love for you in Christ? Do you have the same hope of righteousness for others, including your spouse and children? What would "faith working through love" look like in your relationships?

4) Every relational imperative that isn't rooted in the gospel is not, at heart, Christian. We love God *because* he first loved us; we love others because he first loved us and because he loves them. Read the following verses and distill what they say about God's love for us and our love for others.

    a) 1 John 1:3, 7

    b) 1 John 2:4–6, 8–11

    c) 1 John 3:16–23

    d) 1 John 4:7–11, 16–21

    e) 1 John 5:1

5) Summarize in four or five sentences what you've learned in this chapter.

CHAPTER NINE

The Gospel Story and the Glory Story

For I decided to know nothing among you except Jesus Christ and him crucified.

1 CORINTHIANS 2:2

AS WE SAID IN THE INTRODUCTION, the number of books that offer counsel or advice for living is innumerable. It is right and good that people help one another and desire that their lives and the lives of their friends grow and mature. Among Christians, too, there are many books offering help on practically every topic imaginable. Sadly, many of the secular and even "Christian" self-help books are not all that different from each other. Of course, they differ somewhat because they use diverse source material, but, generally speaking, most counseling or self-help books are very much alike, and they are alike because they all contain what Martin Luther called a "glory story."[1]

This perspective, this "glory story," contains an unstated but deeply held belief that people don't really need a crucified Savior; they just need a little help "getting their act together," and they can attain glory[2] by hard work, self-discipline, and the right list of activities.[3]

People who believe in the glory story put their faith in whatever happens to be this week's "six steps [or seven habits] to success." In doing so, they intrinsically put faith in themselves as people who can follow those steps and develop those habits if they just try hard enough. When it comes to our ability to attain glory from our own efforts, sadly, we are all far too optimistic.

As Michael Horton wrote, the glory story doesn't resonate only in the secular world, but many Christians also are "swimming in a sea of narcissistic moralism."[4] We think we can live happy, perfected lives if we just ferret out the right key to get God to unlock all his treasure and make us healthy, wealthy, and wise. Make no mistake: this moralism—whether for more shallow endeavors such as just having a "good day" or for nobler goals, such as making life better for our families or assuring ourselves that God still smiles on us—is, as Horton writes, narcissistic. It is all about us and all for us and our glory.

Although all true Christians recognize their need for a crucified Savior to *begin* their life of faith, most of them fall back into their innate belief in self-glorification once they get saved.[5] Whether Happy Moralists or Sad, nearly all Christians believe that the answer to their problem is just around the corner. They will have it once they find the secret to their perfect life, once they throw off that distressing habit, once they find the right spouse/child/job/home/church, once they uncover their idols, once they learn how to pray the magic words, and on and on their whole life through.

The Happy Moralist will read one self-help book after another, while the Sad Moralist will seek deeper and deeper self-understanding and repentance. In fact, we are so proud and convinced of our perfectibility that even living in the light of the gospel can be twisted into a secret self-improvement regimen. "If I just get the gospel right," we think, "I know I'll be able to love better." Whether Happy Moralist or Sad, we all believe that we can attain glory through our own efforts. But, in the end, everyone who is honest has to admit that he has failed because the truth is that no matter how hard we try, we are never truly free, never fully trusting, never properly sorry, never consistently loving, and never satisfied with the perfection of our accomplishments or the accolades of others. Our efforts always come up short.

Living for the glory story is like chasing a mirage: it looks so good out there in the distance, but once we attain the sought-after accomplishment, transformation, or acclamation, we see another on the horizon, and the pool we're standing in is not the refreshing spring we thought it would be; it is only a putrid mud hole or another stretch of bone-dry sand.

LAY DOWN YOUR DEADLY DOING

Shall we just give up and not try anymore? Well, yes and no. We should give up our quest for glory here, although doing so runs afoul of all that we believe about ourselves. We must recognize that if the Man of sorrows has taught us anything, it is that this life is filled with humiliation, sin, and sorrow and that we must indeed despair of putting any hope or trust in our ability to reform ourselves. The mere fact of the cross proves that. We should not be surprised by our sin; instead we "must learn to say 'I am a sinner' and to never stop saying it until Christ's return makes it no longer true."[6] Yes, we must give up hope of approving of ourselves or of finally earning grace and proving to God that we really do love him and are worthy of his love.

Utterly despairing of our ability must lead us to Christ and to trust in him to work in us and make us willing and able to serve him (Phil. 2:12). Paul prayed that God would make the Thessalonians "worthy of his calling" and that the Lord would "fulfill every resolve for good and every work of faith *by his power*, so that the name of our Lord Jesus may be glorified in you, and you in him, according to the grace of our God and the Lord Jesus Christ" (2 Thess. 1:11–12).

All our obedience, every resolve to do good, and every work of faith is "by his power" and so that the Lord Jesus would be glorified because of the grace he gives. Yes, we must pursue obedience, but that obedience must always be *cruciform*, formed by Christ's cross. We must seek to obey *because of the cross*, find the grace to obey *because of the cross*, and live free from condemnation whether we succeed or fail in the *light of the cross*. The cross must be our only story, as Paul boldly proclaimed: "For I decided to know nothing among you except Jesus Christ and him crucified" (1 Cor. 2:2).

PETER: A THEOLOGIAN OF GLORY

In Luke 22:14–34[7] we find a perfect portrayal of someone who fully believed the glory story, Peter:

> When the hour came, he reclined at table, and the apostles with him. And he said to them, "I have earnestly desired to eat this Passover with you before I suffer. For I tell you I will not eat it until it is fulfilled in the kingdom of God." And he took a cup, and when he had given thanks he said, "Take this, and divide it among yourselves. For I tell you that from now on I will not drink of the fruit of the vine until the kingdom of God comes." And he took bread, and when he had given thanks, he broke it and gave it to them, saying, "This is my body, which is given for you. Do this in remembrance of me." And likewise the cup after they had eaten, saying, "This cup that is poured out for you is the new covenant in my blood. But behold, the hand of him who betrays me is with me on the table. For the Son of Man goes as it has been determined, but woe to that man by whom he is betrayed!" And they began to question one another, which of them it could be who was going to do this.
>
> A dispute also arose among them, as to which of them was to be regarded as the greatest. And he said to them, "The kings of the Gentiles exercise lordship over them, and those in authority over them are called benefactors. But not so with you. Rather, let the greatest among you become as the youngest, and the leader as one who serves. For who is the greater, one who reclines at table or one who serves? Is it not the one who reclines at table? But I am among you as the one who serves.
>
> "You are those who have stayed with me in my trials, and I assign to you, as my Father assigned to me, a kingdom, that you may eat and drink at my table in my kingdom and sit on thrones judging the twelve tribes of Israel.
>
> "Simon, Simon, behold, Satan demanded to have you, that he might sift you like wheat, but I have prayed for you that your faith may not fail. And when you have turned again, strengthen your brothers." Peter said to him, "Lord, I am ready to go with

you both to prison and to death." Jesus said, "I tell you, Peter, the rooster will not crow this day, until you deny three times that you know me."

That scene is a mirror that reflects our true identity. It also shows the identity of our Savior. Let's take a moment to gaze into this mirror to see our reflection there. What does the theologian of glory believe? What are we like? Since Peter's protestation that he would never deny Jesus was echoed by the rest (Mark 14:31), we see that all of the Twelve are theologians of glory who didn't see their own vulnerability to sin and deception. They had just heard Jesus talk about his suffering, his death, his body, and his blood, but as usual they ignored his "negative" speech.

Even though Peter had been confronted previously by the Lord about his refusal to embrace the truth and give up his glory story—"Get behind me, Satan! You are a hindrance to me. For you are not setting your mind on the things of God, but on the things of man" (Matt. 16:23)—he still hadn't given it up. His heart was still fully engaged in the belief in his own power and glory. So he argued with the other disciples about who might stoop so low as to betray Jesus, and then, while they were busy puffing themselves up and ignoring what Jesus had just said to them about spilled blood and a broken body, they decided they might as well try to figure out who was going to be the greatest.

The Lord foretells his denial, and Peter responds with bluster, denying that Jesus knows anything about what's going to happen. But within a few short hours Peter's fall occurs, and, because he had placed such great confidence in himself, he went out and "wept bitterly" (Matt. 26:75). The unavoidable end of the glory story is always utter despair; *there is no other possibility*.

Now, in light of all that, how do we see Jesus, the one whose entire existence is cruciform, live? Think deeply about his desires, his kindness, and his great heart of love. He reclined at the Passover table with them; he didn't stomp around worrying, angry because they didn't get it. No, he "cozied up" with them. His first recorded sentence is astonishing, "I have earnestly desired to eat this Passover with you before I suffer" (Luke 22:15). This meal wasn't a mere duty for him; he *longed* to eat with them, to strengthen them and receive the comfort of their fellowship, to cherish the final moments they had left together before his suffering. He loved them and loved being with them. He knew what was coming, the terror they would face and their duplicity of soul. He gave them of himself; he was the meal, he was their means of grace.

Next, he took the cup and the bread and said, "Take this, and divide it among yourselves. . . . This is my body, which is given for you. Do this in remembrance of me. . . . This cup that is poured out for you is the new covenant in my blood" (Luke 22:17, 19–20). Don't these words fly right in the face of our glory story? They demonstrate the extent of our helplessness and our defection from him. A death must occur. Blood must be spilt and wrath appeased. We don't need six secret steps to our best life now. We need the God-Man's death and resurrection.

How far does our capacity for right action reach? At most, we can chew, swallow, and remember. In the meantime, what is he doing? He is pouring out his blood and giving his body to be broken because we can't do anything to change ourselves. How frequently do we fail to remember him, even during the Lord's Supper, because we are so focused on our glory story that the story of the cross seems weak, passé, and hackneyed? All we are called to do is to remember, and we can't even do that.

Jesus calmly foretells Judas's betrayal. Jesus doesn't plead with him not to do it; he simply states the truth: the betrayer seeks his own glory, so he will receive wrath. This, too, is according to the Father's predetermined plan. The disciples' response to Jesus' grave words is to turn on one another, a perfect example of the fruit of the glory story. They fight about who is going to fall and who is going to be greatest. They miss the truth completely. Once again the Savior tells them about true greatness: "Be a servant. Be like me." Can't you imagine their eyes glazing over as he speaks about becoming a servant? "Yes, servants are nice," they might have thought, "just as long as we aren't the ones doing the serving. Can't he skip to the part about us and our kingdom?"

How would you have responded to them? Would you have been angry, judgmental, censorious, or impatient? Do you see how responding in that way is simply another fruit of your belief in the glory story? Like them, are you assured of your own worthiness, and do you have confidence that you would have gotten it right? That false assurance is the cause of your self-righteous judgment. Look instead at how the Passover Lamb responds: "You are those who have stayed with me in my trials, and I assign to you, as my Father assigned to me, a kingdom, that you may eat and drink at my table in my kingdom and sit on thrones judging the twelve tribes of Israel" (Luke 22:28–30).

He commends and commissions them! He knows what is in their hearts, and yet he takes time to commend them, saying in essence, "You've stayed with me in my trials." Amazing grace! Of course, he knows that the only reason that they stayed with him was because he inclined their hearts to do so. But still, he brings them words of encouragement. Then he commissions them as those who will eternally eat and drink with him and ultimately judge Israel.

Why would Jesus commission and use this band of men? He did so to demonstrate his grace and to shatter their belief in the glory story. They think that they are being commended and commissioned because they are such winners, but the exact opposite is true:

> God chose what is foolish in the world to shame the wise; God chose what is weak in the world to shame the strong; God chose what is low and despised in the world, even things that are not, to bring to nothing things that are, so that no human being might boast in the presence of God. (1 Cor. 1:27-30)

They weren't chosen because they were good candidates for glory. No, they were chosen so that, at the end, when all masks are removed and all they really were will be clearly seen, no one will give them any accolades.[8] No human being—not the apostles, not the church fathers, not mighty theologians like Martin Luther, not faithful missionaries, not humble mothers training their children— will boast in the presence of God.

> I heard *every creature in heaven and on earth and under the earth and in the sea, and all that is in them*, saying, "*To him who sits on the throne and to the Lamb* be blessing and honor and glory and might forever and ever!" And the four living creatures said, "Amen!" and the elders fell down and worshiped. (Rev. 5:13–14)

And then, as if all this weren't enough to demonstrate our need and destitution, we have the interchange between the Paschal Lamb and Peter, the proud prototype of the man of glory.

> "Simon, Simon, behold, Satan demanded to have you, that he might sift you like wheat, but I have prayed for you that your faith may not fail. And when you have turned again, strengthen your brothers." Peter said to him, "Lord, I am ready to go with you both to prison and to death." Jesus said, "I tell you, Peter, the rooster will not crow this day, until you deny three times that you know me." (Luke 22:31–34)

Here the Lord isn't telling Peter to be careful not to sin. No, he is telling him that he will sin. Peter's proud belief in his personal glory story needed to be shattered. Peter needed to know that he would continue to stand only because his Savior had prayed that his faith would not fail.

Imagine the generous heart of the Lamb, who was facing Calvary, taking time to assure Peter that he had prayed for him! Jesus knew that Peter *would* repent because Jesus had prayed for him. "When [not "if"] you have turned again," he said, "strengthen your brothers." Peter was to use his shameful fall as means of grace to bring strength and hope to his brothers in their failure and sin. In the meantime, Jesus says that he, the faithful suffering Servant, is about to be numbered with "the transgressors" (Luke 22:37). Who are these "transgressors"? For whom has Jesus Christ interceded?

(John 17:11, 15). They are the Father's children, his bride—you and me and all who trust, however feebly, in him and his sacrifice.

After Peter's denial and before the weight of what he had done had fully fallen upon him, his loving Redeemer reestablished contact with him. "And the Lord turned and looked at Peter. And Peter remembered the saying of the Lord. . . . And he went out and wept bitterly" (Luke 22:61–62). The pain that Peter felt as his self-assurance and self-confidence were crushed was evidenced by his violent wails as he glimpsed his soul's poverty in the light of his Savior's loving gaze. But this lesson was not all pain.

The demolition of the glory story and its replacement with simple trust in the cross is also the fountainhead of all freedom from futility and the establishment of all persevering hope. The cross of Christ is the only "staff by means of which [we] might successfully leap over the abyss of despair."[9] Thank God for the demolition of our self-trust and for the kindness and power of our blessed Redeemer who calls us to abandon all hope of personal glory and to embrace his cross instead.

It is only here, beneath the cross of Jesus, that we will taste the true righteousness, peace, and joy that mark members of his kingdom. The cross shouts at us, "Give up your glory story. Let the nails and the blood and the cries free you from your slavery, fear, and despair!"

WHAT HAVE YOU DECIDED TO KNOW?

Have you ever wondered what Paul meant when he said, "For I decided to know nothing among you except Jesus Christ and him crucified" (1 Cor. 2:2)? Did he mean that he was going to empty his mind of every other bit of information? No, Paul meant that he was going to attend solely to Christ as the only hope for mankind. He wasn't going to argue about the Jewish law nor was he going to dispute Greek philosophers. He knew that neither Moses nor Aristotle held out any hope for the salvation of men; neither God's law nor the world's wisdom could salvage a human soul from the despair of our fallen condition.

Additionally, Paul determined to remember a crucified Savior, this weak, beaten, bloody, despised, pierced Man groaning in agony and calling out in despair to his Father. This crucified Messiah was a stumbling block both to Jews, who trusted in their good works, and to Greeks, who trusted in their wisdom. How could a so-called illegitimate, executed criminal push the glory story forward? What foolishness! He couldn't. He wasn't interested in our glory story at all. Instead he demolished it and wrote the story of the cross, the only truly life-transforming story ever written.

Through the gospel story—and only through it—are men and women changed. The story of the cross isn't a story about our goodness, perfectibility, power, wisdom, or perseverance. The story of the cross is a story of suffering and humiliation that ends with our being stripped of all our self-confidence and being clothed in the glory of Another. Next to this story, the glory story fades into absurdity.

Because of God the Son's incarnation, crucifixion, resurrection, and ascension, we know that we are not alone in a hostile and empty universe. We can be assured of his protection, intercession, and care, because he has taken our flesh into heaven and stands there with us before his Father. But the incarnation was neither grand nor proper. His birth was obscure, questionable, and poor. He slept his first night on earth in an animal's feeding trough. His ascension wasn't attended by great fanfare either. There was no glory story there; just some clueless disciples looking up as he disappeared from view.

His earthly life wasn't attended by much glory either. Yes, there were those who saw his miracles and were astonished by his teaching, but even his closest followers failed to understand the message he preached. It wasn't until after the resurrection that they began to really see. And, of course, although his crucifixion was the most glorious act ever witnessed by man, it just seemed to the watching world to be one more execution of some doubtful, pious zealot who had angered other religious zealots, and it seemed to his friends to be an unmitigated, life-shattering disaster. Glory? Hardly.

Because of Christ's sinless life and substitutionary death we can confidently stand before the gaze of him to whom all things are "naked and exposed" and to whom all people will "give account" (Heb. 4:13). On the day when we give account, we will not be foolish enough to talk about how *we* matured, how faithful *we* were, how *we* deserve glory. No, on that day, we will humbly fall before his pierced feet and rest only in his death and righteousness. We will receive the reward *he* has earned, and we will cast it at his feet so that all the glory will go to him because he has done it all for us.

Because of his resurrection, we can live confidently today. We can fight the good "fight of the faith" and seek to "pursue righteousness, godliness, faith, love, steadfastness, gentleness" (1 Tim. 6:11–12) because we know that our Savior's sacrifice has been accepted. We can know that we are accepted because God raised him from the dead. We can also know that the power of sin, to which we have been so enslaved, has been broken. We have been completely and forever redeemed. We are now free to love unashamedly, wildly, confidently, and fully because our ultimate glory is assured. We have been made new. We will not always be as we are now.

> We shall all be changed, in a moment, in the twinkling of an eye, at the last trumpet. For the trumpet will sound, and the dead will be raised imperishable, and we shall be changed. For this perishable body must put on the imperishable, and this mortal body must put on immortality. When the perishable puts on the imperishable, and the mortal puts on immortality, then shall come to pass the saying that is written:
>
> "Death is swallowed up in victory."
>   "O death, where is your victory?
>   O death, where is your sting?"
>
> The sting of death is sin, and the power of sin is the law. But thanks be to God, who gives us the victory through our Lord Jesus Christ. Therefore, my beloved brothers, be steadfast, immovable, always abounding in the work of the Lord, knowing that in the Lord your labor is not in vain. (1 Cor. 15:51–58)

We will be changed because we have been given the victory through our crucified and risen Lord. This victory is ours now but it won't be fully realized until we are finally and completely changed. Sin and the law's condemning demand have been denuded and disarmed, but they still pull at our hearts. The glory story still sounds good to us, but on that day we *will* be completely free from its allure.

So, then, in light of these facts, this assured future and the change that will inevitably be ours, we are called to be "steadfast, immovable, always abounding in the work of the Lord, knowing that in the Lord your labor is not in vain." We can know that our toil is not futile and we can trust that even though we fail miserably, we should continue to fight because our labor is "in the Lord" and nothing in him is in vain.

COUNSEL, THEN, FROM THE CROSS

Whether you have read this book because you want to learn to counsel yourself or to counsel others in the light of the cross, we are glad that you have done so. We are glad that you have persevered to the end of our time together, and we trust that the Lord has used it to make you love him more.

We pray that you will understand, believe, and remember that there really are only two ways to counsel. You can counsel using either the tenets of psychology or even the Bible's imperatives in the light of the glory story, giving helpful hints on how to progress in a personal pursuit of self-perfection, or you can *counsel from the cross.* Either we train ourselves and others to put our trust in our ability and then hope for the best, or we train ourselves and others to self-despair and to live "on in 'naked confidence in the mercy of God.'"[10] We will view God as either the "rewarder of all our 'good' works, the pot of gold at the end of our rainbow of merit,"[11] or as our merciful Father who inexplicably identifies with us, loves and welcomes us, and rewards us with blessing despite our sin and failures.

If we see him in that light, as he truly is, then (and only then), will we have the proper motivation for grateful obedience, not as slaves to the law but as thankful children. *The point is precisely that the power to do good comes only out of this wild claim that everything has already been done.*

We would like to leave you with one last word, and it is simply this: when in your counseling room or when you're visiting with friends, pursuing a door of opportunity with a stranger on a bus, wrestling with your heart's idols and unbelief, determine to know nothing except Jesus Christ and him crucified. Remember what the gospel says about us: we are more sinful and flawed than we ever dared believe but we are also more loved and welcomed than we ever dared hope.

PURSUING COUNSEL FROM THE CROSS

1) Take time to interact with Psalm 115:1, "Not to us, O LORD, not to us, but to your name give glory, for the sake of your steadfast love and your faithfulness!" Does your counsel either to yourself or to others seek to give glory to human beings rather than to God? In what way(s)?

2) What does it mean to believe in the "glory story"?

3) What does it mean to believe in the "gospel story"? How does believing in the gospel story affect our attitudes, affections, aspirations, and relationships with others?

4) What might be some of the obvious ramifications of believing in each one?

5) Summarize in four or five sentences what you have learned in this chapter.

6) After reviewing your summaries of the previous chapters, summarize the truths you are taking away from this book.

Why *Biblical* Counseling?

EVERYONE, AND EVERY counselor in particular, is an anthropologist. An anthropologist studies the nature, origin, and destiny of mankind. Whether we have studied a formal anthropology or any of its subsets—such as psychology, the study of the soul or human mind—or just listened to Dr. Laura on the radio, we are all anthropologists. We have all drawn conclusions about the nature, origin, and destiny of mankind. We have all observed human behavior; we have thought about how we and others think. We just can't avoid it. Make no mistake: whether we get our anthropology or psychology from pop culture sources like *People* magazine or Dr. Phil, from the study of Greek philosophers, or from the Bible, we have firm underlying beliefs about who we are, why we are here, what's wrong with us, and what kind of help we need. We are all anthropologists. We have all studied psychology.

Just think about it: when we sit down with a friend who is struggling in his work or marriage, we bring certain biases or presuppositions about him into the conversation. We bring our psychology. For instance, when a friend complains that his boss is unfair or that his wife is too demanding, we hear him through the grid of our underlying beliefs about who he is and the source of his problem. We counsel and comfort him and prescribe solutions to those problems based on what we believe about him as a human being. Is he a victim? Is he an innocent bystander? Is he responsible? Does he need a better work environment in order to be a better employee? Does he have all the answers he needs within himself? Does he need an outside source? These are some of the questions we'll have already answered before we even start the conversation.

Whether or not we know it, we have all embraced specific anthropological perspectives, and in our day most of these perspectives have been highly influenced both by Darwin's theory of evolution and by the many prominent systems of psychology that have permeated our culture, beginning with Freud's. Unless we have intentionally sought to discern and refuse the presuppositions of Darwinian evolution and Freudian psychology[1] we will unwittingly accept them and, like Jacob, we might be surprised one morning to find out whom we have been in bed with. There is a great gulf between the psychology propounded by atheists like Freud and our Christian beliefs.

All of our anthropologies and methodologies for helping others will flow either out of the Bible or out of the anthropological presuppositions of the men and women who propound and promulgate them. Of course, there are many among us who seek to eclectically combine the truths of the Bible with the tenets of whatever forms of psychology most appeal to us, but in the end, because these systems are in competition with one another, one will eventually consume the other.

Because psychology, unlike chemistry, is not "hard" science, it has failed to produce one overarching, unifying system that deeply and clearly describes man and his problems. Because psychology is a "soft" science, many different psychologies have been developed since the days when Freud first espoused his famous doctrines. Most if not all psychologists will gladly admit that there is no absolute truth when it comes to their field and that the practice of psychology is like eating in a cafeteria—one chooses whatever system happens to appeal to him and then combines it with others. There is not one unified theory that any psychologist can point to and say, "This is absolute truth."

The hundreds of branches or systems of psychology differ from one another, and some are absolutely antithetical to other systems because they are based on the differing beliefs and personalities of their founders.[2] For instance, the Skinnerian behaviorist scorns the dream interpretation of the Freudian psychotherapist. The Gestalt therapist focuses on here-and-now experiences and doesn't care about interpretation, while interpretation is the "main work"[3] of the Jungian psychoanalyst with his archetypes. The warm and caring Person-Centered therapist won't presume to give you any answers but will cordially help you discover your own inward truth on your individual path to self-actualization. Albert Ellis's RET[4] doesn't care a fig about warmth but is "highly cognitive, active-directive, homework-assigning and discipline-oriented."[5]

Of course, in recent years all these therapies (and hundreds of others like them) have been gobbled up by materialistic determinism and the pharmacological giant of biopsychiatry. The materialistic determinist's anthropology is very simple indeed: all you are is a bag of interacting chemicals, and all your problems can be diagnosed and solved by observing and balancing your chemicals. Talk therapy? Nonsense! Take the right pill and you'll feel better![6]

From this perspective it's easy to see that psychology is not a science, but something more akin to a religion or a philosophy. It is man's attempt to define and assist himself, and its systems are as different as every one of the men who developed them. Of course, psychologists will never discover one great unifying truth because they refuse to acknowledge any absolute truth that would inform psychology from outside itself. Therefore, it continues to be created and recreated in a never-ending cycle of darkness and futility.

We should not be surprised that secular man embraces these futile schemes. After all, what else does he have? He is lost, without hope and without God in this world (Eph. 2:12). His entire life is full of trouble (Job 5:7); he works and is never satisfied (Eccl. 6:7), and his foolish heart is darkened (Rom. 1:21). It is not surprising that he tries to construct fig-leaf false identities while hammering away at his personal rendition of the Tower of Babel. What is surprising, though, is how frequently Christians mimic and employ the systems and psychologies of secularists.

It is in light of the overabundance of counseling principles and methods propagated these days that we are presenting the presuppositions and goals of biblical counseling in this appendix.

To begin with, we'd like you to know what we believe about the role of the Bible in counseling. When we say that we are "biblical counselors," what we mean is that we try to consistently allow the Bible to define us—who we are, where our problems come from, and how we can be helped. We believe that the truths of Scripture, when rightly understood and applied, are the answer to every difficulty, trial, and doubt that Christians face. We believe that any diagnosis of or prescription for human problems that contradicts or disregards the worldview revealed in the Bible is bound in the end to lead away from our Creator's good purpose for us: to glorify and enjoy him forever.

WHO GOD SAYS HE IS AND WHO HE SAYS WE ARE

Every counseling construct that does not begin with an understanding and acceptance of God's self-revelation in the Old and New Testaments is not biblical (or even Christian) in nature. God declares that he is the Creator of all peoples and that he has created them in his own image (Gen. 1:26–28) and for his own glory (Rom. 11:36; Rev. 4:11). Because God is man's creator, man owes him his allegiance, obedience, and worship. Because man was created in the image of God, we owe respect and honor to one another.

The counselor who begins with that simple presupposition will embrace a methodology antithetical to the counselor who believes that man evolved into his present state from primordial slime and that his existence is a random occurrence that he must fight to sustain. The "survival of the fittest" fits well into many secular psychologies ("look out for number one," "get your needs met first," "learn to love yourself before you can love others"[7]), but not into biblical Christianity, in which the Fittest laid down his life for the weak. Every psychology from Freud on has been developed in the belief that there is no Creator-God and that man owes no allegiance to anyone besides himself.[8] This is the ultimate fly that spoils the ointment of every modern psychotherapy. Man is not, as Freud and his ilk believe, autonomous. He is a dependent creature in dire need of a help from outside himself.

Because God is our creator, his knowledge of us is perfect and complete (1 Chron. 28:8; Ps. 139:2; John 2:25; Heb. 4:13). Any methodology that has its primary genesis in the mind of fallen man *must* by definition be skewed in some way. Fallen man does not know the heart of man because it is hidden from his perception, and he is darkened in his understanding and deceived by sin (Jer. 17:5; Rom. 1:21; 3:10–11; Eph. 4:18; Heb. 3:13). Due to the noetic effect of sin[9] we must be suspicious of any counseling construct that does not intentionally begin and consistently continue with the Bible's definition of God, man, and our problems. Proverbs 28:26 puts this thought even more bluntly: "Whoever trusts in his own mind is a fool."

Apart from the illumination of God through the Scripture and the Holy Spirit, we would forever stumble in darkness about the cause and ultimate cure of our problems (Prov. 4:19). Hebrews 4:12 gives us hope, however, because it tells us where we can find a clear and accurate diagnosis and understanding of ourselves and others: "The word of God is living and active, sharper than any two-edged sword, piercing to the division of soul and of spirit, of joints and of marrow, and discerning the thoughts and intentions of the heart." Hebrews goes on to observe about the omniscient divine speaker of Scripture: "No creature is hidden from his sight, but all are naked and exposed to the eyes of him to whom we must give account" (4:13). God has told us who we are, and he has told us where we can discover information about ourselves—in Scripture.

In addition, God has clearly stated where all our problems originate. If man had not succumbed to the tempter's lies in the garden, we would not be having a discussion about counseling today. We would have unbridled, free, and delightful fellowship with one another and with our Creator. We would not be saddled with the heavy burden of shame and embarrassment or with difficulties with others and the failures and disappointments that are so common to our lives.

God defines the source of all our problems as sin. In the new heavens and earth where there will be no sin, there will be no "mourning, nor crying, nor pain anymore" (Rev. 21:4). There won't be any need for counseling because there won't be any sin, and the bitter fruit of all sin—mourning, crying, and pain—will be destroyed.

We are not saying that we willfully cause all our own problems (although we do cause many of them). We are saying that sin—in others and in ourselves, and all through life in this sin-cursed world—is the source of all the difficulties we face.[10] The world, the flesh, and the Devil conspire to produce all our sin and suffering. If we refuse to recognize this reality, we cut ourselves off from the only source of lasting relief or help. If we refuse to say that we sin or that those we love sin, we refuse the help of the One who was born to "save his people from their sins" (Matt. 1:21).

We refuse Jesus' help because it isn't the sort of help we want, but he wasn't sent to deliver people from their issues, dysfunctions, or imbalances. He was sent to "seek and to save the lost" (Luke 19:10). It is our lostness, our helplessness, our self-deceived and wandering hearts, our selfishness, our frailty, and our ultimate death that are the root of all our troubles. These are the very troubles that Jesus Christ came to overcome and conquer.

Biblical counselors define man as both created and dependent but also desperately lost and sinful. We see man as being responsible to "give an account of himself to God" (Rom. 14:12), but we also see him as enslaved to sin and unable to save himself (John 8:34; Acts 4:12). So we refuse to point man inward toward himself or outward toward us as counselors. Rather, we direct him to the Scriptures and upward to the Lord of those Scriptures.

The Scriptures' self-testimony is that it was written so that we might have hope (Rom. 15:4), know truth (John 17:17), and have life (John 6:63, 68). Jesus himself, the Word who became flesh (John 1:14), came that we might have life through belief in him (John 10:10; 20:31). He "gave himself for us to redeem us from all lawlessness and to purify for himself a people for his own possession who are zealous for good works" (Titus 2:14).

Any counseling that does not consistently strive to anchor itself in the Scriptures and in the saving work of Jesus Christ for sinners is not Christian. Any anthropology or perspective on man that ignores man's relation to God and his desperate need for a Savior is not Christian. Biblical counselors believe that all the "treasures" of wisdom and knowledge are hidden in Jesus Christ (Col. 2:3). Any so-called wisdom not originating in Scripture and particularly in Jesus Christ is not Christian.[11]

THE GOAL OF BIBLICAL COUNSELING

Biblical counselors also define the goal of their counseling (and all of life) as not merely the alleviation of suffering but the living of life for the glory of God. Although we always hope for alleviation of suffering, we have a higher goal than the here and now. Our goal is that the God who loved us, who gave his Son for us, would be glorified through us, and that the name of Jesus Christ would be praised.

When people finally decide to find a friend or counselor and ask for help, the glory of God is not usually on their wish list. Instead goals such as "feeling better about myself," "getting my husband to love me more," or "having more obedient children" top the list. The biblical counselor does hope, of course, that people will feel better and have better relationships as a result of their meeting together. But that is not his primary objective. No, his primary objective is that the counselee would see her life as having one goal: making the great love, holiness, power, beauty, and majesty of God the Father, Son, and Holy Spirit more evident in her life.[12]

The goal of glorifying God through our lives is, of course, absent from all secular counseling, since secular systems do not acknowledge any higher authority than the human individual, or possibly human society (except one you might create in your mind). The goal of glorifying God is also absent from any system of counseling that does not consciously seek to keep it as its central motivation. A counselor who is a Christian might give tacit acknowledgment to the importance of glorifying God, but if he believes that what his counselee really needs is to have his "love cup" filled up before he can love others or glorify God, then self-fulfillment will become his goal and God's glory will fade into insignificance.

Here we are again with our primary premise: any counseling that does not begin *and consistently stay with* the Bible's revelation about God and man will always slide into man-centeredness. It will always make man and his plans, power, goals, and aspirations the focus of counseling. It is impossible for anything else to happen.

BIBLICAL COUNSELING IS A TRUST TRANSFER

And finally, biblical counseling reflects the "trust transfer" that is part of our Christian faith. Rather than trusting in ourselves as counselors or in our system's power to change lives, we trust in the power of the Holy Spirit. We acknowledge that we are unable to change anyone and that all of our words will amount to only so much hot air unless we bring in Scripture, and thereby the Holy Spirit who inspired that Scripture, to our counselees. So even though we know we are weak, and the bread of the Word seems weak as we break it, we also trust that there is a power great enough to transform lives. We trust in the power of God through the agency of the Holy Spirit.

This trust transfer is actually one of the great benefits of being a counselor who relies on Scripture. Trusting in God and his Word frees us from having to depend on our own wisdom or strength. Of course, God uses means to accomplish his goals in our counselee's life, so we want to be prepared; but even so, we can depend on God who will accomplish the work he wants to do in the lives of those we speak to.

So, to answer the question, "Why *biblical* counseling?" here is our summary: We believe in and practice biblical counseling because we have embraced an anthropology taken from the Bible, and we trust God's evaluation of us and of our condition as our only source of help and our ultimate goal.[13] We are not looking for new systems, because we have embraced the one authoritative and absolute truth. We have embraced the Bible as being "breathed out by God and profitable for teaching, for reproof, for correction, and for training in righteousness, that the man of God may be competent, equipped for every good work" (2 Tim. 3:16–17).

Scripture Passages by Topic for Use in Counseling

WHAT FOLLOWS IS A BRIEF LIST of possible counseling topics with Scriptures that address each one. This kind of list is not unusual in biblical counseling literature, and in fact, many of the references used here were taken from Jay Adams's *Christian Counselor's New Testament*.[1] What may make this list unique, however, is the drawing out of both the declarations and the obligations of Scripture.

This list is not exhaustive, but it will be helpful as a paradigm as you begin to learn how the declarations of the gospel are meant to inform and motivate the obligations of the gospel. This list is certainly not meant to be the only tool to use with someone struggling with any of these problems. It's simply meant to serve as a model as you learn to counsel yourself and others from the full perspective of the cross.

SCRIPTURE PASSAGES BY TOPIC FOR USE IN COUNSELING

TOPIC	PASSAGE	DECLARATION (Because of this . . .)	OBLIGATION (Therefore . . .)
Adultery	I am the LORD your God, who brought you out of the land of Egypt, out of the house of slavery. . . . You shall not commit adultery. (Ex. 20:2, 14)	*Because* I am the Lord your God who brought you out of the land of Egypt, out of the house of slavery . . . *Because* he has been faithful to you to rescue and keep you when you were slaves . . .	*Therefore* you shall not commit adultery. You should be faithful even to those who willfully sin against you, to those who no longer attract you, because I have been faithful to you even when you were my enemy.

TOPIC	PASSAGE	DECLARATION (Because of this . . .)	OBLIGATION (Therefore . . .)
Anger	Be angry and do not sin; do not let the sun go down on your anger, and give no opportunity to the devil. Let no corrupting talk come out of your mouths, but only such as is good for building up, as fits the occasion, that it may give grace to those who hear. And do not grieve the Holy Spirit of God, by whom you were sealed for the day of redemption. Let all bitterness and wrath and anger and clamor and slander be put away from you, along with all malice. Be kind to one another, tenderhearted, forgiving one another, as God in Christ forgave you. (Eph. 4:26–27, 29–32)	*Because* you were graciously sealed for the day of redemption and *because* God in Christ has already forgiven you, *because* you don't need to try to keep everything together by your own strength, and *because* you are completely loved, welcomed, and accepted by God . . .	*Therefore*, don't sin in your anger. Handle problems quickly, as they come up, and don't give Satan a foothold in your heart by defiling your conscience through your anger. *Therefore*, forgive others and be as tenderhearted with them as he has been with you.
Bitterness	See to it that no one fails to obtain the grace of God; that no "root of bitterness" springs up and causes trouble, and by it many become defiled; that no one is sexually immoral or unholy like Esau, who sold his birthright for a single meal. . . . But you have come to Mount Zion and to the city of the living God, the heavenly Jerusalem, and to innumerable angels in festal gathering, and to the assembly of the firstborn who are enrolled in heaven, and to God, the judge of all, and to the spirits of the righteous made perfect, and to Jesus, the mediator of a new covenant, and to the sprinkled blood that speaks a better word than the blood of Abel. (Heb. 12:15–16, 22–24)	*Because* you have come to Mount Zion and to the city of the living God, the heavenly Jerusalem, and to innumerable angels in festal gathering, and to the assembly of the firstborn who are enrolled in heaven, and to God, the judge of all, and to the spirits of the righteous made perfect, and to Jesus, the mediator of a new covenant, and to the sprinkled blood that speaks a better word than the blood of Abel . . . *Because* you are no longer at the terrifying foot of Sinai but have been enrolled in heaven and have been brought to Jesus and sprinkled clean . . .	*Therefore*, see to it that no one fails to obtain the grace of God; that no "root of bitterness" springs up and causes trouble, and by it many become defiled; that no one is sexually immoral or unholy like Esau, who sold his birthright for a single meal. Being bitter, jealous, and coveteous doesn't make sense when you realize what you have been given. *Therefore*, value what you have and trust in Jesus the "mediator of a better covenant" to supply all you need.

TOPIC	PASSAGE	DECLARATION (Because of this . . .)	OBLIGATION (Therefore . . .)
Communication problems	But now you must put them all away: anger, wrath, malice, slander, and obscene talk from your mouth. Do not lie to one another, seeing that you have put off the old self with its practices and have put on the new self, which is being renewed in knowledge after the image of its creator. Here there is not Greek and Jew, circumcised and uncircumcised, barbarian, Scythian, slave, free; but Christ is all, and in all. (Col. 3:8–11)	*Because* . . . you have put off the old self with its practices and have put on the new self, which is being renewed in knowledge after the image of its creator. Here there is not Greek and Jew, circumcised and uncircumcised, barbarian, Scythian, slave, free; but Christ is all, and in all. *Because* you have been made new and are being renewed into the image of your creator and because all class envy and caste distinctions are nullified by the gospel, and all Christians have been made one and equal in Christ. *Because* all the ground for fighting and unkindness to one another, for pride and competition, has been obliterated in Christ, as well as all cause for boasting in one's self-righteousness and resultant judging and criticism and false boasting, we are able to change our speech to be like his.	*Therefore*, you must put them all away: anger, wrath, malice, slander, and obscene talk from your mouth. Do not lie to one another.
Depression or fatigue	Consider him who endured from sinners such hostility against himself, so that you may not grow weary or fainthearted. (Heb. 12:3–4)	*Because* Jesus endured from sinners such hostility against himself . . . *Because* he loved you with such a great love, he willingly endured mankind's hostility from the moment of his birth until his death.	*Therefore*, consider him . . . so that you may not grow weary or fainthearted. Focus your heart and mind on this love as you face the hostility of others and even of your own heart.
Envy	For we ourselves were once foolish, disobedient, led astray, slaves to various passions and pleasures, passing our days in malice and envy, hated by others and hating one another. But when the goodness and loving kindness of God our Savior	*Because* when the goodness and loving kindness of God our Savior appeared, he saved us, not because of works done by us in righteousness, but according to his own mercy, by the washing of regeneration and renewal of the Holy Spirit, whom he poured	*Therefore*, we ourselves were once foolish, disobedient, led astray, slaves to various passions and pleasures, passing our days in malice and envy, hated by others and hating one another. Envy, hatred, foolishness, disobedience, and

195

TOPIC	PASSAGE	DECLARATION (Because of this . . .)	OBLIGATION (Therefore . . .)
Envy (cont.)	appeared, he saved us, not because of works done by us in righteousness, but according to his own mercy, by the washing of regeneration and renewal of the Holy Spirit, whom he poured out on us richly through Jesus Christ our Savior, so that being justified by his grace we might become heirs according to the hope of eternal life. (Titus 3:3–7)	out on us richly through Jesus Christ our Savior, so that being justified by his grace we might become heirs according to the hope of eternal life. *Because* he's done all this for us and has "richly" poured out his mercy and cleansing through Jesus Christ, justifying us by his grace and making us heirs of eternal life.	idolatrous desires are no longer part of our life. We have been made new and when we are tempted to be envious of others we need to remember the great riches that have been given to us in Christ.
Family relationships	Put on then, as God's chosen ones, holy and beloved, compassionate hearts, kindness, humility, meekness, and patience, bearing with one another and, if one has a complaint against another, forgiving each other; as the Lord has forgiven you, so you also must forgive. And above all these put on love, which binds everything together in perfect harmony. . . . Wives, submit to your husbands, as is fitting in the Lord. Husbands, love your wives, and do not be harsh with them. Children, obey your parents in everything, for this pleases the Lord. Fathers, do not provoke your children, lest they become discouraged. . . . You are serving the Lord Christ. (Col. 3:12–14, 18–21, 24)	*Because* you are God's chosen ones, holy and beloved, the Lord has forgiven you. You are in the Lord; you are serving the Lord Christ. *Because* you have been adopted by the Father, and because you've been chosen and forgiven and he calls you "holy and beloved," because you have been given this great grace and mercy.	*Therefore*, put on compassion, kindness, humility, meekness, and patience, bearing with one another and, if one has a complaint against another, forgiving each other; as the Lord has forgiven you, so you also must forgive. And above all these put on love, which binds everything together in perfect harmony. Wives, submit to your husbands, as is fitting in the Lord. Husbands, love your wives, and do not be harsh with them. Children, obey your parents in everything, for this pleases the Lord. Fathers, do not provoke your children, lest they become discouraged. You are serving the Lord Christ. You have been loved, adopted, forgiven, and treated with mercy; *therefore*, treat others in your family with this love and grace. Wives should think about how Jesus submitted to his Father for them and then consciously submit to their husbands. Husbands should consider how gentle, kind, loving, and patient the

Scripture Passages by Topic

TOPIC	PASSAGE	DECLARATION (Because of this . . .)	OBLIGATION (Therefore . . .)
Family relationships (cont.)			Father has been with them and treat their wives and children in the same way. Even children can please the Lord by learning to submit even as Jesus did to his own parents.
Fear	And do not fear those who kill the body but cannot kill the soul. Rather fear him who can destroy both soul and body in hell. Are not two sparrows sold for a penny? And not one of them will fall to the ground apart from your Father. But even the hairs of your head are all numbered. Fear not, therefore; you are of more value than many sparrows. (Matt. 10:28–31)	*Because* not one of them will fall to the ground apart from your Father. Father. . . . Even the hairs of your head are all numbered. . . . You are of more value than many sparrows.	*Therefore*, do not fear those who kill the body but cannot kill the soul. Rather fear him who can destroy both soul and body in hell.
Grief	But we do not want you to be uninformed, brothers, about those who are asleep, that you may not grieve as others do who have no hope. For since we believe that Jesus died and rose again, even so, through Jesus, God will bring with him those who have fallen asleep. For this we declare to you by a word from the Lord, that we who are alive, who are left until the coming of the Lord, will not precede those who have fallen asleep. For the Lord himself will descend from heaven with a cry of command, with the voice of an archangel, and with the sound of the trumpet of God. And the dead in Christ will rise first. Then we who are alive, who are left, will be caught up together with them in the clouds to meet the Lord in the air, and so we will always be	*Because* Jesus died and rose again, even so, through Jesus, God will bring with him those who have fallen asleep. For this we declare to you by a word from the Lord, that we who are alive, who are left until the coming of the Lord, will not precede those who have fallen asleep. For the Lord himself will descend from heaven with a cry of command, with the voice of an archangel, and with the sound of the trumpet of God. And the dead in Christ will rise first. Then we who are alive, who are left, will be caught up together with them in the clouds to meet the Lord in the air, and so we will always be with the Lord.	*Therefore*, do not grieve as those who have no hope, and encourage one another with these words.

TOPIC	PASSAGE	DECLARATION (Because of this . . .)	OBLIGATION (Therefore . . .)
Grief (cont.)	with the Lord. Therefore encourage one another with these words. (1 Thess. 4:13–18)		
Habitual sin	For if we have been united with him in a death like his, we shall certainly be united with him in a resurrection like his. We know that our old self was crucified with him in order that the body of sin might be brought to nothing, so that we would no longer be enslaved to sin. For one who has died has been set free from sin. Now if we have died with Christ, we believe that we will also live with him. We know that Christ, being raised from the dead, will never die again; death no longer has dominion over him. For the death he died he died to sin, once for all, but the life he lives he lives to God. So you also must consider yourselves dead to sin and alive to God in Christ Jesus. Let not sin therefore reign in your mortal body, to make you obey its passions. Do not present your members to sin as instruments for unrighteousness, but present yourselves to God as those who have been brought from death to life, and your members to God as instruments for righteousness. For sin will have no dominion over you, since you are not under law but under grace. (Rom. 6:5–14)	*Because* we have been united with him in a death like his, we shall certainly be united with him in a resurrection like his. We know that our old self was crucified with him in order that the body of sin might be brought to nothing, so that we would no longer be enslaved to sin. For one who has died has been set free from sin. Now if we have died with Christ, we believe that we will also live with him. We know that Christ being raised from the dead will never die again; death no longer has dominion over him. For the death he died he died to sin, once for all, but the life he lives he lives to God.	*Therefore*, you also must consider yourselves dead to sin and alive to God in Christ Jesus. Let not sin therefore reign in your mortal bodies, to make you obey their passions. Do not present your members members to sin as instruments for unrighteousness, but present yourselves to God as those who have been brought from death to life, and your members to God as instruments for righteousness. For sin will have no dominion over you, since you are not under law but under grace.
Life-dominating problems such as drunkenness	At one time you were darkness, but now you are light in the Lord. Walk as children of light (for the fruit of light is found in all	*Because* at one time you were darkness, but now you are light in the Lord.	*Therefore*, walk as children of light (for the fruit of light is found in all that is good and right and true), and try to discern what is pleasing

198

TOPIC	PASSAGE	DECLARATION (Because of this . . .)	OBLIGATION (Therefore . . .)
Life-dominating problems such as drunkenness (cont.)	that is good and right and true), and try to discern what is pleasing to the Lord. Take no part in the unfruitful works of darkness, but instead expose them. . . . And do not get drunk with wine, for that is debauchery, but be filled with the Spirit, addressing one another in psalms and hymns and spiritual songs, singing and making melody to the Lord with your heart, giving thanks always and for everything to God the Father in the name of our Lord Jesus Christ, submitting to one another out of reverence for Christ. (Eph. 5:8–11, 18–21)		to the Lord. Take no part in the unfruitful works of darkness, but instead expose them. And do not get drunk with wine, for that is debauchery, but be filled with the Spirit, addressing one another in psalms and hymns and spiritual songs, singing and making melody to the Lord with your heart, giving thanks always and for everything to God the Father in the name of our Lord Jesus Christ, submitting to one another out of reverence for Christ.
Laziness	Slaves [servants], obey in everything those who are your earthly masters, not by way of eye-service, as people-pleasers, but with sincerity of heart, fearing the Lord. Whatever you do, work heartily, as for the Lord and not for men, knowing that from the Lord you will receive the inheritance as your reward. You are serving the Lord Christ. (Col. 3:22–24)	*Because* from the Lord you will receive the inheritance as your reward. You are serving the Lord Christ.	*Therefore*, slaves [servants], obey in everything those who are your earthly masters, not by way of eye-service, as people-pleasers, but with sincerity of heart, fearing the Lord. Whatever you do, work heartily, as for the Lord and not for men.
Lack of love	Beloved, let us love one another, for love is from God, and whoever loves has been born of God and knows God. Anyone who does not love does not know God, because God is love. In this the love of God was made manifest among us, that God sent his only Son into the world, so that we might live through him.	*Because* in this the love of God was made manifest among us, that God sent his only Son into the world, so that we might live through him. In this is love, not that we have loved God but that he loved us and sent his Son to be the propitiation for our sins. No one has ever seen God; if we love one another, God abides	*Therefore*, beloved, let us love one another, for love is from God, and whoever loves has been born of God and knows God. Anyone who does not love does not know God, because God is love. Beloved, if God so loved us, we also ought to love one another.

TOPIC	PASSAGE	DECLARATION (Because of this . . .)	OBLIGATION (Therefore . . .)
Lack of love (cont.)	In this is love, not that we have loved God but that he loved us and sent his Son to be the propitiation for our sins. Beloved, if God so loved us, we also ought to love one another. No one has ever seen God; if we love one another, God abides in us and his love is perfected in us. (1 John 4:7–12)	in us and his love is perfected in us.	
Lying	If then you have been raised with Christ, seek the things that are above, where Christ is, seated at the right hand of God. Set your minds on things that are above, not on things that are on earth. For you have died, and your life is hidden with Christ in God. When Christ who is your life appears, then you also will appear with him in glory. . . . Do not lie to one another, seeing that you have put off the old self with its practices and have put on the new self, which is being renewed in knowledge after the image of its creator. Here there is not Greek and Jew, circumcised and uncircumcised, barbarian, Scythian, slave, free; but Christ is all, and in all. (Col. 3:1–4, 9–11)	*Because* you have been raised with Christ. . . . You have died, and your life is hidden with Christ in God. When Christ who is your life appears, then you also will appear with him in glory . . . seeing that you have put off the old self with its practices and have put on the new self, which is being renewed in knowledge after the image of its creator. Here there is not Greek and Jew, circumcised and uncircumcised, barbarian, Scythian, slave, free; but Christ is all, and in all.	*Therefore*, seek the things that are above, where Christ is, seated at the right hand of God. Set your minds on things that are above, no on things that are on earth. *Therefore*, do not lie to one another.
Pride	So if there is any encouragement in Christ, any comfort from love, any participation in the Spirit, any affection and sympathy, complete my joy by being of the same mind, having the same love, being in full accord and of one mind. Do nothing from rivalry or conceit, but in humility count others more significant than yourselves. Let each of you look not only to his own interests, but	*Because* yours is the mind of Christ Jesus— who, though he was in the form of God, did not count equality with God a thing to be grasped, but made himself nothing, taking the form of a servant, being born in the likeness of men. And being found in human form, he humbled himself by becoming obedient to the point of death, even death on a cross. Therefore God has highly	*Therefore*, be of the same mind, having the same love, being in full accord and of one mind. Do nothing from rivalry or conceit, but in humility count others more significant than yourselves. Let each of you look not only to his own interests, but also to the interests of others. Have this mind among yourselves . . .

TOPIC	PASSAGE	DECLARATION (Because of this . . .)	OBLIGATION (Therefore . . .)
Pride (cont.)	also to the interests of others. Have this mind among yourselves, which is yours in Christ Jesus, who, though he was in the form of God, did not count equality with God a thing to be grasped, but made himself nothing, taking the form of a servant, being born in the likeness of men. And being found in human form, he humbled himself by becoming obedient to the point of death, even death on a cross. Therefore God has highly exalted him and bestowed on him the name that is above every name, so that at the name of Jesus every knee should bow, in heaven and on earth and under the earth, and every tongue confess that Jesus Christ is Lord, to the glory of God the Father. (Phil. 2:1–11)	exalted him and bestowed on him the name that is above every name, so that at the name of Jesus every knee should bow, in heaven and on earth and under the earth, and every tongue confess that Jesus Christ is Lord, to the glory of God the Father.	
Reconciliation	So if you are offering your gift at the altar and there remember that your brother has something against you, leave your gift there before the altar and go. First be reconciled to your brother, and then come and offer your gift. (Matt. 5:23–24)	*Because* you are offering your gift at the altar . . . *Because* you've been granted the privilege of offering gifts to God, gifts that he has given and access that he has granted . . .	*Therefore*, leave your gift there before the altar and go. First be reconciled to your brother, and then come and offer your gift.
Sexual problems in marriage	Or do you not know that your body is a temple of the Holy Spirit within you, whom you have from God? You are not your own, for you were bought with a price. So glorify God in your body. Now concerning the matters about which you wrote: "It is good for a man not to have sexual relations with a woman." But because of the temptation to sexual immorality, each man should have his own wife and	*Because* your body is a temple of the Holy Spirit within you, whom you have from God, you are not your own, for you were bought with a price.	*Therefore*, the husband should give to his wife her conjugal rights, and likewise the wife to her husband. For the wife does not have authority over her own body, but the husband does. Likewise the husband does not have authority over his own body, but the wife does. Do not deprive one another, except perhaps by agreement for a limited time, that you may devote yourselves to prayer;

TOPIC	PASSAGE	DECLARATION (Because of this . . .)	OBLIGATION (Therefore . . .)
Sexual problems in marriage (cont.)	each woman her own husband. The husband should give to his wife her conjugal rights, and likewise the wife to her husband. For the wife does not have authority over her own body, but the husband does. Likewise the husband does not have authority over his own body, but the wife does. Do not deprive one another, except perhaps by agreement for a limited time, that you may devote yourselves to prayer; but then come together again, so that Satan may not tempt you because of your lack of self-control. (1 Cor. 6:19–7:5)		but then come together again, so that Satan may not tempt you because of your lack of self-control.
Sexual problems outside of marriage	The body is not meant for sexual immorality, but for the Lord, and the Lord for the body. And God raised the Lord and will also raise us up by his power. Do you not know that your bodies are members of Christ? Shall I then take the members of Christ and make them members of a prostitute? Never! Or do you not know that he who is joined to a prostitute becomes one body with her? For, as it is written, "The two will become one flesh." But he who is joined to the Lord becomes one spirit with him. Flee from sexual immorality. Every other sin a person commits is outside the body, but the sexually immoral person sins against his own body. Or do you not know that your body is a temple of the Holy Spirit within you, whom you have from God? You are not your own, for you were bought with a price. So glorify God in your body. (1 Cor. 6:13–20)	*Because* the body is not meant for sexual immorality, but for the Lord, and the Lord for the body, you are not your own, for you were bought with a price.	*Therefore*, glorify God in body. Flee from sexual immorality. Every other sin a person commits is outside the body, but the sexually immoral person sins agast his own body.

TOPIC	PASSAGE	DECLARATION (Because of this . . .)	OBLIGATION (Therefore . . .)
Worry	Rejoice in the Lord always; again I will say, Rejoice. Let your reasonableness be known to everyone. The Lord is at hand; do not be anxious about anything, but in everything by prayer and supplication with thanksgiving let your requests be made known to God. And the peace of God, which surpasses all understanding, will guard your hearts and your minds in Christ Jesus. Finally, brothers, whatever is true, whatever is honorable, whatever is just, whatever is pure, whatever is lovely, whatever is commendable, if there is any excellence, if there is anything worthy of praise, think about these things. (Phil. 4:4–8)	*Because* the Lord is at hand, and the peace of God, which surpasses all understanding, will guard your hearts and your minds in Christ Jesus.	*Therefore*, rejoice in the Lord always; again I will say, Rejoice. Let your reasonableness be known to everyone. Do not be anxious about anything, but in everything by prayer and supplication with thanksgiving let your requests be made known to God. Finally, brothers, whatever is true, whatever is honorable, whatever is just, whatever is pure, whatever is lovely, whatever is commendable, if there is any excellence, if there is anything worthy of praise, think about these things.

The Best News Ever

I (ELYSE) DIDN'T BEGIN TO understand the gospel until the summer before my twenty-first birthday. Although I had attended church from time to time in my childhood, I'll admit that it never really transformed me in any significant way. I was frequently taken to Sunday school where I heard stories about Jesus. I knew, without really understanding, the importance of Christmas and Easter. I remember looking at the beautiful stained-glass windows with their cranberry red and deep cerulean blue and Jesus knocking on a garden door and having a vague sense that being religious was good. But I didn't have the foggiest idea about the gospel.

My strongest memories of adolescence are those of despair and anger. I was consistently in trouble, and I hated everyone who pointed that out. There were nights when I prayed that I would be good, or more specifically, get out of whatever trouble I was in and do better, only to be disappointed and angered by the failures of the following day.

Upon graduation from high school at seventeen, I got married, had a baby, and got divorced all before the second decade of my life ended. It was during the following months and years that I discovered the anesthetizing effects of drugs, alcohol, and illicit relationships. Although I was known as a girl who liked to party, I was utterly lost and joyless, and I was beginning to know it.

At one point, I remember telling a friend that I felt like I was fifty years old which, at that point in my life, was the oldest I could imagine anyone being. I was exhausted and disgusted, so I decided to set about improving myself. I worked a full-time job, took a full course load at a local junior college, and cared for my son. I changed my living arrangements and tried to start over. I didn't know that the Holy Spirit was working in my heart, calling me to the Son. I just knew that something had to change. Don't misunderstand: I was still living a shamefully wicked life; it's just that I felt like I was beginning to wake up to something different.

At this point, Julie entered my life. She was my next-door neighbor and she was a Christian. She was kind to me, and we became fast friends. She had a quality of life about her that attracted me, and she was always talking to me about her Savior, Jesus. She let me know that she was praying for me and would frequently encourage me to "get saved." Although I'd had the Sunday school training, what she had to say was something completely different from what I'd remembered ever hearing. She told me I needed to be "born again."

And so, on a warm night sometime in June of 1971, I knelt down in my tiny apartment and told the Lord that I wanted to be his. At that point, I didn't really understand much about the gospel, but I did understand this: I knew I was desperate, and I desperately believed that the Lord would help me. That prayer on that night changed everything about me. I remember it now, thirty-five years later, as if it were yesterday.

In the words of Scripture, I knew I needed to be saved, and I trusted that Christ could save me. One man who came in contact with some of Jesus' followers asked this question: "What must I do to be saved?" The answer was simple: "Believe in the Lord Jesus, and you will be saved" (Acts 16:30–31).

Very simply, what do you need to believe in order to be a Christian? You need to believe that you need salvation—help or deliverance. It won't work to try to reform yourself or decide that you are going to become a moral person so that God will be impressed. He is completely holy, that is, perfectly moral, so you have to give up any idea that you can be good enough to meet his standard. This is the good *bad* news. It's bad news because it tells you that you are in an impossible situation that you cannot change. But it's also good news because it will free you from endless cycles of self-improvement that end in ultimate failure.

You also need to trust that what you're unable to do—live a perfectly holy life—Christ has done for you. This is the good *good* news. This is the gospel.

Basically, the gospel is the story of how God looked down through the corridors of time and set his love on his people. At a specific point in time, he sent his Son into the world to become fully like us. This is the story you hear about at Christmas. This baby grew to be a man, and after thirty years of obscurity he began to show the people who he was. He did this by performing miracles—healing the sick, raising the dead. He also demonstrated his deity by teaching people what God required of them, and he continually foretold his coming death and resurrection. And he did one more thing: he claimed to be God.

Because of his claim to be God, the leading religious people along with the political powers of the day passed an unjust sentence of death upon him. Although he had never done anything wrong, he was beaten, mocked, and shamefully executed. He died. Even though it looked like he had failed, the truth is that this was God's plan from the very beginning.

His body was taken down from the cross and laid hastily in a rock tomb in a garden. After three days, some of his followers went to properly care for his remains and discovered that he had risen from the dead. They actually saw him, spoke with him, touched him, and ate with him. This is the story that we celebrate at Easter. After another forty days, he was taken back up into heaven, still in his physical form, and his followers were told that he would return to earth in just the same way.

I told you that there are two things you need to believe. The first is that you need more significant help than you or any other mere human could ever supply. The second is that you need to believe that Jesus, the Christ, is the person who will supply that help, and that if you come to him, he will not turn his back on you. You don't need to understand much more than that, and if you really believe these truths, your life will be transformed by his love.

Below are some verses from the Bible for you. As you read them, you can talk to God, just as though he were sitting right by you (because his presence is everywhere!) and ask him for help to understand. Remember, his help isn't based on your ability to perfectly understand or on anything that you can do. If you trust him, he has promised to help you, and that's all you need to know for now.

> For all have sinned and fall short of the glory of God. (Rom. 3:23)

> For the wages of sin is death, but the free gift of God is eternal life in Christ Jesus our Lord. (Rom. 6:23)

> For while we were still weak, at the right time Christ died for the ungodly. For one will scarcely die for a righteous person—though perhaps for a good person one would dare even to die—but God shows his love for us in that while we were still sinners, Christ died for us. (Rom. 5:6–8)

> For our sake he made him to be sin who knew no sin, so that in him we might become the righteousness of God. (2 Cor. 5:21)

> If you confess with your mouth that Jesus is Lord and believe in your heart that God raised him from the dead, you will be saved. For with the heart one believes and is justified, and with the mouth one confesses and is saved. For the Scripture says, "Everyone who believes in him will not be put to shame." . . . The same Lord is Lord of all, bestowing his riches on all who call on him. For "everyone who calls on the name of the Lord will be saved." (Rom. 10:9–13)

> Whoever comes to me I will never cast out. (John 6:37)

> Therefore, if anyone is in Christ, he is a new creation. The old has passed away; behold, the new has come. (2 Cor. 5:17)

Come to me, all who labor and are heavy laden, and I will give you rest. Take my yoke upon you, and learn from me, for I am gentle and lowly in heart, and you will find rest for your souls. (Matt. 11:28–30)

There is therefore now no condemnation for those who are in Christ Jesus. (Rom. 8:1)

If you'd like to, you might pray something like this:

Dear God,

I'll admit that I don't understand everything about this, but I do believe these two things: I need help, and you want to help me. I confess that I'm like Elyse and have pretty much ignored you my whole life, except when I was in trouble or just wanted to feel good about myself. I know that I haven't loved you or my neighbor, so it's true that I deserve to be punished and I really do need help. But I also believe that you've brought me here, right now, to read this page because you are willing to help me and that if I ask you for help, you won't send me away empty-handed. I'm beginning to understand how you punished your Son in my place and how, because of his sacrifice for me, I can have a relationship with you. Father, please guide me to a good church and help me understand your Word. I give my life to you and ask you to make me yours.

In Jesus' name, Amen.

Here are two more thoughts: first, in his kindness, Jesus established his church so that we could encourage and help each other understand and live out these two truths. If you know that you need help and you think that Jesus is able to supply that help, or if you are still questioning but want to know more, please search out a good church in your neighborhood and begin to make relationships there.

A good church is one that recognizes that we cannot save ourselves by our own goodness and that relies wholly on Jesus Christ (and no one else) for this salvation. You can call around and ask these questions or you could even go on the Internet and get a listing of churches in your area. Usually churches will have something called a "Statement of Faith" on their Web site, where you can get information about them.

Mormons (Church of Jesus Christ of Latter Day Saints) and Jehovah's Witnesses (Kingdom Hall) are not Christian churches and they do not believe in the gospel (though they might tell you that they do), so you don't want to go there. Finding a good church is sometimes quite a process, so don't be discouraged if you don't succeed right away. Keep trying and believing that God will help you.

Second, another factor that will help you grow in this new life of faith is to begin to read what God has said about himself and about us in his Word, the Bible. In the New Testament (the last one-third or so of the Bible), there are four Gospels, or narratives, about the life of Jesus. I recommend that you start with the first one, Matthew, and then work your way through the other three. I recommend that you purchase a good modern translation, like the English Standard Version, but you can get any version (though not a paraphrase) that you are comfortable with and then begin to read more right away.

The last request that I have of you is that you contact me through my Web site, www.elysefitzpatrick.com, if you've decided you want to follow Jesus. Thank you for taking time to read this little explanation of the most important news you'll ever hear. You can read this book now and trust that the Lord will help you understand and become what he wants you to be: a person who has been so loved by him that you are transformed in both your identity and life.

Psalm 78

A Maskil of Asaph.
Give ear, O my people, to my teaching;
    incline your ears to the words of my mouth!
I will open my mouth in a parable;
    I will utter dark sayings from of old,
things that we have heard and known,
    that our fathers have told us.
We will not hide them from their children,
    but tell to the coming generation
the glorious deeds of the LORD, and his might,
    and the wonders that he has done.

He established a testimony in Jacob
    and appointed a law in Israel,
which he commanded our fathers
    to teach to their children,
that the next generation might know them,
    the children yet unborn,
and arise and tell them to their children,
    so that they should set their hope in God
and not forget the works of God,
    but keep his commandments;
and that they should not be like their fathers,
    a stubborn and rebellious generation,
a generation whose heart was not steadfast,
    whose spirit was not faithful to God.

The Ephraimites, armed with the bow,
    turned back on the day of battle.

They did not keep God's covenant,
    but refused to walk according to his law.
They forgot his works
    and the wonders that he had shown them.
In the sight of their fathers he performed wonders
    in the land of Egypt, in the fields of Zoan.
He divided the sea and let them pass through it,
    and made the waters stand like a heap.
In the daytime he led them with a cloud,
    and all the night with a fiery light.
He split rocks in the wilderness
    and gave them drink abundantly as from the deep.
He made streams come out of the rock
    and caused waters to flow down like rivers.

Yet they sinned still more against him,
    rebelling against the Most High in the desert.
They tested God in their heart
    by demanding the food they craved.
They spoke against God, saying,
    "Can God spread a table in the wilderness?
He struck the rock so that water gushed out
    and streams overflowed.
Can he also give bread
    or provide meat for his people?"

Therefore, when the LORD heard, he was full of wrath;
    a fire was kindled against Jacob;
    his anger rose against Israel,
because they did not believe in God
    and did not trust his saving power.
Yet he commanded the skies above
    and opened the doors of heaven,
and he rained down on them manna to eat
    and gave them the grain of heaven.
Man ate of the bread of the angels;
    he sent them food in abundance.
He caused the east wind to blow in the heavens,
    and by his power he led out the south wind;
he rained meat on them like dust,

winged birds like the sand of the seas;
    he let them fall in the midst of their camp,
        all around their dwellings.
And they ate and were well filled,
        for he gave them what they craved.
But before they had satisfied their craving,
        while the food was still in their mouths,
the anger of God rose against them,
        and he killed the strongest of them
        and laid low the young men of Israel.

In spite of all this, they still sinned;
        despite his wonders, they did not believe.
So he made their days vanish like a breath,
        and their years in terror.
When he killed them, they sought him;
        they repented and sought God earnestly.
They remembered that God was their rock,
        the Most High God their redeemer.
But they flattered him with their mouths;
        they lied to him with their tongues.
Their heart was not steadfast toward him;
        they were not faithful to his covenant.
Yet he, being compassionate,
        atoned for their iniquity
        and did not destroy them;
he restrained his anger often
        and did not stir up all his wrath.
He remembered that they were but flesh,
        a wind that passes and comes not again.
How often they rebelled against him in the wilderness
        and grieved him in the desert!
They tested God again and again
        and provoked the Holy One of Israel.
They did not remember his power
        or the day when he redeemed them from the foe,
when he performed his signs in Egypt
        and his marvels in the fields of Zoan.
He turned their rivers to blood,
        so that they could not drink of their streams.

He sent among them swarms of flies, which devoured them,
and frogs, which destroyed them.
He gave their crops to the destroying locust
and the fruit of their labor to the locust.
He destroyed their vines with hail
and their sycamores with frost.
He gave over their cattle to the hail
and their flocks to thunderbolts.
He let loose on them his burning anger,
wrath, indignation, and distress,
a company of destroying angels.
He made a path for his anger;
he did not spare them from death,
but gave their lives over to the plague.
He struck down every firstborn in Egypt,
the firstfruits of their strength in the tents of Ham.
Then he led out his people like sheep
and guided them in the wilderness like a flock.
He led them in safety, so that they were not afraid,
but the sea overwhelmed their enemies.
And he brought them to his holy land,
to the mountain which his right hand had won.
He drove out nations before them;
he apportioned them for a possession
and settled the tribes of Israel in their tents.

Yet they tested and rebelled against the Most High God
and did not keep his testimonies,
but turned away and acted treacherously like their fathers;
they twisted like a deceitful bow.
For they provoked him to anger with their high places;
they moved him to jealousy with their idols.
When God heard, he was full of wrath,
and he utterly rejected Israel.
He forsook his dwelling at Shiloh,
the tent where he dwelt among mankind,
and delivered his power to captivity,
his glory to the hand of the foe.
He gave his people over to the sword
and vented his wrath on his heritage.

Fire devoured their young men,
    and their young women had no marriage song.
Their priests fell by the sword,
    and their widows made no lamentation.
Then the Lord awoke as from sleep,
    like a strong man shouting because of wine.
And he put his adversaries to rout;
    he put them to everlasting shame.

He rejected the tent of Joseph;
    he did not choose the tribe of Ephraim,
but he chose the tribe of Judah,
    Mount Zion, which he loves.
He built his sanctuary like the high heavens,
    like the earth, which he has founded forever.
He chose David his servant
    and took him from the sheepfolds;
from following the nursing ewes he brought him
    to shepherd Jacob his people,
    Israel his inheritance.
With upright heart he shepherded them
    and guided them with his skillful hand.

Notes

Acknowledgments

1. *Covenant, Justification, and Pastoral Ministry* (Phillipsburg, NJ: P&R, 2007).

Introduction

1. B. B. Warfield, "'Miserable-Sinner Christianity' in the Hands of the Rationalists," *The Works of Benjamin B. Warfield*, vol. 7 (Grand Rapids, MI: Baker, 1931), 113ff.

Chapter 1: What Do You See?

1. Of course, none of us can do what Jesus did. He served his Father with complete purity, always seeking to please him and always knowing exactly what would please him. In addition, he made sacrificial atonement for our sin, something we could never do. Although I suppose that the impetus behind the WWJD movement is increased obedience, it neglects the unique work of the Savior and calls us to a form of moralism that will always eventuate in self-condemnation and/or pride.

2. It should be obvious that we're not saying that attending conferences, reading books meant to help us in our Christian walk, and seeking out biblical counsel are somehow wrong or futile. What we are saying is that most of us are thirsting for a drink of gospel truth, and we are searching for the soul-satisfaction that only a vigorous remembering of Jesus' work can accomplish.

3. All the people and circumstances we describe in this book are fictitious. They might resemble, in one small way or another, people we have known or presently know, but they are simply a conglomeration of our experiences over twenty years of counseling, as well as a representation of the sins and struggles of our own hearts. Any resemblance to anyone you know is purely coincidental. Also, due to space constraints, we have flattened out both the description of each circumstance and the gospel declarations and obligations that would apply to each problem. But, just to be clear, we don't believe that gospel declarations are magic elixirs that instantaneously deliver us from our struggle with sin, the sins of others against us, or life in a sin-cursed world. The gospel does indeed transform us but it isn't a gimmick to use like the latest self-help fad. It transforms us slowly, over time and in conjunction with a maturing of our faith, and, like everything else, our sanctification is subject to God's sovereign will.

4. In Jesus' parable of the welcoming father (often mislabeled "the prodigal son") both sons are prodigals because both treat their father with contempt. The libertine can't wait for his father to die so he can get what he wants; he takes his inheritance and off he goes to celebrate his freedom, only to find himself dining with swine when the money runs out. The moralist is bound by grinding duty, self-righteousness, and pride to obey his father but hates him all the same. Neither son loves his father; they only love what he can give them. He isn't their beloved father; he is simply a means to an end. Astonish-

ing in this parable are the father's responses to both his sons. Listen to these words of welcome and love for both the law-breaking younger brother and the law-keeping older one. Let your heart drink of this mercy:

> But while he was still a long way off, his father saw him and felt compassion, and ran and embraced him and kissed him. . . .
> But the father said to his servants, "Bring quickly the best robe, and put it on him, and put a ring on his hand, and shoes on his feet. And bring the fattened calf and kill it, and let us eat and celebrate. For this my son was dead, and is alive again; he was lost, and is found." And they began to celebrate. . . . And he said to him, "Son, you are always with me, and all that is mine is yours." (Luke 15:20, 22–24, 31)

The father goes out *twice* to bring in *both* estranged sons to feast at his table.

5. This doesn't excuse us from diligently training our children in the nurture and discipline of the Lord. God does use means, and he may use our efforts as means to save our children. But we must remember that our children's hearts are in the hands of the Lord.

6. Of course, Madeline may not be at fault for contributing to Hannah's sin. Hannah bears her own responsibility for her rebellion against God's Word and her parents. But Madeline will no doubt wrestle eventually with the questions, "What did I do wrong? What should I have done differently with Hannah?" Only the deep assurance of God's fatherly love can bring Madeline to a place where she finds the safety to face honestly the question whether her parenting approach and expectations of her daughter were contributing factors in Hannah's sin.

Chapter 2: Seeing Your Savior

1. Both God's art in creation and man's art in designing beautiful buildings in which to worship him do allow us to see something of God's glory but are not sufficient to transform our minds and hearts. In addition, any art that seeks to depict God in any visual way is a violation of the second commandment (Ex. 20:4–6). We can hardly expect God to bless, as an avenue for personal transformation into godliness, a method that he has expressly forbidden!

2. In fact, although many today dismiss preaching as boring and irrelevant, godly pastors and theologians, in a time more attuned to the gospel, noted: "The Spirit of God maketh the reading, but *especially the preaching* of the Word, an effectual means of enlightening, convincing, and humbling sinners; of driving them out of themselves, and drawing them unto Christ; of conforming them to his image, and subduing them to his will; of strengthening them against temptations and corruptions; of building them up in grace, and establishing their hearts in holiness and comfort through faith unto salvation" (Westminster Larger Catechism, answer 155 [emphasis added]).

3. Heidelberg Catechism with Scripture Texts (1563; repr., Grand Rapids, MI: Faith Alive Christian Resources, 1989), answer 69.

4. William Romaine, *The Life, Walk and Triumph of Faith* (Cambridge, UK: James Clarke, 1970), 90. Romaine writes, "No sin can be crucified either in heart or life unless it first be pardoned in conscience, because there will be want of faith to receive the strength of Jesus, by whom alone it can be crucified. If it be not mortified in its guilt, it cannot be subdued in its power. If the believer does not see his perfect deadness to sin in Jesus, he will open a wide door to unbelief, and if he be not persuaded of his complete-

ness in Christ, he gives room for the attacks of self-righteousness and legal tempers. . . . The more clearly and steadfastly he believes this, as the apostle did—'I am crucified with Christ,' in proportion will he cleave to Christ, and receive from Him greater power to crucify sin. This believing view of his absolute mortification in Christ is *the true gospel method* of mortifying sin in our own persons" (p. 280; emphasis added).

5. The Heidelberg Catechism, question 70.

6. Ibid., question 75.

7. Although biblical fellowship is clearly commanded, it is seldom seen within the local church community. Most Christians have only superficial relationships with one another or have been in coercive, manipulating relationships with others who demand accountability and repentance. For a more balanced approach to biblical fellowship, see C. J. Mahaney and Greg Somerville, eds., *Why Small Groups?* (Gaithersburg, MD: Sovereign Grace Ministries, 1996); Timothy S. Lane and Paul D. Tripp, *Relationships: A Mess Worth Making* (Burlington, NC: New Growth Press, 2006).

8. Timothy Keller, "The Centrality of the Gospel." Available from Redeemer Presbyterian Church, http://download.redeemer.com/pdf/learn/resources/Centrality_of_the_Gospel-Keller.pdf, p. 3.

Chapter 3: God's Immeasurable Love

1. Contrary to modern pop psychology, none of us needs to learn to love himself more. Our problem, even when we experience self-loathing, is that we love ourselves too much and just can't believe that we are so flawed. If we really hated ourselves, we wouldn't care at all about ourselves or our reputation, failures, or imperfections. In one sense, we do need to love our souls and learn how to properly care for them by continually exposing them to the means of grace, but when Jesus commanded us to love God and our neighbor as ourselves, he assumed that we already do a good job loving ourselves. There are two, not three, commands in Matthew 22:37–40: "He said to him, 'You shall love the Lord your God with all your heart and with all your soul and with all your mind. This is the great and first commandment. And a second is like it: You shall love your neighbor as yourself. On these *two* commandments depend all the Law and the Prophets.'"

2. Of course, it's always better to try to act in a loving manner, even when we don't feel much love for God or others. But God's command isn't to merely *act* as though we love; the command is to love deeply, warmly, and purely (1 Pet. 1:22). Acting in a loving manner (when we don't really love) does less harm to others than being unkind, but it's a hollow facsimile of the real thing. We must act in a loving manner, even when we don't love, all the while confessing our inexcusable lovelessness and pleading for faith to believe that God is as good as he says he is.

3. William Romaine, *The Life, Walk and Triumph of Faith* (Cambridge, UK: James Clarke, 1970), 117.

4. He uses the exact description, "merciful and gracious, slow to anger, and abounding in steadfast love and faithfulness" (Ex. 34:6), at least six more times in the Old Testament (Neh. 9:17; Pss. 86:15; 103:8; 145:8; Joel 2:13; Jonah 4:2). Note also that John 1:14 and James 5:11 are, probably, New Testament echoes of the Lord's self-description in Exodus 34:6.

5. "Paul personifies love as a person who acts in the ways Christians should imitate. The total picture suggests a description of Christ Himself." *The Reformation Study Bible*, ESV (Orlando, FL: Ligonier Ministries, 2005), note on 1 Corinthians 13:4–7, p. 1661.

6. Dan. 2:44–45; Rev. 19:15.

7. "Covenant Eyes" is an accountability software program that monitors Internet use and automatically sends e-mail reports to people you select. Information about this program is available at www.covenanteyes.com. Pure Life Ministries offers distinctly biblical counseling and resources for men and women who struggle with sexual sin including, but not limited to, pornography, at www.purelifeministries.org. Harvest USA, a ministry begun by Tenth Presbyterian Church in Philadelphia to bring the power of the gospel to homosexuals, has now expanded its ministry geographically (to other regions of the U.S.) and addresses those enslaved to other sexual sins, including pornography. The Web site is: http://www.harvestusa.org/.

8. Martin Luther, *Galatians*, The Crossway Classic Commentaries, ed. Alister McGrath and J. I. Packer (Wheaton, IL: Crossway, 1998), 40–41.

Chapter 4: God's Love and Our Hearts

1. Even in Old Testament times, there were people who were confident that God was obligated to bless them because they were keeping his laws pretty well. See Ps. 50:7–16; Isa. 29:13; Mal. 2:17.

2. Beginning in the mid to late 1960s the belief in the necessity of having good self-esteem became a given. By the 1980s it became institutionalized in our school systems as the long sought-after vaccine against failure, crime, and irresponsibility. Affirmation became the goal of every conscientious parent who embraced the duty to tell little Johnnie and Janie what great kids they were and that they were doing a good job (no matter how they were actually doing).

Sadly, the church bought into this hypothetical need for good self-esteem and searched through Scripture to try to find a verse that would prove that God wanted us to love ourselves. Since the Bible is silent about the command to love and appreciate one's self, verses were pulled apart to try to find biblical warrant for doing so. Matthew 22:39 was used: "You shall love your neighbor as yourself." Ignoring the fact that Jesus explicitly taught that there are only two commands that summarize the Law and the Prophets, we were told that there are really three, and the real meaning of the verse is that we cannot love God or others until we have loved ourselves.

The fruit of this misguided emphasis has been quite bitter, not the least of it being churches that overflow with shallow, self-satisfied, self-focused consumers who continually look for the magic elixir that will finally make them into the wonderful people they think they must be. Emotional problems have resulted as well: people don't feel valued as they think they should be, so anxiety, depression, and addictions have become commonplace. But by far the most disheartening fruit is the lack of a zealous joy and a blindness to how amazing grace is.

3. See Alfred J. Poirier, "The Cross and Criticism," *Journal of Biblical Counseling*, vol. 17, no. 3 (Spring 1999), http://bookstore.peacemaker.net/html/artic10.htm.

4. *Luther's Works*, ed. Jaroslav Pelikan and Helmut T. Lehmann (Philadelphia: Fortress Press, 1958–1972), 42:7–14.

5. George Whitefield, *The Method of Grace*, http://www.bartleby.com/268/3/20; emphasis added.

6. Distilled from Jonathan Edwards, David Brainerd, and Sereno Edwards Dwight, *The Works of President Edwards with a Memoir of His Life* (New York: G&C&H Carvill, 1830), 36, 38, 43.

7. "It Is Finished!" James Proctor, lyrics; Ira D. Sankey, music (1840–1908).

8. Ira Sankey, *My Life and the Story of Gospel Hymns and of Sacred Songs and Solos* (Stationer's Hall: London: Sunday School Times, 1906), 189; emphasis added.

9. "What is sanctification? A. Sanctification is the work of God's free grace, whereby we are renewed in the whole man after the image of God, and are enabled more and more to die unto sin, and live unto righteousness." Westminster Shorter Catechism, answer 35 (emphasis added). Reference also Westminster Shorter Catechism on justification: "Justification is an act of God's free grace, wherein he pardoneth all our sins, and accepteth us as righteous in his sight, only for the righteousness of Christ imputed to us, and received by faith alone." Westminster Shorter Catechism, answer 33.

10. Westminster Shorter Catechism on justification, answer 33.

11. "No one in this life can obey the Ten Commandments perfectly; why then does God want them preached so pointedly? A. First, so that the longer we live the more we may come to know our sinfulness and the more eagerly look to Christ for forgiveness of sins and righteousness. Second, so that, while praying to God for the grace of the Holy Spirit, we may never stop striving to be renewed more and more after God's image, until after this life we reach our goal: perfection." Heidelberg Catechism, answer 115.

12. Martin Luther, *Galatians,* The Crossway Classic Commentaries, ed. Alister McGrath and J. I. Packer (Wheaton, IL: Crossway, 1998), 177.

13. George Herbert, "Love (3)" in *The Complete English Works* (New York: Alfred A. Knopf, 1995), 184.

Chapter 5: Gospel-centered Counseling

1. See Appendix 1: "Why *Biblical* Counseling?" for a fuller explanation of why we believe the Bible, in particular the law/gospel dynamic, is so imperative for helping people change.

2. Even though we desire to completely rely on and draw from Scripture, it is impossible for us to perfectly do so, because of the noetic effect of sin. It is, however, our desire to grow in our discernment of the ways in which humanistic philosophies have influenced our thinking and to continually strive to think and counsel in the light of Scripture, without importing remnants of worldviews that contradict God's truth.

3. In *The Reason for God: Belief in an Age of Skepticism* (New York: Dutton, 2008), Pastor Tim Keller, Redeemer Presbyterian Church, New York, confesses: "When my own personal grasp of the gospel was very weak, my self-view swung wildly between two poles. When I was performing up to my standards—in academic work, professional achievement, or relationships—I felt confident but not humble. I was likely to be proud and unsympathetic to failing people. When I was not living up to standards, I felt humble but not confident, a failure. I discovered, however, that the gospel contained the resources to build a unique identity. In Christ I could know I was accepted by grace not only despite my flaws, but because I was willing to admit them. The Christian gospel is that I am so flawed that Jesus had to die for me, yet I am so loved and valued that Jesus was glad to die for me. This leads to deep humility and deep confidence at the same time. It undermines both swaggering and sniveling" (pp. 180–81).

4. Of course, if the gospel is being presented in its fullness, it will breed love for God and neighbor, the fulfilling of the law. But simplistic "Jesus is nice and loves you just because you're you" won't create the holy fear and humility that is at the heart of true obedience.

5. Even beyond the gospel/indicative clues in verses 22–24, when these verses are read in their larger context the fact that our response is based on Christ's prior work for us is

even clearer. In verse 20 Paul begins speaking of "the way you learned *Christ*," and he goes on to speak of the fact "that you have heard about *him* and were taught in *him*, as the truth is in *Jesus*." Moreover, although most English versions such as the ESV that we are using interpret the Greek infinitives in verses 22–24 ("to put off," "to be renewed," "to put on") as having the force of imperatives (expressing our obligations), responsible New Testament scholars have argued that they should actually be viewed as indicative declarations. Such a reading looks like this: "You were taught in Jesus that you have put off the old self, you are being renewed in the spirit of your minds, and you have put on the new self, created after the likeness of God." See Daniel Wallace, *Greek Grammar Beyond the Basics: An Exegetical Syntax of the New Testament* (Grand Rapids: Zondervan, 1996), 605. This understanding of the indicative force of the infinitives in Ephesians 4:22–24 coincides precisely with the indicative significance of the same verbs, which appear as participles in Colossians 3:9–10, correctly translated in the ESV: "Do not lie to one another, seeing that *you have put off* the old self . . . and *have put on* the new self, which *is being renewed*." Even if the Greek verbs in Ephesians 4:22–24 are understood as implied commands, however, their grounding in the gospel is shown in other ways, as we argue above.

6. Our obligation to put off the evil patterns that characterized our lives "in Adam" and put on the motives and practices that fit our new identity "in Christ" is clearly taught in Ephesians 4, even if (as Dennis believes) Daniel Wallace is correct to view Ephesians 4:22–24 as declarations of truth about our new identity in Christ. The succeeding verses (4:25–5:2 and beyond) contain one command after another, starting with the clearly imperative sequence, "Having put away falsehood, let each one of you speak the truth. . . . Be angry and do not sin. . . . Let the thief no longer steal" and so on.

7. It's quite obvious that secular talk therapies have failed. Had they been successful, the pharmaceutical industry would not have been able to almost completely capture that market. People no longer worry about being dysfunctional, codependent victims. They have moved on to imbalances in brain chemicals, hormones, and faulty genes. We are not saying that the psychotropic pharmaceutical proponents are correct in their assumptions (or methods). We are merely saying that secular "talk therapy" really wasn't very helpful, so people became disillusioned and turned to medicine for help. See Elyse Fitzpatrick and Laura Hendrickson, *Will Medicine Stop the Pain? Finding God's Healing for Your Troubling Emotions* (Chicago, IL: Moody, 2006).

8. Because psychology tends to blend scientific observation of human behavior with worldview-laden theoretical constructions regarding the causes of emotions and actions, there are many distinct schools of thought, all with different answers to the questions, Who are we? and How are we helped?

9. Please don't misunderstand. We are not saying that remembering such passages isn't part of the process of responding in a biblical way to temptation to sin. We are just saying that we shouldn't get to them before we have gotten to gospel declarations.

10. Of course, the "ten item" rule for the express lane was determined by the store, not the Lord; but observing it is a matter of loving our neighbors as ourselves—and that is God's law!

11. The Greek word is even stronger: "All these years I've *slaved* for you."

12. According to Hebrews 10:5–10, these words capture the mind-set of the Son of God as he entered the world and acquired our human nature for the sake of our salvation.

Chapter 6: The Gospel and Our Sanctification

1. It does seem strange that the method some employ to give people truth is the hiding of it.

2. Westminster Shorter Catechism, answer 35.

3. See John Murray, "Definitive Sanctification," in *Collected Writings of John Murray*, vol. 2: *Select Lectures in Systematic Theology* (Edinburgh: Banner of Truth, 1977), 277–84.

4. This is one point where we need to understand the difference between justification and sanctification. Although justification is equal for all of us, sanctification is not.

5. Bryan Chapell, *Holiness by Grace: Delighting in the Joy That Is Our Strength* (Wheaton, IL: Crossway, 2001), 41.

6. Ibid., 50–51.

7. It's very tempting to think that God will be more impressed with us if we prove how serious we are about our sin by being sad and grief-stricken all the time. In some of us, the temptation to become morose and introspective can become a work in itself: a way to make ourselves more worthy of God's love and acceptance. This self-focused grieving is rooted in too high of an opinion of oneself and too low of an opinion of the work and merit of Jesus Christ. The restrictions on the Day of Atonement tell us that we are not to try to strengthen ourselves in ourselves, nor are we to offer our work to God when it comes to our acceptance with him.

8. "Religious joy, properly tempered with continual dependence on the help of God, meekness of mind, and self-diffidence, is a powerful means of strengthening the soul. In such a state every duty is practicable, and every duty delightful. In such a frame of mind no man ever fell, and in such a state of mind the general health of the body is much improved; a cheerful heart is not only a continual feast, but also a continual medicine." Adam Clarke's *Commentary on the Bible*, electronic database. Copyright © 1996, 2003 by Biblesoft. All rights reserved.

9. C. F. Keil and F. Delitzsch, *Commentary on the Old Testament*: New Updated Edition, electronic database. Copyright © 1996 by Hendrickson Publishers. All rights reserved.

10. Martin Luther, *Galatians*, The Crossway Classic Commentaries, ed. Alister McGrath and J. I. Packer (Wheaton, IL: Crossway, 1998), 169.

Chapter 7: The Gospel and Our Emotions

1. Richard Baxter, *A Christian Directory* (1673; repr., Morgan, PA: Soli Deo Gloria, 1996), 125.

2. For a more in-depth discussion of emotions see Elyse Fitzpatrick and Laura Hendrickson, *Will Medicine Stop the Pain? Finding God's Healing for Depression, Anxiety and Other Troubling Emotions* (Chicago, IL: Moody, 2006); Edward Welch, *Blame It on the Brain? Distinguishing Chemical Imbalances, Brain Disorders, and Disobedience* (Phillipsburg, NJ: P&R, 1998).

3. Obviously materialistic determinism is completely antithetical to biblical anthropology. The Bible declares that man is, in fact, responsible for his thoughts, words, and deeds, and that his activity has grave consequences. "So then each of us will give an account of himself to God" (Rom. 14:12).

4. Please don't misunderstand what we're saying here. We're not saying that certain drugs such as antidepressants or anti-anxiety medications can't affect mood. In many cases they can and do. We are also not saying that it is sinful to resort to these medicines, especially when feelings have become so overwhelming that violence is being contemplated. What we are saying is that the philosophy underlying the development and prescription of these drugs is antithetical to biblical truth, which declares that we are responsible before God for the way in which we live our lives. In some cases use of these drugs can help a person quell their most painful feelings for a time so that real change can be effected. In other cases, such as in psychotic brain disorders like bipolar 1 or schizophrenia, a more permanent use of psychotropic medications is recommended. Even in these cases, however, gospel-centered biblical counseling will be helpful.

5. "Hyperthyroidism is the term for overactive tissue within the thyroid gland, resulting in overproduction and thus an excess of circulating free thyroid hormones: thyroxine (T_4), triiodothyronine (T_3), or both. . . . In excess it overstimulates, causing 'speeding up' of various body systems, and thus symptoms: Fast heart beat results in palpitations, a fast nervous system in tremor and anxiety symptoms, a fast digestive system in weight loss and diarrhea. *Lack* of functioning thyroid tissue results in a symptomatic lack of thyroid hormone, termed hypothyroidism" (http://en.wikipedia.org/wiki/Hyperthyroidism). Cushing's syndrome symptoms "include rapid weight gain, particularly of the trunk and face with sparing of the limbs (central obesity), a round face often referred to as a 'moon face,' excess sweating, telangiectasia (dilation of capillaries), thinning of the skin (which causes easy bruising) and other mucous membranes, purple or red striae (the weight gain in Cushing's stretches the skin, which is thin and weakened, causing it to hemorrhage) on the trunk, buttocks, arms, legs or breasts, proximal muscle weakness (hips, shoulders), and hirsutism (facial male-pattern hair growth). A common sign is the growth of fat pads along the collar bone and on the back of the neck (buffalo hump) (known as a lipodystrophy). The excess cortisol may also affect other endocrine systems and cause, for example, insomnia, reduced libido, impotence, amenorrhoea and infertility. Patients frequently suffer various psychological disturbances, ranging from euphoria to psychosis. Depression and anxiety are also common" (http://en.wikipedia.org/wiki/Cushing%27s_disease).

6. Although we are not usually aware that we have two parts, we say things like, "My legs are so slow today," or "I wanted to run faster but my body wouldn't respond." We all know instinctively that we are not just a physical body. We also see this when someone dies, and even unbelievers, when looking at the body, say, "That's not really her. She's gone on."

7. Our words and deeds also reveal our hearts. "For out of the abundance of the heart the mouth speaks. The good person out of his good treasure brings forth good, and the evil person out of his evil treasure brings forth evil" (Matt. 12:34–35).

8. When Pastor Jack went to his doctor for help, the doctor put him on antidepressants. Jack felt better immediately, but this change in mood wasn't from the drugs. Antidepressants won't affect mood until they have been in the bloodstream for several weeks. What Jack experienced was a well-known phenomenon called the placebo effect. Because the doctor had assured Jack that he would get better on these drugs, and because the cause of his depression was now seen to be something outside of his mind or soul (in his physical body), he didn't condemn himself for it, and he had hope that he could change. Just giving Jack a diagnosis and a remedy lifted his depression for a time, even before the medication could work.

9. I (Elyse) am saying "initially" here because I see within myself a propensity to coddle these painful emotions. I personally have used depression, anxiety, and even anger as a way to excuse myself from my obligations, to garner pity from others, and to protect myself from difficult realities. I'm not saying that everyone is like me. I know that many people really do despise their painful emotions, but I also know that the human heart is desperately wicked and will use even its pain for selfish purposes.

10. For more on this topic see Elyse Fitzpatrick, *Overcoming Fear, Worry, and Anxiety: Becoming a Woman of Faith and Confidence* (Eugene, OR: Harvest House, 2001).

11. David was sinfully angry with Nabal (1 Sam. 25:13ff.); he was sinfully afraid and ordered the execution of Uriah to cover his sin with Bathsheba (2 Sam. 11:15ff.); he was full of sinful self-pity and sorrow about Absalom's death (2 Sam. 18:33).

12. See note 8, this chapter, for a discussion of the placebo effect.

13. We don't ever want to assume that every problem in every relationship is because someone is willfully sinning. Sally may, in fact, have an anemia that saps her energy. She may also need help balancing hormones that might be out of kilter since her last delivery. Chad may be struggling with hyperthyroidism and interpreting all of his feelings of depression as problems in his marriage.

14. Richard Baxter, *A Christian Directory*, 89.

Chapter 8: The Gospel and Our Relationships

1. Of course, none of us (aside from the Savior) has ever done this perfectly. John is not teaching that we earn our salvation by loving others, nor is he saying that our ongoing salvation is predicated upon our perfect love for others. He is saying that the love of others will be the fruit of loving God and seeing how we have been loved by him. If we don't have this fruit, we should question whether we really do love God or have come to "know and to believe" (1 John 4:16) the love he has for us.

2. These are the books that are based on Scripture where the author has tried to be faithful to biblical truth. There are myriads of other books that are based primarily on psychological tenets, such as getting the needs of one's inner child met in order to have a good marriage, that have been marketed as Christian books but are not distinctly "Christian."

3. Of late there have been several books on the family written from a gospel-centered perspective, such as Dave Harvey, *When Sinners Say "I Do": Discovering the Power of the Gospel for Marriage* (Wapwallopen, PA: Shepherd Press, 2007); Gary Ricucci, C. J. Mahaney, et al., *Love That Lasts: When Marriage Meets Grace* (Wheaton, IL: Crossway Books, 2006); C. J. Mahaney and Carolyn Mahaney, *Sex, Romance, and the Glory of God: What Every Christian Husband Needs to Know* (Wheaton, IL: Crossway Books, 2004); and Bryan Chapell and Kathy Chapell, *Each for the Other: Marriage as It's Meant to Be* (Grand Rapids: Baker, 2006).

4. We are not saying that we have innate psychological "needs" that have to be met before we can be happy. What we are saying is that we have an appropriate God-given desire for relationship and, because of sin, we have turned that desire into a self-focused craving—an idol. These selfish cravings are frequently given legitimacy in our culture by calling them "needs."

5. We have to be wise about what kinds of sin we confess to our children. For instance, it wouldn't be wise or loving to confess that you are having a hard time loving one of them or that you are tempted to sexual sin by a secretary at work. It would be acceptable to confess sin that they are aware of and can easily relate to. If you struggle with

the sin of anger or impatience with them or if you have a hard time disciplining your time in front of the computer or television, it would be helpful to them if you were to confess this and ask for prayer.

Chapter 9: The Gospel Story and the Glory Story

1. For more on Luther's "Theology of Glory" see Gerhard O. Forde, *On Being a Theologian of the Cross: Reflections on Luther's Heidelberg Disputation, 1518* (Grand Rapids, MI: Eerdmans), 1997.

2. We are using "glory" here not to speak of heaven *per se,* but rather self-perfection.

3. That our whole culture believes the glory story is so very obvious by the people we idolize: athletes who overcome great adversity by hard work, superheroes who fight against great odds and still win. The glory story seems to be inbred in all of us: hard work, discipline, and perseverance will always capture the prize of self-glorification. In its essence the glory story can be summarized this way: "We came from glory and we are bound for glory. Of course, in between we seem somehow to have gotten derailed—whether by design or accident we don't quite know—but that is only a temporary inconvenience to be fixed by proper religious effort. What we need is to get back on 'the glory road.'" Forde, *On Being a Theologian of the Cross,* 5.

4. http://www.wscal.edu/faculty/wscwritings/horton.osteen/glorystory.php.

5. I (Elyse) have even had Christians question whether the injunction in Hebrews 6:1 to "leave the elementary doctrine of Christ" isn't proof that we shouldn't revisit the truths of the gospel on a daily basis. In fact, however, the author to the Hebrews is referring to a preoccupation with foundational Old Testament doctrines (repentance from dead works, faith toward God, resurrection of the dead, eternal judgment) and ceremonies (washings, laying on of hands [on sacrificial animals, with confession of sins]), which were distracting the Hebrew Christians from living in the privileges now opened to them through the sacrifice and priestly intercession of Jesus, the great, final, and eternal high priest. They and we will "go on to maturity" only as they and we go ever more deeply into the central truth of the gospel and the primary point of this epistle—the high priestly sacrifice and heavenly intercession of Jesus (Heb. 8:1).

6. Forde, *On Being a Theologian of the Cross,* 17.

7. I (Elyse) first heard this passage preached in light of the glory story by my former pastor, Mark Lauterbach.

8. Earlier Jesus had responded to the joy of seventy-two disciples, who had seen demons expelled by the power of Jesus' name, that their greater joy should be in the fact that their names are written in heaven, and he followed this amazing statement with a prayer that extolled the sheer grace by which anyone can be received by the Father and given insight into his truth: "I thank you, Father, Lord of heaven and earth, that you have hidden these things from the wise and understanding and revealed them to little children [note the humiliating term that Jesus applies to his demon-defeating disciples!]; yes, Father, for such was your gracious will" (Luke 10:17–21).

9. F. W. Krummacher, *The Suffering Savior* (1856; repr., Carlisle, PA: Banner of Truth, 2004), 91.

10. Luther's *Works,* quoted in Forde, *On Being a Theologian of the* Cross, 36.

11. Forde, *On Being a Theologian,* 85.

Appendix 1

1. In the same way that we recognize that Darwinian evolution has evolved over time, we also recognize that Freudian psychotherapy has changed and splintered into hundreds of other systems, many of them in competition with each other. We are simply using Freud as shorthand for the hundreds of psychotherapies that have been developed over the last century.

2. "Theories of personality and their psychotherapeutic systems can be seen as direct extensions of their [Freud, Jung, Adler] personalities." Raymond J. Corsini, ed., *Current Psychotherapies*, 3rd ed. (Itasca, IL: F. E. Peacock, 1984), 9.

3. Ibid., 125.

4. Rational-emotive therapy.

5. Corsini, *Current Psychotherapies*, 197.

6. See Elyse Fitzpatrick and Laura Hendrickson, *Will Medicine Stop the Pain? Finding God's Healing for Depression, Anxiety, and Other Troubling Emotions* (Chicago, IL: Moody, 2006).

7. Other pseudo-psychotherapies, such as neurodevelopmentalism, find their origin in a basic belief that man evolved and therefore children must evolve in their development if they are to be successful. Abraham Maslow's "Hierarchy of Needs" (where we get our teaching on the importance of self-esteem) also flows from this evolutionary perspective.

8. The doctrines of religion, Freud wrote, "bear the imprint of the times in which they arose, the ignorant times of the childhood of humanity." He asserted that "the religions of mankind must be classed among the mass delusions," and that "when a man has once brought himself to accept uncritically all the absurdities that religious doctrines put before him . . . we need not be greatly surprised at the weakness of his intellect" (Armand M. Nicholi, *The Question of God: C. S. Lewis and Sigmund Freud Debate God, Love, Sex, and the Meaning of Life* [New York: Free Press, 2003], http://www.hno.harvard.edu/gazette/2002/09.19/09-god.html.). Speaking for Jungian Analytical Psychotherapists (probably the most "spiritual" of the major psychological systems), Yoram Kaufmann writes, "*It is a basic tenet of Jungian therapy that all products of the unconscious are symbolic* and can be taken as guiding messages. . . . By doggedly following the wisdom of the unconscious, the patient learns to accept that within himself there exists a guiding force, the Self, that points the way, painful though it might be, to a mode of being more meaningful and more whole" (Corsini, *Current Psychotherapies*, 108, 124; emphasis in original). Harold A. Mosak, a practitioner of Adlerian Psychotherapy, writes, "Life has no intrinsic meaning. *We* give meaning to life, each of us in his own fashion" (ibid., 60, emphasis in original.) Carl R. Rogers's Person-Centered Therapy trusts in the innate potential within each person to grow and mature in an environment of unconditional positive regard without interference from any outside source. He defines *psychotherapy* as the "releasing of an already existing capacity in a potentially competent individual." He writes, "Positive regard is not an intellectual attitude nor a saccharine optimism toward humanity. It is a reality-based trust in the actualizing potential of the individual and is expressed in an unwillingness to interfere, direct or evaluate the ongoing processes of another human being" (ibid., 143, 164). Although behavior therapy is a diverse system with various approaches, B. F. Skinner's applied behavior analysis states that "behavior is a function of its consequences" (ibid., 239) and can be most easily understood by the motivational paradigm of the donkey, the carrot, and the stick. For Skinner, man's problem originates outside of himself in his

environment, and his thoughts are not really of much interest. In the neobehavioristic mediational stimulus-response model, "desensitization and covert conditioning techniques such as covert sensitization" are integral. "The rationale behind all these methods is that covert processes follow the laws of learning that govern overt behaviors" (ibid., 240).

9. The effect of sin on our ability to think and understand.

10. Of course, sometimes our problems do originate in our physical bodies. Illness may or may not be the result of a specific sin but it is always the result of living in sin-cursed bodies (Rom. 5:12).

11. Many would argue that, because the image of God in man was severely damaged but not utterly destroyed by the fall into sin, there is wisdom outside of the wisdom that can be found in Scripture. They might call this wisdom *general revelation*—the insights that one can gain from observing the world without the special revelation needed to understand and embrace salvation—and its perception is the result of God's *common grace*, extended both to believers and to unbelievers. It is true that unbelievers can figure out how to change a carburetor or perform brain surgery, and Scripture even attributes significant theological and ethical insights to pagans whose hearts are not captive to Christ's grace (Acts 17:27–28; 1 Cor. 5:1; Titus 1:12). See Dennis E. Johnson, "Spiritual Antithesis, Common Grace, and Practical Theology," *Westminster Theological Journal* 64 (2002): 73–94. But non-Christians cannot accurately diagnose the problems in a man's soul nor effect true heart change apart from the work of Jesus Christ in conjunction with the Bible and the Spirit. The Bible has been given to us to answer the very questions that psychology seeks to answer: who is man, what is his problem, how can he be helped? The answers to these questions will be found either in the philosophies of fallen man or in the Bible.

Of course, none of us is consistently biblical. Try as we might, we all bring our presuppositions to Scripture. It is for this reason that we must be very careful and must also ask for help from others to enable us to see where we fail to consistently listen to the Bible's theology and anthropology.

12. That we are created to glorify God and that his glory is to be the ultimate goal of our lives is, of course, completely missed in secular psychological systems, since they are agnostic at best. Sadly too, though, it is also often missed in the awareness of Christians. In case the thought of living life to the glory of God is new to you, we have included a series of Scripture verses for you to peruse:

> Glory in his holy name; let the hearts of those who seek the LORD rejoice! Declare his glory among the nations, his marvelous works among all the peoples! For great is the LORD, and greatly to be praised, and he is to be held in awe above all gods. For all the gods of the peoples are idols, but the LORD made the heavens. Splendor and majesty are before him; strength and joy are in his place. Ascribe to the LORD, O clans of the peoples, ascribe to the LORD glory and strength! Ascribe to the LORD the glory due his name. (1 Chron. 16:10, 24–29)

> Declare his glory among the nations, his marvelous works among all the peoples! For great is the LORD, and greatly to be praised; he is to be feared above all gods. For all the gods of the peoples are worthless idols, but the LORD made the heavens. Splendor and majesty are before him; strength and beauty are in his sanctuary. (Ps. 96:3–6)

Not to us, O Lᴏʀᴅ, not to us, but to your name give glory, for the sake of your steadfast love and your faithfulness! (Ps. 115:1)

For from him and through him and to him are all things. To him be glory forever. Amen. (Rom. 11:36)

Therefore welcome one another as Christ has welcomed you, for the glory of God. (Rom. 15:7)

To the only wise God be glory forevermore through Jesus Christ! Amen. (Rom. 16:27)

So, whether you eat or drink, or whatever you do, do all to the glory of God. (1 Cor. 10:31)

For all the promises of God find their Yes in him. That is why it is through him that we utter our Amen to God for his glory. (2 Cor. 1:20)

Grace to you and peace from God our Father and the Lord Jesus Christ, who gave himself for our sins to deliver us from the present evil age, according to the will of our God and Father, to whom be the glory forever and ever. Amen. (Gal. 1:3–5)

. . . so that we who were the first to hope in Christ might be to the praise of his glory. (Eph. 1:12)

To him be glory in the church and in Christ Jesus throughout all generations, forever and ever. Amen. (Eph. 3:21)

. . . filled with the fruit of righteousness that comes through Jesus Christ, to the glory and praise of God. (Phil. 1:11)

. . . and every tongue confess that Jesus Christ is Lord, to the glory of God the Father. (Phil. 2:11)

To our God and Father be glory forever and ever. Amen. (Phil. 4:20)

The Lord will rescue me from every evil deed and bring me safely into his heavenly kingdom. To him be the glory forever and ever. Amen. (2 Tim. 4:18)

. . . equip you with everything good that you may do his will, working in us that which is pleasing in his sight, through Jesus Christ, to whom be glory forever and ever. Amen. (Heb. 13:21)

. . . in order that in everything God may be glorified through Jesus Christ. To him belong glory and dominion forever and ever. Amen. (1 Pet. 4:11)

But grow in the grace and knowledge of our Lord and Savior Jesus Christ. To him be the glory both now and to the day of eternity. Amen. (2 Pet. 3:18)

To the only God, our Savior, through Jesus Christ our Lord, be glory, majesty, dominion, and authority, before all time and now and forever. Amen. (Jude 25)

. . . and made us a kingdom, priests to his God and Father, to him be glory and dominion forever and ever. Amen. (Rev. 1:6–7)

Worthy are you, our Lord and God, to receive glory and honor and power, for you created all things, and by your will they existed and were created. (Rev. 4:11).

13. Of course, there is much more that can be said about the principles and practice of biblical counseling. For a fuller explanation see Elyse Fitzpatrick and Carol Cornish, *Women Helping Women* (Eugene, OR: Harvest House, 1997); Paul David Tripp, *Instruments in the Redeemer's Hands: People in Need of Change Helping People in Need of Change* (Phillipsburg, NJ: P&R, 2002); David Powlison, *Seeing with New Eyes: Counseling and the Human Condition through the Lens of Scripture* (Phillipsburg, NJ: P&R, 2003); Paul D. Tripp and Timothy S. Lane, *How People Change* (Burlington, NC: New Growth Press, 2008); John MacArthur, Wayne Mack, et al., *Counseling: How to Counsel Biblically* (Nashville: Thomas Nelson, 2005); Jay E. Adams, *A Theology of Christian Counseling* (Grand Rapids, MI: Zondervan, 1986); Jay E. Adams, *The Christian Counselor's Manual* (Grand Rapids, MI: Zondervan, 1986).

Appendix 2

1. Jay E. Adams, *The Christian Counselor's New Testament: A New Translation in Everyday English with Notations, Marginal References, and Supplemental Helps* (Grand Rapids, MI: Baker), 1977.

Index

man/woman: as both body and soul, 133–35, 224n6; as created in the likeness/image of God, 96, 228n11; inner and outer, 131

materialistic determinism, 130, 185, 223n3

Mormons, 210

Moses, 39–40, 58; transformation of by God's glory, 51; as witness to the glory of God, 50–52

Nehemiah, 117, 119, 127

neurodevelopmentalism, 227n7

new covenant, superiority of over the old covenant, 51

New Jerusalem, 84

Nicodemus, 74

Noah, 44

obedience, 24, 27–28, 31, 44, 45, 66, 75, 76, 83, 85, 92, 98, 123, 127, 158–59, 165, 181, 221n4; as a burden or delight, 102, 104–5, 108; cruciform obedience, 171–72; ethical, 96; of Jesus, 89, 107, 122. *See also* Jacob

parable of the welcoming father, 32, 103–4, 217–18n4

patience, 101

Paul, 88, 96, 142, 171, 172, 177–78, 219n5; counsel of to the Corinthians, 38–39; counsel of to parents, 164;

on grace, 47; on husbands and wives, 154; passion of to honor Christ, 39

Peter, 47; as a theologian of glory, 172–77

pornography, 69–70, 220n7

preaching, 41–43, 218n2

pride, 101

Proctor, James, 81

psychology, 187, 222n8; Alderian Psychotherapy, 227–28n8; behavior therapy, 227–28n8; "Christian," 99; different branches of, 184–85; Freudian, 184; humanistic, 98; Jungian therapy, 227–28n8; Person-Centered Therapy, 227–28n8; psychotherapy, 227–28n8; rational-emotive therapy (RET), 185; secular "talk therapy" methods of, 222n7

purity, 76

Rachel, 102

Reformation, the, 121–22

rejoicing, in God's goodness, 118–21, 142

revelation, general, 228n11

Rodgers, Carl, 227–28n8

Romaine, William, 44, 218–19n4

Sad Moralists, 79–82, 88, 106, 112–13, 118, 170; Luther as, 122

To

Richard Rastn

from

Martin R.
Bensman

12/1983

BROADCAST REGULATION

Selected Cases and Decisions

Marvin R. Bensman, J.D., Ph.D.

UNIVERSITY
PRESS OF
AMERICA

LANHAM • NEW YORK • LONDON

PREFACE

With the rapid technological advances in national and global communications; entertainment and communications have become very specialized fields. Within copyright, contracts, tax, labor law, antitrust and tort law are considerable issues which will affect the electronic media. These issues are of increasing import to decision-making management, media practioners, and students for they will impact upon custom and practice in the electronic media industry.

Managers and their staffs must rely upon each other knowing, understanding and applying the myriad legal principles that are imposed upon daily operations. Such reliance may be misplaced and lack of understanding may create a problem that recognition would have prevented. This book is designed to provide up-to-date information, but is not a rendering of legal services.

To best utilize this work it might be useful in a class setting to pose a series of questions which deal with an issue in a problem area. The answer can then be sought by reading the various cases which deal with that problem. The organization of this work lends itself to an historical overview of the development of legal principles as well as to supplying the quick answer and reference. Basic public policy issues underlying the areas treated can be covered from a supplemental text or lecture material.

Citations are from court decisions, FCC Reports, various loose-leaf services such as Pike and Fischer <u>Radio Regulations</u> (RR) and trade and copyright reporting services. It is hoped that enough references are cited over a wide-range of available material so that even modest libraries can provide research facilities if further in-depth material is desired, but the book is designed to stand alone if necessary.

Appreciation is expressed to Lawrence W. Lichty and Joseph R. Ripley for introducing me to broadcast regulation at the University of Wisconsin-Madison where early material originally compiled by students of Harrison B. Summers of Ohio State University was utilized.

This work would not have been possible without the assistance and support of my wife, Harriet and my children; David and Lauren.

Marvin R. Bensman, J.D., Ph.D.
Memphis State University
Department of Theatre and
    Communication Arts
Memphis, Tennessee 38152

1983

i

BROADCAST REGULATION
SELECTED CASES, OPINIONS, MEMORANDA, ETC. OF NOTE

Citations

1. WOR Music Copyright Decision, Non-sponsored B'casts are
    'Performance for Profit,' Witmark. v. Bamberger, 291 Fed.
    776, (D-N. Jer., 1923)

2. 1912 Death Knell, Sec. of Commerce no authority over
    frequency, power, etc., U.S. v. Zenith Radio Corp, 12 F.
    2d 614, (1926)

3. Congress's Right to Establish Radio Regulatory Agency,
    G.E. v. Fed. Radio Commission, 31 F. 2d 630, (App. D.C.
    1929)

4. All Radio Transmissions are Interstate Commerce,
    'Federal Radio Commission has power over intrastate
    radio as ancillary to authority over interstate radio,
    which devolves from the commerce clause of the consti-
    tution, because radio waves inside a state could affect
    radio waves crossing state lines,' FRC v. Nelson Bros.,
    289 US 266, (1933)

5. WCOT License Renewal Refusal for Editorial Practices,
    FRC., 2nd Annual Report, p. 152-3, (1928; Arno Press
    re-print)

6. WCRW License Renewal Refusal for Overcommercialization,
    See (Blue Book), Fed. Communications Commission, Public
    Service Responsibility of Broadcast Licensees., p. 41,
    (1946)

7. Great Lakes Application Opinion, 'Need for Balanced
    Program Structure, Service to Entire Public,' Great
    Lakes v. FRC (D. 4900, 1928), see P&F, Digest (2)
    ¶53:253, 254

8. FRC Assertion of Right to Consider Program Service, FRC
    2nd Annual Report, (1928)

9. Schaeffer Case, 'Licensee Responsibility for Content of
    Sponsored P'g'ms, Profanity utterance punishable under
    Act of 1927,' Duncan v. U.S., 48 F. 2d 128, (Cir. Ct.
    App. 9th, 1931)

10. Brinkley Case, 'License Renewal refusal for undesireable
    programs, et. al., FRC has right to consider past

1

performance, engaging in personal communication not within purview of Radio Broadcasts, defines 1927 no censorship Sec. §109 clause (applies to Sec. §326-Act of 1934)'; KFKB v. FRC, 47 F. 2d 670, App. D.C., (1931)

11. Baker Case, 'FRC License Renewal denial on basis of attacks, undesireable program content,' FRC 5th Ann. Report, p. 78, (1931) & Baker v. U.S., 115 F. 2d 533, (1940)

12. Shuler Case, 'FRC License Renewal denial on basis of attacks, Ct. of App. upheld FRC action as not 'censorship,' Trinity Methodist Church, S. v. FRC, 62 F. 2d 850, (App. D.C. 1932)

13. KVOS News Piracy Case, 'Rights of newsgathering agencies to news they provide, damages not substantiated,' Associated Press v. KVOS, 299 U.S. 269, (1936)

14. KMBC Defamation on Network Program, 'Affiliated station liable for defamation carried in network program,' Coffey v. Midland, 8 F. Supp., 889, (West D-Mo., 1934)

15. KFEQ Astrologer Opinion, 'Advice programs undesireable, if point-to-point,' Scroggin v. FCC, 1 FCC 194, (1935)

16. WMCA 'Birconjel' Advertising Contraceptives, 'Adv. contraceptives offensive also misleading advertising,' Knickerbocker, 2 FCC 76, (1935)

17. WAAT 'Code Message' B'c's, 'Codes, not understandable by all listeners are private communication, not broadcasting,' Bremer, 2 FCC 79, (1935)

18. WARD 'Foreign Lang. B'c's, 'Foreign Language B'c's Private communication; illegal transfer of control to buyer of block time,' United States B'c'g Co. 2 FCC 208, (1935)

19. WWAE Pur Erb Fraudulent Adv., 'Carrying ads for product under Post Office Fraud Order,' Hammond Calumet B'c'g, 2 FCC 321, (1936)

20. WOCL Baseball Recreation, 'Recreation not re-broadcasting,' Newton, 2 FCC 281, (1936)

21. WGBZ Texas Crystals & Speculative Stock Adv., 'License revocation based in part on fraudulent advertising,' WGBZ, 2 FCC 599, (1936)

22. <u>KFRC</u> <u>Marmola</u> <u>Adv.</u>, 'Station's Responsibility to investigate accuracy of ad claims,' Don Lee B'c'g Co., 2 FCC 642, (1936)

23. <u>WRBL</u> <u>Information</u> <u>Concerning</u> <u>Lottery</u>, 'Broadcasting information concerning lottery violation of Act, (Changed, see 294),' WRBL, 2 FCC 687, (1936)

24. <u>Vandenburg</u> <u>Political</u> 'Debate,' 'Station has right to reject, or censor, political speech by non-candidate,' News stories: Broadcasting, 1 Nov. 87, (1936).

25. <u>Athens</u> <u>Chiropractor</u> <u>Application</u>, 'Rejection of applications of Dr. who advertises own service,' Liberty B'c'g, 3 FCC 218, (1936)

26. <u>KTWI</u> <u>Advice</u> <u>Program</u>, 'Advice programs mislead public, objectionable, followed previous conclusion not in public interest,' B'c'g Corp., 4 FCC 125, (1937)

27. <u>Louis-Farr</u> <u>Rights</u> <u>to</u> <u>Fight</u> <u>B'c'st</u>, 'Unauthorized use of information and exclusive rights sold to others,' 20th Cent. Sporting Club v. Transradio, 300 NYS 159, (1937)

28. <u>Mae</u> <u>West</u> <u>Objectionable</u> <u>Language</u>, 'Network and Stations Responsibility for objectionable language,' News stories: Broadcasting, 20 Dec. (1937), 25 Jan. (1938)

29. <u>KVOS</u> <u>Licensee</u> <u>Control</u> <u>over</u> <u>News</u> <u>Programs</u>, 'Possible transfer of control over contents of news programming,' KVOS, 6 FCC 22, (1938)

30. <u>WMBQ Merchants Association Lottery Drawing</u>, 'License renewal denied, in part, due to carrying information concerning lottery,' Metro, 5 FCC 501, (1938)

31. <u>Beyond the Horizon Profane Language Incident</u>, 'Use of profane language in network broadcast,' News Story: Broadcasting, 15 Oct. p. 22, (1938)

32. <u>Philadelphia Young People's Gospel Association Denial</u>, 'Propaganda stations not in public interest,' YPGA for Propagation of Gospel, 6 FCC 178, (1938)

33. <u>KMPC 'Basic Science' Institute</u>, 'Re station's responsibility to check accuracy of advertising claims,' KMPC, 6 FCC 729; 7 FCC 449, (1939)

34. <u>FCC 1939 Memo</u>, 'Re Undesireable Program Materials,' Variety, 8 March p. 40 (1939), for alcholic beverage

3

advertising see Letter to Senator Edwin C. Johnson, released, 43 FCC 446, (Aug. 5, 1949)

35. <u>Mau Privacy Decision</u>, 'Right of individual to privacy re news events no longer news,' Mau v. Rio Rande Oil Co., 28 F. Supp. 845, (1939)

36. <u>WMBD 'Mu$ico' Lottery</u>, 'Defines lottery as applied to radio,' News story: Broadcasting, 29 Aug. (1939)

37. <u>Jolson Ad-Lib Defamation</u>, 'No network liability for ad-libbed defamation on sponsored program if due care taken to prevent,' Summit Hotel v. NBC, 336 Penn. 182, (1939)

38. <u>Sander's Bros. Economic Injury</u>, 'Right of FCC to consider economic injury to station in granting another's license,'

39. <u>WSAL Misrepresentations in Application</u>, 'Deletion', 8 FCC 34, (1940)

40. <u>KIEV Promise v. Performance</u>, 'FCC calls for programming in line with application promises,' Cannon System Lyd., 8 FCC 207, (1940)

41. <u>'Painted Dreams' Rights to Soap Opera</u>, 'In the absence of any definite contractual provision to the contrary, literary materials developed by Irna Phillips, employee, on co. time are considered property of employer,' Phillips v. WGN, 307 Ill. App. 1, 29 NE 2d 849, (1940)

42. <u>'Mayflower' Editorializing Opinion</u>, (changed, see 80), Mayflower, 8 FCC 333, (1941)

43. <u>Mr. District Attorney Rights</u>, 'Rights to program developed by employee prior to employment,' Cole v. Phillips H. Lord, 28 NYS 2d 404, (1941)

44. <u>Muzak 'World Series' Feed</u>, 'Unfair competition violates property rights using play-by-play materials already broadcast,' Mutual v. Muzak, 30 NYS 2d 419, (1941)

45. <u>The Sting of the Written Word is Its Permanence</u>, 'Extraneous defamatory remarks in radio script are slander, not libel,' (changed, see 401)' Locke v. Gibbons, 164 NY Misc. 877, (1937)

46. <u>The Privileged Broadcast</u>, 'District Attorney's remarks in broadcast of actual murder trial are privileged and not actionable slander,' Irwin v. Ashurst, 158 Ore. 61, (1938)

4

47. WMCA Qualified Privilege Claim, 'Sponsorship insufficient for station to claim qualified privilege,' 15 NY Supp. 2d 193, (1939)

48. WELL Management Contract, 'Transfer of control aspects of management contract,' Federated Publications, 9 FCC 150, (1942)

49. Voliva Advance Script Requirement, 'Station's right to require advance script,' (changed, see 258) Voliva v. WCBD, 313 Ill. App. 177, (1942)

50. FCC Network Regulation Test Case, 'FCC has right to exercise control over network-station relations,' NBC v. U.S., 47 F. Supr. 940, (1942), 319 US 190, (1943)

51. Blue Network Sale, 'Duopoly Rule forced NBC to sell 'Blue'; Sale conditions: No Policy barring sale of time for controversy,' RCA and ABS, 10 FCC 212, (1943)

52. WHKC Labor Union Sponsorship of Controversy, 'There should be no policy barring sale of time to unions for discussions of controversial issues as, absent a compelling state interest a corporation cannot be barred from influencing a public issue. However, neither may compel members or employees to contribute money,' (see 121) United B'c'g, 10 FCC 515 (1945); First National Bank of Boston v. Belloti, 435 U.S. 765, (1978)

53. WPEN Sale of Time for Religious Programs, 'Station has right to determine to whom time is to be sold or given,' FCC letter to Carl McIntire, 24 Apl 1945; McIntire v. William Penn B'c'g, 151 F. 2d 597, (1945); 327 US 779, cert. denied, (1946)

54. WDSU Equal Facilities for Candidates, 'Equal opportunities means equal quality as well as quantity,' Stephens, 11 FCC 61, 3 RR 1, (1945)

55. AVCO Rule, 'FCC procedures re transfer to new owners,' Crosby, 11 FCC 3, 3 RR 6, (1945)

56. Blue Book, 'Public Interest Requirements,' FCC Memo, entitled Public Service Responsibility of Broadcast Licensees,' Mar. (1946)

57. Elmhurst News Figure Privacy, 'Person involved in newsworthy event does not retain right of privacy,' Elmhurst v. Pearson, et. al., 153 F. 2d 467, (1946)

58. <u>Scott Atheist Time Demand</u>, 'Station obligation to air unpopular views,' 'later modification,' Scott, 3 RR 259; 5 RR 59, 11 FCC 377, (1946)

59. <u>Ft. Smith Newspaper Application Denial</u>, 'Desireability of diversity of ownership,' Arkansas-Oklahoma Co., 3 RR 479, (1946)

60. <u>WOKO Ownership Concealed Revocation</u>, 'FCC right to revoke license for false statements,' WOKO v. FCC, 153 F. 2d 623, 329 US 223, reversed; 3 RR 1061, (1946)

61. <u>KOB Political Sponsorship Identification</u>, 'Requirement of Sponsor ID of Political Broadcasts, Station's Obligation to Carry Political B'c's,' Albuquerque, 3 RR 1820, (1946)

62. <u>KOB, Time Reservation As Control</u>, 'Station's Right, regardless of contract provisions, to control of time,' Regents-N.M., 158 F. 2d 900; 5 RR 976; 6 RR 131, (1947)

63. <u>WOV Transfer Denial</u>, 'Denial based on Purchaser's Character Qualifications, Ct. upheld FCC's right to refuse transfer of license,' Arde Bulova, Transferor, Mester Bros. Transferees, 11 FCC 137, (1946); Mester v. FCC, 70 F. Supp. 118; Mester et. al. v. US, 392 US 749, cert. denied, affirmed 332 US 749, rehearing denied, 332 US 820, (1947)

64. <u>WTOL Overcommercialization</u>, 'Undesireability of Over-commercialization and Incentive Pay Contracts,' Community, 12 FCC 85, 3 RR 1360, (1947)

65. <u>TQN Right to Limit Amount of Political Time</u>, 'Station's right to limit amount of time Used by Political Candidates,' Homer P. Rainey, 11 FCC 898, 3 RR 737, (1947)

66. <u>KTSL-TV, Right to Televise Boxing Match</u>, 'Promoter's Right to give B'c's rights to TV fight Upheld,' Chavez v. Hollywood Post 45 & Don Lee Sts., 16 USL Week 2362, (Cal. Superior Ct.)

67. <u>Port Huron Ruling</u>, 'Station does not have right to censor talk by Political Candidate even if defamatory and not liable for such remarks,' Port Huron B'c'g, 12 FCC 1069, 4 RR 1, (1948)

68. <u>Non-newspaper given Preference over Newspaper applicant</u>, 'Daily News-NY loses license in comparative hearing because newspaper ownership, FCC goal is diversity, also

residents of community preferred, etc.' News Syndicate, 12 FCC 805, 4 RR 205, (1948)

69. **WWDC Racetrack Broadcasts**, 'Racetrack broadcasts not desireable programming,' Capitol, 4 RR 21, 12 FCC 648, (1948)

70. **WSAY Network Service Right**, 'Station cannot compel network to provide service,' Federal B'c'g Co. v. ABC, 167 F. 2d 349, 4 RR 2019, 335 US 821, (1948)

71. **KRLD Primary v. Regular Elections**, 'Equal opportunities applies only to same office and same election,' Sam Morris, 4 RR 885, (1948)

72. **WADC Proposed Use of Network Programs Denial**, 'Can't ride the network all the time--station which proposed less network wins,' Simmons, 169 F.2d 670, 4 RR 2023; 335 US 846, cert. denied, (1948)

73. **WTTM Defamation by Sponsored Newscaster**, 'Unless due care proof offered, station liable for remarks made by sponsored newsman,' Kelly v. Hoffman, 137 NJL 695 (NJ Ct. App.), 4 RR 2047, (1948)

74. **Paramount Pictures Monopoly Case**, 'Included radio as part of press, ergo, under 1st Amendment,' US v. Paramount Pictures, 334 US 131, 4 RR 2022, (1948)

75. **Brockton Application**, 'Applicant offering 60% limit on Sponsored Time Superior,' Bay State v. FCC, 171 F. 2d 826, 4 RR 2109, (1948)

76. **Grant Based on Superior Local Program Service**, 'Past record and local program service Superior,' Kentucky B'c'g v. FCC, 12 FCC 282, 3 RR 1547, (1947); 174 F. 2d 38, 4 RR 2126, (1949)

77. **WAAT Rights to Program Title**, 'Rival Station Restrained from using Title of Program Identified with WAAT,' Bremer B'c'g v. NJ B'c'g, (NJ Supp. Ct), Docket C-793-49, (1949)

78. **Birmingham Program Plans Decision**, 'FCC Not Engaged in Censorship when comparing plans of Rival Applicants,' Johnston B'c'g, 3 RR 1784, (1947); 175 F. 2d 351, 4 RR 2138, (1949)

79. **Peterson Privacy Case**, 'No Violation of Employed Entertainer Property Rights by Broadcast of Film of Entertainment Act,' (see 324), Peterson v. KMTR, LA Sup. Ct. 557555, (1949)

80. Mayflower Opinion Reversed, 'Broadcasters May Editorialize on Condition Facilities Available to Spokesman of
Opposing Viewpoints,' 13 FCC 1246, 1 RR 91, 201, (1949)

81. WCAM Refusal to Sell Religious Program Time, 'Licensee
can refuse to sell time; can restrict free time for
religious programs,' NJ Council of Churches, 5 RR 1014a,
14 FCC 370, (1949)

82. Mansfield Unfair Ad Practices of Newspaper, 'FCC has
right to consider monopolistic and unfair ad practices
of newspaper applicant, 'Fostoria, 3 RR 2014a, (1948);
Mansfield v. FCC, 180 F. 2d 28, 5 RR 2074e, 13 FCC 23,
(1950)

83. WGST Management Contract, 'Management Contract illegal
transfer of control; when contract cancelled to preserve
license, licensee liable for contract violation,'
Georgia Tech, 3 RR 47, (1945), Regents of Georgia v.
Carrol, 338 US 586, 11 FCC 71, 5 RR 2083, (1950)

84. Cullman Economic Injury, 'FCC refused to consider possible results of competition,' (see 137), Voice of
Cullman, 6 RR 164, (1950)

85. O'Brien Privacy Decision, 'Inaccurate Depicting of Event
invades Privacy,' News Story, Variety, 8 Mar. (1950)

86. WLIB Seek Out Opinion, 'Licensee obligated to 'Seek Out
and Encourage' Opposing viewpoints when Editorializing,'
New B'c'g, 6 RR 258, (1950)

87. Screen Test Rights to Title, 'Rights to Title Abandoned
after 4 years Non-use,' Screen Test, Inc., v. ABC, 97
NYS 2d 372, (1950)

88. WWJ Issues of a Strike Controversy, 'Station has no
right to insist on two-sided discussion of controversy
where one side refuses to air its viewpoint,' Detroit
Evening News, 6 RR 282, (1950)

89. Hollywood Preview Property Rights in Format, 'Property
Right of Program Format development protected by common
law,' Stanley v. Columbia B'c'g, 221 P. 2d 73, (Calif.
1950)

90. WLAW Censorship of Religious Program, 'Licensee has
right to refuse to broadcast programs it considers
unsuitable; must reserve final decision as to what
programs best serve the Public Interest,' Mass.

Universalist v. Hildreth, 183 F.d 497, 5 RR 2073, see also 87 F Supp. 822, 5 RR 2070, (1950)

91. Dewey 'Report to the People', 'Reports by Officials not automatically entitling opponents to time for reply,' Fitzpatrick, 6 RR 543, (1950)

92. WTUX Racetrack Program, 'Racetrack Information aiding Illegal Gambling may be grounds for Revocation,' Port Frere B'c'g, 5 RR 1137, (1950)

93. Sharkey 'Privacy of Entertainer,' 'Broadcasting old fight film not dissemination of news; former professional boxer has not completely lost right of privacy, can challenge unauthorized use of name and picture for ad purposes,' Sharkey v. NBC, 93 F. Supp. 986, 6 RR 2070, (1950)

94. Pennsylvania No Censorship of Films on TV, 'State censors cannot have right to pass on films shown over TV,' DuMont v. Carroll, 5 RR 2053, (1949); 6 RR 2045, (1950); 86 F. Supp. 813, affirmed 184 F. 2d 153, (1950), 340 US 939, cert. denied, (1951)

95. Felix Political Defamation, 'Section 315 applies to candidate personally,' Felix v. Westinghouse Radio, 6 RR 2014, (1950); 6 RR 2086, (1950); West. v. Felix, 341 US 909, cert. denied, (1951), 89 F. Supp. 740, reversed 186 F. 2d 1, (1950)

96. Scripps-Howard Diversification of Control, 'FCC consideration of Diversification in Mass Media within scope of agency,' Scripps-Howard, 4 RR 525, (1949); 189 F. 2d 677, Scripps v. FCC, 342 US 830, cert. denied, 13 FCC 473, (1951)

97. WBAL Upgraded Programming Saved License, 'Cited in Blue Book, short-term license renewal, challenged for license, upgraded programming, renewal given on ability to render a 'well-rounded program presentation', Hearst, 6 RR 994, 15 FCC 1149, (1951)

98. WIBK Attacks on Religious Groups Revocation, 'Misrepresentations, plus attacks on other religious groups on other station's programs; license denied, 'Independent B'c'g 6 RR 383, (1950); 193 F. 2d 900, (1951); 344 US 837, 14 FCC 72, (1949)

99. WLRD Broadcast Muzak Service Ruling, 'Muzak Service without identifications violates requirements,' WLRD, 7 RR 66, (1951)

100. Bride and Groom Rights, 'Damages for owner of program format which is pirated,' News Story in Variety, 25 July, (1951)

101. Richards News Slanting Case, 'News Slanting, proven, reflects on character qualifications,' Frances S. Richards, KMPC, 7 RR 788, (1951); see 73:24(D)

102. KSFO Right of Communist to Political Time, 'Only known instance of ruling that candidate who is (a) communist, (b) in jail (c) could not appear in person still had right to time as candidate,' Yates v. Associated B'c'g, 7 RR 2088, (1951)

103. Lorain Newspaper Unfair Competition, 'Injunction against unfair competitive methods not violation of Freedom of Press,' WEOL v. Lorain Jr., 92 F. Supp. 794, 6 RR 2037, (1950); US v. Lorain Jr., 342 US 143, 7 RR 2078, (1951)

104. Haas Socialist Candidate Right to Speak, 'Candidate cannot be censored for talk which does not deal with candidacy,' WMCA, 7 RR 1132, (1952)

105. KGNS Candidates Report to Constituents, 'Once Candidate has announced for re-election equal time provision in effect including 'reports' if opponent makes request within one week of broadcast,' KGNS, 7 RR 1130, (1952)

106. WWJ-TV Unreasonable Refusal to Allow Rebroadcast, 'Affiliate cannot refuse to permit rebroadcast for no reason, or upon unreasonable grounds,' In Re Amendment of FCC Rules (Docket 9808), 1 RR 91: 1131, (1952)

107. Schneider Fringe Candidate, 'Even fringe candidate with less than 1% of primary vote entitled to equal time,' CBS, 7 RR 1189, (1952)

108. Sally Rand Ad-Lib Defamation, 'NBC neither malicious nor negligent in ad-lib defamation, ergo, removed from action.' Wagner v. Finkelstein (Rand) (N. D-Ill., 1952); 8 RR 2016, (1952)

109. Rosenberg Advance Script Ruling, 'If all candidates treated alike, advance script may be required, refuse to allow extemporaneous speeches, and recording allowed in advance,' (changed, see 258) Rosenberg Letter, 11 RR 236, (1952)

110. Gautier Commercial Use of Picture, 'Sponsorship does not per se constitute use for ad purposes; picture and act must be connected with commercial itself,' Gautier v.

Pro-Football, Inc., 304 NY 354, 107 NE 2d 485; 6 RR 2024, 8 RR 2001, (1952)

111. Kefauver Crime Commission Hearings, Witness Right of Privacy, 'Two cases-two Cts.--different decisions-one Yes-invasion of privacy to cover on TV--atmosphere created lack of decorum; other-No,' US v. Kleinman, 107 F. Supp. 407, 8 RR 2031, (1952); and US v. Moran, 194 F. 2d 623, (1952)

112. Belt Talent Hunt Program Format Rights, 'Person can have right to idea even though not patentable nor subject to copyright if reduced to concrete detailed form and in some way novel,' Belt v. Hamilton Bank, 108 F. Supp. 689, 8 RR 2046, (1952), (see 295)

113. Texas Auto Race Recreation, 'Summary of race transmitted by phone by staff member listening to station which bought rights to race; recreated at station is OK as became part of history upon happening,' Loeb v. Turner, 9 RR 2018, (1953)

114. Double or Nothing Format Rights, 'Unsolicited submission of program idea without contractual agreement covering confidential basis of submission cannot be basis for recovery if idea or parts of idea are by another with no connection,' Carneval v. William Morris Agency, 9 RR 2048, (1953)

115. Marciano Recreation of Boxing Match Shown on Theatre TV, 'May do recreation if news summaries and at end of each round,' Int. Boxing v. Wodaam, 9 RR 2050, (1953)

116. Charlie Chaplin Right of Privacy, 'Gossip program informational and Chaplin public figure,' Chaplin v. NBC, 9 RR 2051, (1953), (see 450)

117. KELP Recreations of Major League Baseball, 'Recreations not rebroadcasts says FCC, McClendon sues Major Leagues for stopping his recreations--settled out of court,' Liberty Broadcasting System v. National League Baseball, 7 RR 2164, (1952); Trinity, 10 RR 279, (1954)

118. Lottery Rule, 'Supreme Ct. ruled that consideration was payment of money in any way or thing of value, but not postcard or listening to station,' ABC v. US, 110 F. Supp. 374, (1953); FCC v. ABC, 347 US 284, (1954)

119. Autry-Rogers Television Rights for Theatrical Film, 'Actor's Right to Restrict Use of Film for Television Depends on Contract Provisions,' Rogers v. Republic

11

Pictures., US Dist. Ct., (S.D.-Calif.), 7 RR 2072; Autry., (CA 9th), 213 F. (2d) 662, 10 RR 2059, (1954); Autry., 213 F. 2d 667, 10 RR 2063, (1954); Rogers., 348 US 858, cert. denied, (1954)

120. <u>Bernstein Right of Privacy of Former Convict,</u> 'Widely publicized criminal proceeding does not lose its status as matter of legitimate Public Interest even after eight years; dramatization permitted,' Bernstein v. NBC, 129 F. Supp. 817, 11 RR 2091, (1954)

121. <u>WJBK-TV, Appearance of Candidate Sponsored by Union,</u> 'Union dues cannot be used to influence electorate, but union members may contribute to a fund as state is barred from restraining labor unions and others from expressing viewpoints,' Fed. Corrupt Practices Act, US v. UAW, 138 F. Supp. 53, reversed 352 U.S. 567; 15 RR 2018, (1957)

122. <u>Fass Pirating of Baseball Play-by-Play,</u> 'Broadcast of play-by-play cannot be used or resold as would violate property rights,' National Exhibition v. Fass, 143 NYS 2d 767, 11 RR 2086, (1955)

123. <u>Mobile Sponsored Religious Programs,</u> 'Commercial sponsorship of religious programs not inherently objectionable or against Public Interest,' WKRG, 10 RR 225, (1955)

124. <u>Jacova Privacy of Spectator Decision,</u> 'Spectator of news-worthy event loses right of privacy,' Jacova v. Southern, 83 So. 2d 34, 13 RR 2001, (1955)

125. <u>Ettore Right of Privacy,</u> 'Public Performance does not remove all rights of privacy,' Ettore v. Philco, 229 F. 2d 481, 13 RR 2107, 351 US 926, cert. denied, (1956)

126. <u>McClatchy Newspaper Applicant Discrimination,</u> 'Apparently, even superior performance as owner insufficient for newspaper applicant in competitive hearing,' McClatchy, 9 RR 1190, (1954); 239 F. 2d 15, 13 RR 2067, (1956); 353 US 918, cert. denied, (1957)

127. <u>Legality of FCC Multiple-Ownership Regulations,</u> 'FCC has right to limit number of stations owned by one owner,' Storer, 220 F. 2d 204, 11 RR 2053, (1955); US v. Storer, 351 US 192; 13 RR 2161, (1956)

128. <u>Eisenhower Talk During Political Campaign,</u> 'State paper-type talk does not entitle opponents to Equal Time even during Campaign,' CBS, 14 RR 720, (1956)

129. **Kansas City Star Anti-trust Violations,** 'Newspaper guilty of unfair practices divested of b'c'g stations,' Kansas City Star, 240 F. 2d 643, (1957); 354 US 923, cert. denied. (1957)

130. **Blondy Equal Time for News-Film,** 'No right to Equal Time on basis of appearance by candidate in News-Film if not initiated by candidate,' Letter to Blondy, 6 Feb. (1957)

131. **Play Marco Lottery Decision,** 'Calling at place of business does not constitute consideration,' Caples, 13 RR 1154, (1956); Caples v. US, 15 RR 2005, (1957)

132. **Albany Transfer of Network Affiliation,** 'Change in Affiliation not contrary to Anti-Trust Act,' Van Curler v. FCC., (Ct. App. D.C.), 12 RR 2040, (1955); Rosenblum, 22 FCC 1432; 11 RR 825, 12 RR 283; 13 RR 49, (1957)

133. **Wyatt Earp Name Rights,** 'Commercial Values in Name Created by TV series belong to owners of series,' W. Earp Enterprises v. Sachman, (S.D-N.Y.), 16 RR 2034, (1958)

134. **WSAY Blanket Rebroadcasting Right,** 'Station has right to refuse blanket rebroadcasting permission,' 24 FCC 147, (1958); 26 FCC 178, (1959); 225 F. 2d 560, (1955); 14 RR 150, (1959)

135. **Jack Benny Gaslight Burlesque,** 'TV Parody of Play, is a copyright infringement,'Loew's v. CBS, 131 F. Supp. 165, 12 RR 2077, (1955); CBS v. Loew's, (C.A. 9th,) 239 F. 2d 532, 14 RR 2075, (1956); CBS v. Loew's, 356 US 43, all affirmed (1958)

136. **Anti-Pay TV Editorials,** 'Don't broadcast editorials without offering time to opponents; Don't use own employees to support opponents points when editorializing,' Alabama B'c'g Sts, Inc., 17 RR 273, (1958)

137. **Carroll Economic Injury,** 'Effect of a new station upon the quality of service provided listeners considered. Sander's (38) Economic Injury was based upon effect of new station upon other stations. Ct. of App. remanded case to FCC, which determined that burden of proof lies with protester and was a heavy one. Both industry and FCC unhappy at widening of considerations into economic comparison of business operations,' 27 FCC 161, (1959), Carroll v. FCC, 258 F. 2d 440, (1958)

138. **Lamb Defamation in Candidate's Talk,** 'Station Not Liable for Talk by Candidate,' Lamb v. Sutton, *et. al.,*

13

(M.D-Tenn.), 164 F. Supp. 928, 17 RR 2099, (1958), (see 145)

139. Patterson-Harris B'cast as News, 'Right to Broadcast Fight 'Summaries' from Press Association as News,' WOR, WINS, WOV, News. Story: Broadcasting, 25 Aug. p. 60, (1958)

140. Non-ID of Supplied Kohler Strike Films, 'Station's should have ID'd source of films of strike,' KSTP, 17 RR 553; Storer, 17 RR 556a; Westinghouse, 17 RR 556d, (1958)

141. Candidate Must Appear in Person, 'Candidate A newscaster, Candidate B applies for Equal Time; FCC gives time equal to all (several weeks) as used by A; B can't use all; FCC says must use personally, no representative,' Grace, 17 RR 697, (1958)

142. Gaines Revocation, 'Violation of Regulations while Manager of 'Other' Station reflects on character,' 25 FCC 1387, 16 RR 159; 17 RR 163, (1958)

143. Radio 'price-fixing' Decision, 'Association of Station's setting rates is price-fixing,' US v. Phil. Radio & TV Broadcaster's Assoc., (E.D. Pa.), 18 RR 2009, (1958)

144. Hintz Privacy of Witness in Congressional Hearing, 'No right of privacy in Congressional Hearings,' US v. Hintz, 193 F. Supp. 325; 21 RR 2021, (1961)

145. WDAY-TV Libel By Candidate, 'Supreme Ct. Decision-- Station Cannot Be Liable for Broadcast by Political Candidate,' Farmers' Union v. Townley, (N.D. Dist. Ct.), (1957); 15 RR 2058, (1957) Farmer's v. WDAY, (N.D. Sup. Ct.), 89 NW 2d 102, 17 RR 2001, (1958); Farmer's v. WDAY, 360 US 525, 18 RR 2135, (1959), (see 216)

146. FCC Political Rules Amendments, 'Requests for Equal Time must be submitted within one week of day Reply proposed; must prove legally qualified candidate,' Rule 73.120; 1940(e)

147. Price is Right Property Rights, 'Royalties on Program Property Used Must be Paid,' News Story: Variety, 15 July p. 35, (1959)

148. FCC Ban on Teaser Announcements, 'FCC Memo: Teaser Ads must carry sponsor ID,' 18 RR 1860, (1959)

149. NBC Signs Consent Decree on Anti-Trust, 'Consent Decree Signed and NBC gives up Phil. stations acquired to avoid losing all licenses if lost anti-trust action,' US v. RCA, (Dist. Ct. E. D. Pa.), 17 RR 764, (1959)

150. One-sided Presentation of Labor Controversy, 'Station expected to 'Seek Out' Opposition even when editorial by outsider,' Metro, 19 RR 602, (1959)

151. FTC Action on Rigged Commercials, 'Use of Visual Deception in TV Commercials Cease and Desist Order,' News Story: Broadcasting, 22 Feb., p. 34, (1960)

152. FCC Payola Action, 'Required ID of free recordings, etc., Sponsor ID of all Broadcast Materials,' 19 RR 1569, FCC Rept & Order 601-1141, 21 Sept (1960)

153. KWTX Weather Reports by Candidate, 'Candidate, also Weatherman, in Performance of Job as Weatherman comes under Section 315--News exemption; Opponent Not Entitled to Equal Time,' KWTX, 19 RR 1075; Bingham v. FCC, 276 F. 2d 828, (Ct. App); 19 RR 2068, (1960)

154. WCLG Sheriff's Reports by Candidate, 'Report by Sheriff-Candidate for re-election not News Program; Opponent entitled to Equal Time,' Freed, 19 RR 1391, (1960)

155. WREC Advertising as Part of Program Balance, 'FCC has right to consider advertising as part of programming in Public Interest,' WREC, 10 RR 1323; 14 RR 1262; 22 FCC 1572, (1960)

156. KIMN DJ Smut, 'Broadcasts of indecent language in DJ program caused hearing order,' Mile High Stations, 28 FCC 795; 20 RR 345, (1960)

157. Political Sale of Time, 'Station not required to sell time to one candidate if hasn't sold time to other candidates for same office,' Grommelin, 19 RR 1392, (1960)

158. Miami Ex Parte License Revocation, 'FCC Commissioner involved in Ex Parte Contacts causes extensive hearings and revocation after remand,' WKAT, 22 FCC 117, (1957); WKAT v. FCC (Ct. App. DC) 258 F. 2d 418, (1958); 17 RR 997, (1960); 296 F. 2d 375, (1961); 368 US 841, cert. denied, (1961)

159. Eisenhower Talk and Fairness, 'Equal Time not applicable to noncandidate but station has obligation to afford reasonable presentation of opposing viewpoints under

Fairness Doctrine,' Calif. Demo. State Central Comm., 20 RR 867, (1960)

160. Short Term License, 'Licensee Failure to Give Enough Supervision,' Eaton, 20 RR 1074, (1960)

161. KDWB Fine, 'Fine of $2,500 marks FCC's first use of that power; failure to reduce power at night,' Crowell-Collier, 21 RR 921, (1961)

162. Ascertainment of Community Needs is Public Service Responsiblity, 'License grant refused on basis of failure to ascertain or survey community needs and Ct. ruled FCC has statutory authority to require survey,' Suburban, 112 US App DC 247, 302 F. 2d 191, 371 US 821, 83 S. Ct 37, cert. denied; 20 RR 951, (1961-62)

163. CATV Use of TV Programs, 'TV stations have no property rights in programs they broadcast other than those covered in Copyright Act,' Intermountain, 196 F. Supp. 315, 21 RR 2084, (1961)

164. KORD Promise v. Performance, 'Stations put on Notice that FCC to give license would look at Promises made versus Performance made,' (see 183) KORD, 21 RR 781; 31 FCC 85, (1961)

165. WHAS-TV Economic Injury to UHF Stations, 'FCC refusal to grant tower height increase based almost entirely upon probable economic injury to existing UHF stations in proposed coverage area,' WHAS, 31 FCC 273; 21 RR 929, (1961)

166. Indianapolis TV CP Revocation, 'Revocation based on Concentration in Media of Mass Communications,' Indianapolis B'c'g, 22 FCC 421, (1957); WIBC, 104 US App. DC 126, 259 F.2d 941, cert. denied. 359 U.S. 920, 22 RR 425, (1961)

167. WESY Overcommercialization, 'Excessive Commercials (av. 15 per hour); lack of program balance gets short-term license renewal,' Miss-Ark B'c'g, 22 RR 305, (1961)

168. No Need Application Denial, 'Contrary to precedent, FCC denied application in non-competitive hearing for interference and for Failure to Establish Need for a Third Station in Market of 18,000,' Dixie Radio, 22 RR 345, (1961)

169. WOGA Secondary Boycott by Union Ruling, 'Precedent Shattering Ruling by NLRB permitted secondary boycott to

take place on grounds that the radio station, by adding its labor, capitol and service to a product manufactured by someone else, becomes one of the producers of that product rather than merely an agency carrying the advertising for the producer. With a station a joint producer with every manufacturer whose products or services it advertises, boycotting the station's advertisers and the station is primary boycott permitted under Landrum-Griffith Act. Strikers were engineers of station,' (changed, see 182), Local 662, IBEW, Middle S., 133 NLRB 165, (1961)

170. KRLA License Revocation, 'Licensee negligent, guilty of fraud in conduct of promo contests and logs altered with intent to deceive FCC,' Eleven Ten B'c'g, 32 FCC 706, 33 FCC 92, (1962); 11-10 v. FCC, 25 RR 2128a, 320 F. 2d 795 (D.C. Cir.), cert. denied, 375 US 904, (1963)

171. State Advertising Statute applies Across State Lines, 'New Mexico station must obey New Mexico statute even when carrying ads for nearby Texas firm,' New Mex. Bo. of Examiners v. Roberts, 23 RR 2042; 70 NM 90; 370 P. 2d 811, aff.; 25 RR 2087; 374 US 424, (1962)

172. Conspiracy Suit over Network Affiliation, 'Cancelling affiliation to transfer to new network owned station no violation of anti-trust laws,' Poller, WCAN-TV v. CBS, 22 RR 2080, 174 F. Supp. 802, affirmed 109 US App DC 170, 284 F. 2d 599, rev. 368 US 464, (1962)

173. Colgate, Ted Bates Use of Mock-Ups on TV Commercials, 'Not permitted to use Mock-up to deceive viewer; substitution due to photographic process is OK,' FTC, 22 RR 2043; 24 RR 2058; 310 F. 2d 89; 380 US 374; see 6 RR(2d) 2024, (1965)

174. CBS TV Network Compensation Plan, 'More pay the more programs carried declared violation of prohibition of exclusive affiliation by FCC after pressure from Justice Dept.,' CBS, 23 RR 769, (1961); 24 RR 513, (1962)

175. CBS v. Amana Sponsorship Case, 'Sponsorship of TV program not sale of commodity within meaning of Robinson-Patman Anti-Trust law; discounts do not have to be equal for all advertisers, (see 368)' CBS v. Amana., (C.A. 7th); 22 RR 2019; 295 F. 2d 375, (1961)

176. Block Booking on TV, 'Block bookings of motion pictures for TV is violation of Anti-Trust laws,' US v. Loew's, 24 RR 2032; 371 US 38, (1962)

177. **CBS Plagiarism on Playhouse 90,** 'Network used article published by Life in 1949, Ct. awarded damages of $50,000,' News Story: Broadcasting, 25 June p. 76. (1962)

178. **WDKD Smut Broadcast License Denial,** 'Indecent Materials cause denial,' Palmetto, 23 RR 483, (1962); 33 FCC 250, (1962)

179. **CBS, NBC Coverage of Debate Not News,** 'Coverage of Debate by Candidates invited by Press Association not News Coverage, Equal Time Applies,' (changed, see 303), 24 RR 401, (1962)

180. **'Sidewinder' Rights to Name,** 'Character created while employee owned by station, however, former employee has right to portray character,' News Story: Broadcasting, 20 Aug. p. 76 (1962)

181. **WLLE Playing One Song All Day and Smutty Remarks,** 'Letter was Sent to all licensees noting WLLE playing of one song all day when call letters changed and remarks made between record were discordant and did not qualify as inventive or in the Public Interest,' Raleigh-Durham, 24 RR 221, (1962)

182. **KXTV Union Secondary Boycott,** 'TV station not simply carrier of advertising, but by adding labor and service producer of products (see 352) said NLRB, but Dist. Ct. overturned and remanded,' News Story: Broadcasting, 19 Nov p. 72, (1962)

183. **WWL-TV Promise v. Performance,** '(see 164) Short-term renewal granted to Loyola University commercial station for not meeting promises,' Loyola, 24 RR 766, (1962)

184. **Cullman Doctrine,** 'When presenting one side of an issue, sponsored, licensee cannot reject a presentation of the other side simply on the ground that he cannot obtain paid sponsorship for that presentation and thus leave the public uninformed,' Cullman B'c'g, 25 RR 895, (1963)

185. **WCLM-FM License Revoked for Aiding Illegal Gambling,** 'SCA Multiplex channel of FM station used to broadcast horse race results to be received by bookmaker's,' Carol Music, 3 RR 2d 477, (1963), 8 RR 2d 93, cert. denied. (1966)

186. **KWK Fraudulent Promotion Revocation,** 'Treasure not hid,' KWK, 25 RR 577, 1 RR 2d 457, (1963), 34 FCC 1039, 35 FCC 561, 2 RR 2d 2071, US App DC, (1964)

187. <u>KHOB State Control of Interstate Advertising</u>, 'Sup. Ct. ruled that state ct. and legislature retained jurisdiction over advertising, even though ads distributed on an interstate basis; 'indirect effect on commerce of country',' Head v. New Mexico Bd., 23 RR 2042, (1962); 25 RR 2087, 374 US 424, (1963)

188. <u>WBTW Privacy in Rape Case</u>, 'Names not used of victims, but pictures of car which was readily identifiable and occupations. Ct. ruled 'name' in S. Carolina statute should be interpreted as equivalent of 'identity',' Nappier, 1 RR 2d 2012, 322 F.2d 502, (1963)

189. <u>KYW Defamation in Documentary</u>, 'Name and Place of business of man found guilty of crime broadcast, but appeal had conviction overturned just prior to broadcast; damages found,' Purcell v. Westinghouse, 1 RR 2d 2016, (1963)

190. <u>FCC Attempts to Limit Commercial Time</u>, 'FCC issued Notice of Proposed Rulemaking limiting commercial time, but Congress upset over issue; so FCC released Policy Statement which became basis for §0.281(7) (i,ii,iii). Commercial AM & FM stations exceeding 18 minutes per hour, or in excess of 20 minutes per hour for 10% or more of total weekly hours of operation and which, during political campaigns or seasonal business markets exceed 22 minutes for 10% of total hours of operation cannot be renewed routinely by FCC staff; the applications must be submitted to full commission. TV stations cannot exceed 16 minutes per hour, but during high demand political campaigns can go in excess of 20 minutes for 10% of total hours of operation,' 36 FCC 45, (1964); (changed, see 442)

191. <u>TV Option Time Prohibited</u>, 'Networks can not option time in Station-Network Contracts,' FCC Rept. & Order, 34 FCC 1103, 25 RR 1951, (1963)

192. <u>Essaness Minority Program Proposal</u>, 'Chicago station proposes program only for Minority Groups; FCC states must program to all groups in service area,' Essaness Assoc. 25 RR 479, (1963)

193. <u>NBC v. FCC and Withdrawal Payments</u>, 'FCC Rules they must approve payment for expenses incurred when competing applicant withdraws--becomes Rule §73.3525 of Title 47 CFR,' 25 RR 67, (1963)

194. <u>Standard Criteria for Competing Applications</u>, 'Review of the Standard Criteria utilized for judging competing

19

applications,' 1 RR 2d 237, (1963) See also, 1965 Policy Statement on Comparative Hearings, 5 RR 2d 1901, (1965)

195. Double Billing Ruling, 'FCC rules against Double Billing (§73:1205) Practices,' 23 RR 175, (1962), 1 FCC 2d 1068 (1965) 38 FCC 2d 1051, 25 RR 2d 1759, (1972)

196. Imitation of Advertising is Unfair Competition, 'Company used the slogan, 'Where there's life. . . there's bugs' in advertising combination floor-wax-insecticide, imitating Budweiser slogan, 'Where there's life. . . there's Bud' in which over $40 million had been invested.   Ct. granted injunction against wax co. not-with-standing the fact the products were noncompetitive,' 306 F. 2d 433 (5th Cir. 1962), cert. denied 372 US 965, 83 S. Ct. 1089, (1963)

197. Quorum for FCC, 'FCC rules four members quorum, 3-1 vote legal,' Jefferson Standard, 1 RR 2d 423, (1963)

198. Local Tax on Programming, 'Opinion of Att. Gen. Kentucky: Can't put local tax on TV programs & advertising,' 1 RR 2d 2058, (1963)

199. WMOZ Falsification of Logs, 'License revoked for false logs,'WMOZ, 36 FCC 201, 1 RR 2d 801, (1964)

200. Announcer's Property Rights, 'Record included one-minute excerpt of CBS announcer's voice during Kennedy assassination.   No Property Rights in News, but in announcer voice and style,' CBS v. Docu. Ltd, (NY Sup. Ct.), 2 RR 2d 2011, (1964)

201. Experience Counts, 'FCC stated where on quantitative basis applicants equal, the qualitative comparison based on broadcast experience becomes decisive,' Rockland B'c'g, 2 RR 2d 39, 36 FCC 303, (1964)

202. Use of Newspaper for News, 'Use by station of newspaper items for newscast may be unfair competition if station competing with newspaper for advertisers or 'subscribers' and news is fresh and of commercial value to paper.   Practice not encouraged,' Comm B'c'g, 6 RR 2d 589, (1965) and, Pottstown Case, 'State has jurisdiction concerning unfair competition but even if copyrighted news, use does not violate copyright act if factual content only,' 6 RR 2d 2027, 247 F.Supp 578 (ED Pa. 1965)

203. Malice Not Needed, 'Nothing in 1st Amendment requires showing of malice as prerequisite to recovery for

violation of right of Privacy of person not public official,' Yousoupoff v. CBS, 265 NYS 2d 754, (NY Sup. Ct.) 6 RR 2d 2033, (1965)

204. Jurisdiction in Copyright Case, 'Entering affiliation agreements in state is systematic activity subjecting network to jurisdiction of state in copyright case,' Scott v. WKJG, (ND Ind.), 5 RR 2d 2065, (1965)

205. Public Disclosure of Records, 'Sup. Ct. required public disclosure except where FCC determines not in public interest,' MCA v. FCC, 85 S. Ct. 1459; 381 US 279, (1965)

206. WMAY Newscaster as Candidate, 'Appearance of employee-candidate is use under Equal Time rule,' WMAY, 4 RR 2d 849, (1965)

207. Billy Sol Estes, 'TV Coverage of trial prejudicial; sentence reversed under Due Process Clause of 14th Amendment,' 381 US 532; 85 S. Ct. 1628; 6 RR 2d 2104, (1965)

208. Sheppard Case, 'Jury exposure to massive publicity of information not introduced at trial required new trial,' Sheppard v. Maxwell, 384 US 333, 86 S. Ct. 1507, (1966)

209. Copyright-responsibility for, 'If station has either actual or constructive knowledge of copyright infringement, but proceedes to advertise illegal copy, without making adequate investigation held liable for infringement,' Screen Gems-Columbia v. Mark-Fi Records, 256 F.Supp. 399, (SD NY), 7 RR 2d 2191, (1966)

210. Capone Invasion of Privacy, 'Capone, deceased, has no right to Privacy and right cannot be asserted by next of kin,' Maritote v. Desilu, 345 F. 2d 418; 5 RR 2d 2077, (1965)

211. Subscription TV, 'In 1963 Calif. voters out-lawed Pay-TV. Cal Sup. Ct. overturned as unconstitutional,' Weaver v. Jordan, 411 P.2d 289, cert. denied, 385 US 844;7 RR 2d 2166, (1966)

212. WLBT-Standing Case, 'Responsible spokesman for representative groups in listening community pursuing broad public interest have standing as petitioners to deny license renewal. FCC has interpreted as allowing single individual to ask for license revocation,' Office of Comm. of United Church of Christ v. FCC, 359 F 2d 994, (1966), and Harrea B'C'g, 52 FCC 2d 998, 33 RR 2d 1075, (1975)

213. <u>Need to Do Ed Programs</u>, 'Commercial stations are obligated to carry programs which fulfill educational needs whether or not non-commercial stations exist in the community of license,' UHF Channel Assignment, 2 FCC 2d 527, 6 RR 2d 1643, (1966)

214. <u>License Control</u>, 'Broadcast that 'amoeba was loose,' caused substantial disturbance and licensee should have maintained greater control,' WIST, 2 FCC 2d 597, 6 RR 2d 793, (1966)

215. <u>Parent Co. Liable</u>, 'FCC has jurisdiction over parent co. although not licensee as it was sole owner of subsidiary,' Federated Pub., 6 FCC 2d 279, 9 RR 2d 252, (1967)

216. <u>Sec. 315 Immunity</u>, 'Licensees' immune from civil action for libelous statements made by candidate extended to statements made by those appearing on program with candidate,' Gray Comm., 14 FCC 2d 766, 14 RR 2d 353, (1968)

217. <u>Fortnightly v. United Artists</u>, 'Sup. Ct. reversed lower Cts. and held that CATV did not do performance within meaning of 1909 Copyright Act and therefore no copyright infringement,(see 295 and 302)' 88 S. Ct. 2084; 392 US 390; 13 RR 2d 2045, (1968)

218. <u>Southwestern Cable</u>, 'Affirmed FCC's jurisdiction over all CATV systems,' Midwest TV v. Southwestern Cable, 88 S. Ct. 1994; 392 US 157; 13 RR 2d 2045, (1968)

219. <u>Anti-Smoking Commercial decisions</u>, 'Banzhaf petitioned FCC to take off cigarette ads; FCC ruled equal time for anti-smoking spots not required, but fair balance on controversial issue needed,' Banzhaf v. FCC, 405 F. 2d 1082, (1968), 14 RR 2d 2061 & <u>Congress Rules Cigarette Ads Off-Air</u>,' law bans cigarette ads on TV-Radio, 15 U.S.C. 1335, (1/2/71)

220. <u>Examples of Station ID violations</u>, 'Public Notice,' 10 FCC 2d 399, 11 RR 2d 1607, ¶53:1201, (1967)

221. <u>Dual Network Operation</u>, 'FCC waives Rule §73.137 to permit ABC to operate four radio networks,' (see 312) 11 FCC 2d 163, 12 RR 2d 72, (1967), 17 FCC 2d 508, 16 RR 2d 84, (1969)

222. <u>Personal Attacks and Fairness Doctrine</u>, 'When a station broadcasts personal attacks they must allow a response from individual attacked. Unlike newspapers which are

not required to allow reply (<u>Miami Herald v. Tornillo</u>, Sup. Ct. 418 US 241, 1974) broadcast frequencies are scarce and there are legitimate claims by those unable without government assistance to gain access. Broadcaster's 1st Amendment rights are abridgeable, as different,' Red Lion v. FCC, Sup. Ct. 395 US 367; 16 RR 2d 2029, (1969); see also Wis. Assoc. of Nursing Homes v. Jr. Co., 285 N.W. 2d 891, (1979).

223. <u>Policy is Control</u>, 'Network-owned TV station broadcast a pot party, prearranged by one of its reporters. Lack of policy deprived licensee of control,' WBBM, 15 RR 2d 140, (1969)

224. <u>No Fairness Doctrine for ads</u>, 'Licensee has right to refuse carrying ads and not accepting ads from union urging boycott did not violate Fairness Doctrine,' Oil, Chemical & Atomic Workers Union, 18 FCC 2d 501, 17 RR 2d 153; 20 RR 2d 2005; 48 FCC 2d 1, 30 RR 2d 1261, 436 F.2d 248, (1969)

225. <u>Broadcasting of Lottery Information</u>, 'Public Notice,' 21 FCC 2d 846, 18 RR 2d 1915, (1970)

226. <u>Sound Effects in Announcements</u>, 'Public Notice,' 20 RR 2d 98, (1970)

227. <u>Zapple Doctrine or Quasi-Equal Opportunities</u>, 'When a station sells time to supporters or spokespersons of a candidate during an election campaign, the licensee must afford comparable time to the spokesperson for an opponent,' Nicholas Zapple, 23 FCC 2d 707, 19 RR 2d 421, (1970)

228. <u>Use of Broadcast Facilities by Candidates for Public Office</u>, 'Public Notice,' 24 FCC 2d 832, 19 RR 2d 1913, (1970)

229. <u>Competition and Responsibility in Network TV Broadcasting</u>, Public Notice which eliminated networks from distribution and profit-sharing in domestic syndication and restricted their activities in foreign markets to distribution of programs of which they were the sole producers,' Amended 73.658 (j), 23 FCC 2d 382, 18 RR 2d 1825, (1970), (see 264)

230. <u>License Revocation on Renewal</u>, 'Herald-Traveler station in Boston filed against by group which promised better programming, integration and diversity of local media control. Newspaper claimed not fair as only promises and paper would fold. FCC revoked license and newspaper

ceased publication shortly thereafter,' WHDH, (US Ct. App. DC) 444 F. 2d 841, (1970); 403 US 923, cert. denied, 15 RR 2d 411, (1971)

231. Policy Statement Concerning Comparative Hearings Involving Regular Renewal Applicants, 'FCC devised policy to lay to rest WHDH effect on license renewals,' 22 FCC 2d 424, 18 RR 2d 1901, (1970)

232. Policy Statement Overturned, 'Ct. of App. DC overturned FCC stating that full comparative hearing must be held, with license judged on evidence, all relevant criteria, including integration of minority groups into station operation. 'Superior' performance to be plus of major significance and means 'far above average.' It includes elimination of excessive and loud advertising, quality programs, re-investment of profit, diversification and independence from governmental influence to promote 1st Amendment objectives,' Citizens Communications Cntr v. FCC, (US Ct. App. DC) 447 F. 2d 1201; 24 RR 2d 2045, (1971), (see 343)

233. Licensee Discretion, 'Refusal to show integrated situations (black man and white woman kissing) would be discriminatory, however no evidence violated licensee discretion,' Citizens Communication Cntr, 22 FCC 2d 705, 20 RR 2d 19, (1970)

234. Cavett Interview Edited, 'Network edited interview stemmed from appropriate concern of effect on a pending trial. FCC will not intrude in this sensitive area if good faith application by licensee,' Letter to Ottinger, 31 FCC 2d 852, 18 RR 2d 1031, (1970)

235. Religious Fairness, 'Presentation of evolution theory material does not itself raise Fairness Doctrine issue unless Biblical creation story and evolution were topics of controversy in community,' Tillson, 24 FCC 2d 297; 18 RR 2d 189, (1970)

236. FTC Controls Misleading Ads, 'FCC has not made, and does not intend to make, judgments whether particular ads are false and misleading-will defer to FTC as per formal memorandum of understanding,' Reply to Center for Law and Social Policy, 23 RR 2d 187, (1971); see also Deceptive Advertising, 'Public Notice' 32 FCC 2d 360, 23 RR 2d 1550, (1971)

237. Negotiating with Public Interest Groups, 'A licensee is not obligated to participate in negotiations concerning employment practices and programming,' WKBN, 30 FCC 2d 958, 22 RR 2d 609, (1971)

238. Fairness Doctrine, 'Ct. of App. DC rules that Banzhaf decision can be extended to other issues even though FCC stated was 'unique' situation. Must decide whether licensee has otherwise met its fairness obligations,' Friends of the Earth v. FCC, (Ct. App. DC) 449 F 2d 1164; 22 RR 2d 2145, (1971)

239. Fairness for Public Service Spots, 'Public Service messages for Armed Services not subject to Fairness Doctrine; however may be if one side of controversial issue presented,' Jelinek, 24 FCC 2d 156, 19 RR 2d 501, (1970), affirmed Green v. FCC, 477 F. 2d 323; 22 RR 2d 2022, (1971)

240. Fairness Against President, 'Some time must be afforded for appropriate spokesman to reply to Presidential speeches on Viet Nam,' Comm. for Fair Broadcasting of Controversial Issues, 19 RR 2d 1103, (1970), reversed on other grounds, CBS v. FCC, 454 F. 2d 1018; 23 RR 2d 2019, (1971)

241. Fairness for Public Service Spots, 'United Appeal Public Spots deemed subject to Fairness Doctrine,' AVCO, 32 FCC 2d 124, 23 RR 2d 111, (1971), (see 421)

242. Use of Broadcast and Cablecast Facilities by Candidates, 'Public Notice,' 37 Fed. Reg. 5796; 23 RR 2d 1901, (1972)

243. Minority Service, 'Ct. did not decide whether licensee has primary obligation to serve its city of license or full service area but petition to deny for not serving 90% black Washington, D.C. denied as black population is 10% of full-service area,' WMAL-Stone v. FCC, 24 RR 2d 2105, 466 F. 2d 316, (1972)

244. Handling of Public Issues Under the Fairness Doctrine and the Public Interest Standards of the Communications Act--1st Report, 36 FCC 2d 40, 24 RR 2d 1917, (1972)

245. Federal Politicians Better than Local, 'Sec. §312 amended adding (a)(7), requiring broadcasters to allow reasonable access to or permit purchase of reasonable amounts of time by a legally qualified candidate for Federal Elective Office on behalf of his candidacy,' P.L. 92-225 (1972)

246. Carroll Doctrine--WLVA-TV, 'In ascertaining a Carroll (see 137) issue applicant must prove factual data to make a *prima facie* case that the economic consequences

of the challenged application will lead to a derogation of service to the public. Three interdependent aspects: 1) revenue potential of market; 2) effect of economic loss on public service programming; 3) loss will not be offset by applicants proposed increased non-network programming,' (Ct. App. DC) 459 F. 2d 1286; 23 RR 2d 2081, (1972)

247. Astrology Policy, 'NBC had policy (as did other nets) banning non-news material presented for purpose of fostering belief in astrology, following NAB Code. However, WFMY-TV, CBS and NAB sued by astrological forecasting service for antitrust conspiracy to limit access for program featuring forecasts. Motion to dismiss denied as ct. found sufficient cause of action on theory of state action and First Amendment rights. Settled out of court,' Mark v. NBC, 25 RR 2d 2083, 468 F. 2d 66 (Cal. 1972); letter, 34 FCC 2d 434 (1972); Gemini v WFMY, 70 F. Supp. 559 (MD. NC 1979)

248. Smothers' Bros. Censorship Not State Action, 'Program producers cannot sue network because of its censorship under the Communication Act of 1934 unless network activities constituted 'governmental or state action,' Smothers v. CBS, (CD Calif.), 25 RR 2d 2099, (1972), (see 304)

249. Right to Reply, 'Automatic right of reply by spokesman of opposing party to Presidential addresses rejected,' Democratic National Committee v. FCC, 460 F. 2d 891, cert. denied, 409 US 843; 23 RR 2d 2165, (1972)

250. Lottery, 'Congress by enacting 18 USC §1304 empowering FCC and Justice Dept. to regulate and enforce Federal Lottery Laws had preempted state law in field,' Miss. B'c'r's Assoc. v. Danforth, (Mo. Cir. Ct.) 26 RR 2d 967, (1973)

251. Diversity, 'It is upon ownership that diversity of content rests and greater weight should have been accorded minority ownership; remanded to FCC. Dealt with issues of experience, participation in local affairs, etc.', (US Ct. App. DC), 495 F. 2d 929, (1973); 419 US 986, cert. denied; 28 RR 2d 1115, (1973), 69 FCC 2d 607, 43 RR 2d 811, (1978)

252. Primer on Ascertainment of Community Problems by Broadcast Applicants, 27 FCC 2d 650, 21 RR 2d 1507, (1971), clarified, 47 FCC 2d 519, 29 RR 2d 1739.

253. FCC Expert Body, 'The FCC does not think the public interest would be better served by a policy that

substituted open bidding for licenses for the reasoned
decision-making of an expert body accountable in its
actions to Congress,' Letter to Hon. William Proxmire,
27 RR 2d 1321, (1973), (see 452)

254. Code Communication Broadcasting, 'A radio station may
not transmit announcements asking a Dr. (identified by
code number) to call the Physician's Bureau. This is
point-to-point communication, not broadcasting and no
urgent need shown,' KFAB, 1 RR 2d 403, (1963), and see
WANV, 27 RR 2d 1607, (1973)

255. Selling Time Not Required, 'Broadcast licensee's general
policy of not selling ads to individuals or groups wishing to speak out on issues they consider important does
not violate the FCC Act or 1st Amendment. The Ct. will
not apply the Fairness Doctrine to editorial advertising; however if such time sold Fairness Doctrine and
Cullman aspect must be observed,' CBS v. Democratic
National Committee, 412 US 94, (Sup. Ct. 1973); 19 RR
2d 977, (1970); 27 RR 2d 907, (1973)

256. Right to Reply FCC Decision Upheld, 'FCC upheld when
denied DNC right to some time to reply to Presidential
addresses on economic policy,' (Ct. App. DC), 481 F. 2d
543, (1973)

257. 'Clipping' of Net Programs, 'Public Notice,' 40 FCC 2d
136, 26 RR 2d 1253, (1973)

258. Political Advance Copy Not Permissible, 'Improper for
station to request candidate submit copy of speech
before broadcast,' Western Comm. B'c'g, 43 FCC 2d 730,
28 RR 2d 1091, (1973)

259. Program Length Commercials, 'Public Notice,' 44 FCC 2d
985, 29 RR 2d 469, (1974), (changed, see 442)

260. Playing Radio in Business May Be Performance of © Music,
'Small Restaurant did not 'perform' copyrighted music
when playing radio through less than four speakers.
However, new © Act §110(5) imposes liability where
proprietor has commercial system installed or converts
standard home receiver into equivalent of commercial
sound system. Another factor is whether establishment
of sufficient size to justify subscription to commercial
background music service,' 20th Century v. Aiken, 422
US 151 (CA 3d 1975), 30 RR 2d 1053, (1974) and Sailor
Music v. Gap Stores, cert. denied, 1982; and 668 F.2d 84
(2d Cir. 1981); BMI v. US Shoe, 678 F.2d 816 (1982)

261. **Not Carrying Religious Program Fair**, 'Station did not violate Fairness Doctrine by refusing to carry religious program,' RKO General, 46 FCC 2d 240, 29 RR 2d 1459, (1974)

262. **Licensee Discretion**, 'Deleting Crest's name from Johnny Carson monologue for humorous but critical comment is licensee decision,' National Citizens Comm., 49 FCC 2d 83, 31 RR 2d 293, (1974)

263. **What is Public Figure**, 'Absent clear evidence of general fame or notoriety an individual should not be deemed a public personality for all aspects of his life; damages for actual injury that can be proven,' Gertz v. Robert Welch, 418 US 323, (1974)

264. **Network Antitrust action resolved by Consent Decree**, 'Consent judgments have been entered against ABC and CBS to restrain monopolization of prime time TV entertainment programs in violations of §1 and 2 of Sherman Antitrust Act, based on NBC consent decree entered into earlier. The affiliated stations and owned-and-operated stations of the networks were found to depend upon the networks for virtually all their entertainment programming. The commercial value of such control over programming, in addition to the first network showing, includes stripping (broadcasting program series episodes more than once a week after initial network exhibition), syndication, foreign distribution, merchandizing, literary and musical rights, etc. During the 1950's many advertisers purchased programs from independent suppliers (producers and production companies) for showing on networks. By 1967 only 11% were advertiser supplied and today no prime-time shows are advertiser supplied. The FCC, in response to network dominance of production or subsidiary rights adopted rules forbidding networks from demanding financial interests or syndication rights from producers before putting on the network (§73:658(j), but networks continued to seek such rights as long-term renewal options with preset license fee escalation rates; exclusive options on spinoffs; creative program control; right to all profits from network exhibition; and right of first refusal at end of option period, (see 229).

The consent judgment, certain provisions of which will be in effect for 10 years and others for 15 years, enjoins networks from acquiring syndication and other distribution rights or profit shares in non-network exploitation of entertainment programs produced by others. Domestic syndication is prohibited by the networks but would allow network-produced and certain foreign programs to be distributed in foreign markets. In order to increase competition networks may produce no more than 2 1/2 hours per week in prime time (with similar restrictions in other time periods). Other practices prohibited are purchasing exhibition rights other than those incident to network licensing and use; a ban on requiring program supplier having to use network production facilities; a prohibition against purchasing another network's programs with the condition that the other network purchase similar rights; and no exclusive yearly options for more than a total of 4 years.

The networks may not have exclusive rights in connection with exhibition of feature films either theatrically, nontheatrically, on discs, cartridges or cassettes, or on closed circuit TV in certain situations. The networks are barred from retaining rights to option program pilots not selected for broadcast beyond 35% of the pilots produced so as to allow other networks and stations access to remaining product. If a spinoff depicts a noncontinuing character, the network may contract only for first negotiation and a limited first refusal right and the use of repeat broadcasts of series episodes is curtailed.

With respect to talent agreements, individuals performing continuing or essential creative services on a prime time series licensed to a network are barred from entering agreements which prevent them from providing their services to the series if it is later licensed elsewhere.

The judgment does not affect network ability to acquire certain rights for nonnetwork broadcast (49 RR 2d 1343; 1981) distribution of programs abroad and they may recover money advanced for development,' US v. CBS, Civil Action No. 74-3599-RJK; US v. ABC No. 74-3600-RJK (C.D. Calif. 1980); US v. NBC, 74-3601-RJK (C.D. Calif. 1977); 'Ct. of Appeals has ruled that $2.3 million may be awarded to Columbia Pictures, Gulf & Western, MCA, 20th Century-Fox and Warner Communication from ABC and CBS to repay costs studios incurred in responding to pretrial discovery supoenas,' 666 F.2d 364 (1982), Sup. Ct. appeal denied

265. Documentaries and Fairness, 'Reversed FCC decision that 'Pensions-Broken Promises' violated Fairness Doctrine. The Fairness Doctrine requires a demonstrated analysis of imbalance on controversial issues,' NBC v. FCC, (Ct. App. DC), 516 F. 2d 1101, (1974); vacated as moot, 424 US 910, cert. denied, (1976)

266. How to Get the Broadcaster, 'The FCC publishes a manual to inform the public of procedures available such as

Fairness Doctrine complaints, personal attacks, equal opportunity, petitions to deny, petitions for rule-making, and informal complaints,' Broadcast Procedure Manual, (1972), 37 FCC 2d 286, 25 RR 2d 1901 and revised 49 FCC 2d 1, 31 RR 2d 224, (1974)

267. Documentary Freedom, 'ABC cannot be enjoined (prior restraint) from showing crib burning in documentary on fire safety. The basic concept of freedom of speech and press applies to the broadcast industry,' ABC v. Smith Cabinet, (CA Ind.) 30 RR 2d 837, (1974)

268. Concerning Licensees Responsibility Under Amendments to the Communication Act Made by the Federal Election Campaign Act of 1971,' Public Notice,' 47 FCC 516; 30 RR 2d 567, (1974)

269. Courtroom Sketching, 'Orders of a Federal District Judge which not only forbade in court sketching, but publications of sketches wherever made constitutionally overbroad. Sketching not shown obtrusive or disruptive,' US v. CBS, 497 F.2d 102 (CA 5th), 30 RR 2d 1349, (1974)

270. Policy Statement on Fairness Doctrine, 'The present rule is that product advertising per se is not a statement on a controversial issue so long as the ad merely extols the virtues of the product and takes no explicit position on matters of public controversy. No scheme of government-dictated access (free or paid) for discussion of public issues practicable or desireable,' 48 FCC 2d 1; 30 RR 2d 1261, (1974)

271. Agreement Between Broadcast Licensees and the Public, 'Policy Statement,'57 FCC 2d 42, 35 RR 2d 1177; (1975)

272. Applicability of Sponsorship ID Rules, 'Public Notice on Sec.§73.1212,' (1975); see Gaylord, 67 FCC 2d 25, 40 RR 2d 830, (1977); Silverman, 63 FCC 2d 233, 39 RR 2d 1713, (1977); US Postal, 41 RR 2d 877, (1977); Dept. of Justice, 41 RR 2d 881, (1977); and 52 FCC 2d 701, 33 RR 2d 975, (1977)

273. Deceptive Advertising, 'FTC given clear regulatory power over deceptive advertising reaching down to local level,' Magnuson-Moss Act, PL 93-637, 88 Stat. 2183, (1975)

274. Past Programming Challenge, 'To successfully challenge past programming, petitioner must make specific allegations of fact, which, if true, would establish that

overall programming could not have reasonably met needs and interests of community including substantial minority. Licensee not required to program in proportion to minority numbers in population,' Newhouse, 53 FCC 2d 966, 33 RR 2d 1514, (1975)

275. Editorializing, 'Licensees are under no obligation to editorialize,' McPherson B'c'g, 54 FCC 2d 565, 34 RR 2d 785, (1975)

276. Primer on Ascertainment of Community Problems by Broadcast Renewal Applicants, 57 FCC 2d 418, 35 RR 2d 1555, (1975); modified, 61 FCC 2d 1, 38 RR 2d 885

277. Renewal on Past Performance, 'RKO-General, KHJ-TV, filed against by Fidelity was heard in comparative hearing in 1966. In 1967 Justice Dept. filed anti-trust action against RKO-General for fixing prices on tires. FCC said would take into consideration when finally decided on. Consent decree signed 1970 so not factor, but Fidelity requested adding as issue. ALJ found that RKO was lacking in past performance in programming and community relations; 'presenting old films of excessive violence.' RKO station WNAC-TV Boston subsequent to decision challenged also. FCC reversed ALJ on KHJ and granted renewal based on; RKO had promised in 1962 renewal old films and had provided old films. RKO was one of many stations in market and credit should be given to existing service. App. Ct. DC reviewed and stated 'FCC when faced with a fairly and evenly balanced record may, on the basis of the renewal applicants past performance, award him the license.' RKO had agreed to sell WNAC upon condition FCC renewed license, 1978. Decision was that FCC could determine that both applicants were poor or minimally acceptable,' Fidelity TV v. FCC, (US Ct. App. DC) 515 F 2d 684, (1975); 44 FCC 2d 149, 16 RR 2d 1181, (1969); 32 RR 2d 1607, (US Ct. App. DC, 1975) (see 417); Case led to following Policy Statement

278. Formulation of Policies Relating to the Broadcast Renewal Applicant, Stemming from the Comparative Hearing Process, 'Until Congress acts no quantitative standards will be adopted and applicant must continue to run on its record measured by whether programming was sound, favorable, and substantially above a level of mediocre service. Case-by-case basis.' FCC Report & Order, 66 FCC 2d 419, 40 RR 2d 763, (1977); Aff'd, 44 RR 2d 547 (US App DC)

279. Violence Not Indecent, 'Violence and mayhem are not obscene, indecent or profane as defined in Sec. 303 (m) (1) (D) of the Act, or 18 USC §1464,' Polite Society, 35 RR 2d 39 and see Pacifica, 56 FCC 2d 94, 32 RR 2d 1331, (1975)

280. Topless Radio, 'On March 27, 1973 FCC announced inquiry into broadcast of obscene, indecent or profane material. $2000 forfeiture levied on Sonderling, 27 RR 2d 1508, (1973). Citizens Committee and Am. Civil Liberties Union filed petition for remission and reconsideration. Radio shows asked sexual questions on talk-in shows. Ct. affirmed FCC on merits, but upheld standing of appellant's as public interest in free flow of information would not be vindicated if licensee finds burden too great to contest FCC action,' Illinois Citizens Comm., v. FCC, 31 RR 2d 1523, (1974) 515 F. 2d 397, (Ct. App. DC, 1975)

281. Drug Lyrics Confusion, 'FCC issues Public Notice, 28 FCC 2d 409, (1971), stating that licensees must make reasonable efforts to determine before broadcast the meaning of music containing drug oriented lyrics. After many complaints about prior censorship and procedures which would be considered reasonable FCC issues second Memorandum and Order, 31 FCC 2d 377, (1971), clarifying and modifying; (1) FCC not prohibiting playing songs, (2) no reprisals against stations which did play drug oriented songs, but (3) licensee responsibility to know content and make judgment regarding wisdom of playing such songs. Appealed to Ct. App. DC, which stated that purpose and actual result was to remind the industry of a pre-existing duty to assume responsibility for all material which is broadcast over their facility and no case had yet been presented of license revocation on issue. Petition for writ of certiorari denied by Sup. Ct,' Yale Broadcasting v. FCC, (Ct. App. DC) 478 F. 2d 594, (1973); 414 US 914, cert. denied, (1973); 28 RR 2d 938; 21 RR 2d 1576; 21 RR 2d 1698; 31 FCC 2d 385, 22 RR 2d 1808, (1971)

282. Prime Time Access Rule Constitutional, 'Prime-time Access Rule adopted in 1970 prohibits networks from using more than 3 hours of prime-time each night in order to get independent producers prime-time access. Held constitutional and consistent with FCC obligations under 1st Amendment to promote diversity of program sources,' Mt. Mansfield v. FCC, 442 F. 2d 470; 21 RR 2d 2087, (1971); National Assoc. of Ind. TV Producers and Directors v. FCC, 516 F. 2d 526, (1975); Ct. remanded for rule changes, 33 RR 2d 2087, (1975)

283. Prime Time Access Rule Changes, 'Rule §73.658(k); Exemptions and Waivers,' 50 FCC 2d 829, 32 RR 2d 697, 1975; 2nd Report and Order, FCC; 53 FCC 2d 335, 33 RR 2d 1089, (1975)

284. Suburban Modified, 'Presumption of service to larger community will only be considered in comparative hearings on renewal,' 54 FCC 2d 1, 34 RR 2d 603, (1975); clarified, 59 FCC 2d 9, 35 RR 2d 666

285. What does it take to Lose, 'License is renewed short-term where broadcast unsubstantiated weather reports, lottery promotion, contest disrupted traffic, violated technical rules, failed to supervise, lacked due care in correspondence with FCC. Revocation too harsh as broadcast significant public service programming,' Action Radio, 51 FCC 2d 803, 33 RR 2d 51, (1975)

286. Broadcasting Rape Victim Name, 'No liability for truthfully publishing the name of rape victim released to the public in official court records,' Cox v. Cohn, 420 US 469; 32 RR 2d 1511, (1975)

287. Loud Commericals, 'Public Notice,' July 12, 1965 and 1975, 5 RR 1621; 1 FCC 2d 10, 5 RR 2d 1631, (1975)

288. Contests, 'New Rule §73:1216, 60 FCC 2d 1072, 38 RR 2d 828, (1976) on Licensee Conducted Contests,' Some examples: Causing damage to public & private property, McLendon, 3 RR 2d 817, (1964); Caused trespassing, traffic congestion, SIS, 6 RR 2d 792, (1966); Broadcast of Station Contests, 37 RR 2d 260, (1976)

289. Fraudulent Billing Rule Amended, 'Rule §73.1205,' 59 FCC 2d 1268, 37 RR 2d 715, (1976)

290. Change in Station ID Announcement Requirements, 'Rule §73.1201(d),' (1976), 61 FCC 2d 149, 37 RR 2d 1223

291. Programming Minimums, 'Official amounts of certain programming would be censorship,' Hubbard, 48 FCC 2d 517, (1974); but unofficial processing guidelines for FCC Staff were: Non-entertainment must be more than 8%, 6% and 10% respectively for commercial AM, FM, TV. TV must show more than 5% local programming and 5% or more informational programming--6 a.m. to 12 midnight,' FCC Report No. 14173, May 12, 1976, see 37 RR 2d 144, (1976), (changed, see 442)

292. Personal Attack Rule, 'Personal attack rule does not apply to every personal attack, but only to a personal

33

attack broadcast during the presentation of views on a controversial issue of public importance,' Straus v. FCC, 530 F 2d 1001; 35 RR 2d 1649, (1976)

293. Section 315-Political, 'Amendment; 45 days before primary election and 60 days before federal or special election station can only charge political candidate lowest unit charge for same class and amount of time for the same period,' 47 USCA 315(b), Pub. L. 93-225, Current Service: 10:315(b) of RR, (1972)

294. Lottery, 'Announcing a winning number is news on day drawn and can be so broadcast.' Congress changed law, 18 USCA §1307, (1976), to exempt broadcast in state or adjacent state if own state has lottery. Can do advertising, prize list, or information. Sup. Ct. remanded case back to determine if decision was moot in case in light of Congressional action. Case declared not moot and affirmed original ruling. Therefore, allows states without lottery or adjacent to lottery state to broadcast about lottery as news,' NJ State Lottery Comm. v. US, 29 RR 2d 157, 491 F.2d 219 (CA 3d, 1974); 34 RR 2d 825

295. Copyright Law Revised, 'PL 94-553; Oct. covers cable TV, etc. Lifetime of copyright owner plus 50 years,' Effective 1978; USCA Title 17, (1976)

296. State Can Broadcast Religion, 'The State of Oregon, licensee of TV station, is not barred by the Constitution from broadcasting religious programs,' Corvallis TV, 59 FCC 2d 1282, 37 RR 2d 1045, (1976)

297. No News OK, 'Failure to broadcast any news programming in its previous license term did not constitute failure as promised no news. Economic consideration for FM stations, but now station should reevaluate,' Patrick Henry, 62 FCC 2d 293, 39 RR 2d 671, (1976)

298. Lottery Consideration, 'Consideration is not: postage, watching, writing for tickets, going to station, going to business, etc,' KCOP TV, 59 FCC 2d 1321, 37 RR 2d 1051, (1976)

299. Misuse of Survey Results: Hypoing, 'Unfair trade practice complaints on use of survey and hypoing will be sent to FTC,' §73.4035; §73.4040; 58 FCC 2d 513, 36 RR 2d 938, (1976)

300. Fairness Doctrine Review, 'When reviewing a Fairness Doctrine complaint, the FCC looks to overall performance

and good faith efforts, not simply one program or series of programs,' Storer B'c'g, 60 FCC 2d 1097, 38 RR 2d 669, (1976)

301. Announcement Charge, 'There is no rule or policy which prescribes the type announcement for which a licensee may charge--obituary-dedication, etc,' La Fiesta, 59 FCC 2d 1175, 37 RR 2d 983, (1976)

302. CATV Report and Order, 'Regulation of CATV, Copyright Agreement--cable to pay reviewed by Ct. The Channel Capability and Access Channel requirements were held to exceed FCC jurisdiction,' Cable TV Report and Order, 36 FCC 2d 143, 24 RR 2d 1501, (1972); 25 RR 2d 1501, (1972); 37 RR 2d 213, (1976); and RR 2d 1637, (1978) F. 2d 1025, 42 RR 2d 659, 45 RR 2d 581, 25

303. Press Conferences and Debates as News, '(see 179), Press Conferences and debates of candidates are exempt 'news events' where broadcast live, in entirety, and not sponsored or controlled by licensee or candidate. Allowed Carter-Ford debates,' Aspen Institute, 55 FCC 2d 697, (1975), affirmed Chisholm v. FCC, 538 F. 2d 349, (Ct. App. DC); cert denied, 429 US 890, (1976); 36 RR 2d 1437, (1976), (see 387 and 429)

304. Family Viewing Policy, 'In 1975, the NAB adopted a family viewing policy providing that entertainment programming inappropriate for viewing by a general family audience should not be broadcast during the first hour of network programming in prime time and in the immediately preceding hour. The policy also required the use of advisories to alert viewers to any prime time programs containing material that might significantly disturb significant segments of the audience. The three major TV networks had previously indicated their willingness to comply with such a policy. The Writers Guild, Directors Guild, Screen Actors Guild and Norman Lear's Tandem Productions brought actions against the NAB, three networks and FCC challenging the adoption of the policy. The plaintiffs contended that the policy violated the First Amendment, Administrative Procedure Act, antitrust laws, and Section §326 of the FCC Act. They sought declaratory and injunctive relief, and Tandem sought damages as 'All in the Family' was moved to a less desireable time slot due to the policy.
   A Federal District Ct. in California concluded that the family viewing policy had been adopted by the NAB and networks in response to threats, influence and pressure of the Chairman of the FCC; that the improper pressure was a per se violation of the 1st Amendment;

that the FCC had violated the Administrative Procedure
Act by using 'the raised eyebrow' to implement public
policy instead of procedure; that action by the networks
and NAB was 'governmental action' under the 1st Amendment claim because of the pressure and because the networks, NAB and FCC had participated in an unprecedented
joint venture to effect the independent judgements of
other broadcast licensees; and networks and NAB had
violated the 1st Amendment by becoming surrogates in the
enforcement of government policy.

However, a Federal Ct. of Appeals in California has
vacated the opinion on the ground that the doctrine of
primary jurisdiction requires the FCC to consider the
claims prior to any court action. The claims are being
held in abeyance pending administrative proceedings
before the FCC.   The doctrine of primary jurisdiction
generally applies when a court is presented with issues
involving a regulatory scheme. The judicial process is
suspended pending referral of such issues to the appropriate administrative body, presumably in order to
achieve uniformity and consistency in regulation and to
allow the court to benefit from the expertise and insight of the agency. A similar doctrine, requiring the
exhaustion of administrative remedies prior to judicial
review, applies when a claim may be heard in the first
instance by an administrative agency alone.   The
District Ct. had felt that the FCC was already biased
and it would not serve any purpose for the FCC to review
their own pressure efforts.   The Ct. of Appeals has
disagreed and utilized the doctrine of primary jurisdiction to obtain a determination by the FCC of whether it
had properly walked the tightrope. The Ct. also noted
that informal procedures of a government agency resulting in self-regulation by an industry often avoided the
need for formal government intervention. Even if such
procedures were characterized as official action by the
agency, the Ct. of Appeals concluded the District Ct.
should not have thrust itself so hastily into the deli-
cately balanced system of broadcast regulation and
should have deferred initially to the FCC,' Writers
Guild of America, West v. FCC, (US Dist. Ct. Cal.) 423
F. Supp. 1064, (1976), 36 RR 2d 711 (oral opinion); 38
RR 2d 1409, (written opinion); 46 RR 2d 813, (CA 9th,
1979), overruled and remanded to FCC. Sup. Ct, appeal
denied

305. Adequate Coverage of Controversial Issues of Public
Importance, 'W. Virginia station did not adequately
cover the locally 'critical issue' of national strip
mining legislation. The FCC is not powerless to insist
that they give adequate and fair attention to public

issues,' Rep. Patsy Mink, 59 FCC 2d 987, 37 RR 2d 744, (1976)

306. Off-Air Concert Promotion, 'Station promotions of non-broadcast off-air concerts while other non-station connected concerts are not nearly so well advertised may be unfair competition,' Radio WCMQ, 62 FCC 2d 487, 39 RR 2d 506, (1976)

307. Citizen-Broadcaster Agreements, 'Rules will not be adopted to require the reporting and FCC enforcement of Citizen-Broadcaster agreements,' National Black Media Coalition, 61 FCC 2d 1112, 38 RR 2d 263, (1976)

308. Prior Restraint Unconstitutional, 'Prior restraint prohibiting broadcasting facts strongly implicative of confessions unconstitutional,' Nebraska Press Assoc. v. Stuart, 427 US 539, (1976)

309. Report and Order in the Matter of Nondiscrimination in the Employment Policies and Practices of Broadcast Licensees, '10-point model program suggesting steps for licensee to follow in developing equal employment opportunity plans,' 62 FCC 2d 708, 39 RR 2d 421, (1976)

310. Women in Programming, 'FCC will not be drawn into controversy over treatment of women in programming,' CBS, 59 FCC 2d 1127, 37 RR 2d 972, (1976); see also, NOW v. FCC, 40 RR 2d 679, (US Ct. App. DC.) 555 F. 2d 1002 (1977)

311. Public Figure Redefined, 'Time Magazine erroneously reported divorce had been granted on grounds of adultery as well as extreme cruelty. Mrs. Firestone was not a public figure because she had not thrust herself to the forefront of any particular public controversy,' Time v. Firestone, 424 US 448, (1976)

312. Statement of Policy on Network Radio, 'Report and Order allowing multiple networking; §73:132; 1977 Report & Order, March 23, 42 FR 16415, 63 FCC 2d 674, 40 RR 2d 80, (1977)

313. Personal Attack But Not Defamatory, '$1000 fine for personal attack on landlord as 'slum-lord,' etc. News Documentary is not exempt from personal attack rules as broadcast over 3 times in a year,' WNET, Ed. B'c'g Corp, 65 FCC 2d 152, 40 RR 2d 1676 (1977); however, 'in similar case, referring to a land-lord as a 'slum-lord' is not strictly defamatory under the innocent construction rule. Term can be construed to mean a person who owned

buildings in a poor-dirty neighborhood. Under innocent construction rule, allegedly libelous statements must be taken as a whole, and if capable of any innocent construction, the statement is not defamatory,' Rasky v. CBS, 431 N.E. 2d 1055, (Ill, App. 1982)

314. Processing Standard for Equal Employment Opportunity, 'The FCC will look first to station's employment profiles as reported on Form 395. Processing quides, (latest) used will be: Stations with fewer than five full-time employees will be exempt from written EEO program; stations with five to 10 employees will have EEO program reviewed if minority group or women do not number, in comparison with local workforce, 50% over-all and 25% in top four job categories (officials, manager, professionals, technicians, sales); stations with 11 or more full-time employees must reach 50% parity over-all and in top four categories; stations with 50 or more employees will receive complete review of EEO programs at renewal,' (1977 & 1980)

315. Federal-State Laws in Area of Broadcasting, 'Public Notice with respect to pre-emption of local laws by the Communications Act of 1934, as amended,' 41 RR 2d 248, (1977); Example: 'FCC's pre-emption of regulation of special pay cable programming rendered invalid NY price regulation on such programming,' Brookhaven Cable TV v. Kelley, 573 F2d 765, 42 RR 2d 1185, (CA 2d 1978)

316. Persistent Violations Revocation, '(see 285) Refusal to renew license, 34 RR 2d 1465, affirmed by US Ct. App. DC on the ground that long history of persistent violations of FCC operating rules was sufficient,' United v. FCC, 55 FCC 2d 416, 40 RR 2d 1646, (1977)

317. Advertising--Fairness Doctrine Reconsidered, 'Handling of Public Issues Under the Fairness Doctrine and the Public Interest Standards, Public Notice of some importance, 58 FCC 2d 691 (1977); exempted from the Fairness Doctrine product commercials which do not obviously and meaningfully address a controversial issue of public importance. This policy was upheld by the Ct. of App DC which noted, 'that merely advocating the use of a product does not of itself raise a controversial issue, even if the product is controversial in the minds of some viewers. Nothing in the Supreme Ct's decision upholding the constitutionality of the political editorializing and political attack rules suggests that the obligation to present opposing points of view must be applied to all constitutionally protected speech. Advertisements in the editorial category, which consists

of direct and substantial commentary on controversial
issues of public importance continue to be under the
Fairness Doctrine,' National Citizens Comm. for
Broadcasting v. FCC, 567 F. 2d 1095, (1977); cert.
denied, 98 S. Ct 2820, (1978).

318. Children's TV Report and Policy Statement, 'ACT petition.
FCC refused to limit ads on children's programs, but
adopted other items,' 50 FCC 2d 1, 31 RR 2d 1228,
(1974), affirmed 564 F. 2d 458 (1977), 40 RR 2d 1577,
(1977); also refused to adopt 14 hr a week minimum for
children's programs; no reconsideration, 546 F. Supp.
872, (D.D.C. 1982)

319. Children's Programming, 'FCC will not redefine children's programming to include programs viewed by, although not designed for, children,' 63 FCC 2d 26, 39 RR
2d 1032, (1977)

320. Ads with Premiums, 'FTC declines to adopt prohibition on
all ads directed to or viewed by children which contain
premium offers,' 40 RR 2d 1, (FTC, 1977)

321. Controversial Ads, 'Ad constituted one side of a controversial issue,' Energy Action Comm., 64 FCC 2d 787, 40
RR 2d 511, (1977)

322. Home Video Recording of TV violates Copyright Act, 'The
Federal Court of Appeals has ruled that off-the-air
video tape recording of TV broadcasts--even for private,
non-commercial uses--violates the © Act. The 1971 Sound
Recording Act states that Congress did not intend to
restrain home audio recording where it is for private
use and with no purpose of reproducing or otherwise
capitalizing commercially. However, home video recording was not a common practice in 1971 and no statutory
or legislative language indicates that video recording
was an exception to the general rule that copyright
owners have an exclusive right to copy their own
material,' Universal Studios v. Sony Corporation, 659 F.
2d 963, (9th Cir. 1981)

323. Pay Cable TV, 'FCC cannot restrict pay cable programming
or bar cablecasters from showing commercials on channels
on which programs are presented for a direct charge,'
Home Box Office v. FCC, (Ct. App. DC) 567 F. 2d 9,
(1977), 40 RR 2d 283, 434 US 829, cert denied, (1978)

324. Entire Act Not News, '1st Amendment does not immunize
the media from liability for damages when they broad-

cast a performer's entire Human Cannonball Act without consent,' Zacchini v. Scripps-Howard, 433 US 562, 40 RR 2d 1485, (1977)

325. Use of Stolen Information, 'Though government may deny access to information and punish its theft, government may not prohibit or punish the publication of that information once it falls into the hands of the press, unless the need for secrecy is overwhelming,' Landmark Comm. v. Virginia, 435 US 829, 98 St. Ct. 2588, (1978)

326. Press Access Not Greater Than Public's, 'Press not entitled to access to prison conditions any more than general public,' Houchins v. KQED, 438 US 1, (1978)

327. Newsroom Security, 'Legislation passed Congress (10/1/80) requiring all federal, state and local law enforcement agencies to obtain a supoena before searching newsroom or newsperson unless person involved is suspected of crime; information necessary to prevent death or serious bodily injury; imminent destruction or concealment of material not produced in response to a ct. order or if contraband material. Law came about because of Zucker v. Stanford Daily, 436 US 547, (1978)

328. Watergate Tapes, 'Common law right of access to judicial records did not entitle TV networks and others to copy White House tapes used in criminal trial of Watergate defendants,' Nixon v. Warner Communication, 435 US 589, (1978)

329. Forfeiture Ceiling Raised, 'Sec. §503(b) (2) (A) amended raising fine power of FCC to $20,000 maximum for willful or repeated violations,' also see Lenawee B'c'g, 42 RR 2d 390, (1978), Pub. L. 95-234.

330. Primer on Political Broadcasting and Cablecasting, 69 FCC 2d 2209, 43 RR 2d 1353, (1978)

331. Minority Programming, 'All minority programming done just on Sunday morning--licensee should present when reasonably could be expected to be effective,' Sonderling B'c'g, 68 FCC 2d 752, 43 RR 2d 573, (1978)

332. Don't Promise Too Much, 'Where an applicant proposed 36.3% local programming the opponent raised question of whether licensee could afford to so program. A slight demerit was given for failure to dispel inherent doubts. Case also dealt with community needs and ascertainment. The key factor was that the premise that local needs can be met only through programming produced locally was rejected by the FCC,' WPIX, 68 FCC 2d 381, 43 RR 2d 278, (1978)

333. Don't lie--to anyone, 'The submission of a misleading and untruthful response to an interrogatory served by competing applicant is as serious as lying to the FCC as ultimately it deceives the FCC,' WNST, 70 FCC 2d 1036, 44 RR 2d 492, (1978)

334. 'Clipping' Revocation, 'License revoked for clipping parts of network shows to insert local ads, misrepresentation to network and FCC. Not excusable that corporate licensee did not know--manager of station was officer and on board of directors to achieve local integration,' Las Vegas Valley, 589 F2d 594 44 RR 2d 683, (US Ct. App. DC 1978)

335. Network Control of Owned Station, 'Short-term license renewal of CBS owned station because Network misrepresented 'winner-take-all' tennis matches. Network misrepresentation hereafter attributed to licensee corporation operating network and could result in revocation or hearing for all their licensed stations,' CBS, 69 FCC 2d 1082, 43 RR 2d 1085, (1978)

336. Double-Billing Revocation, Berlin Communication, Inc., 68 FCC 2d 923, 42 RR 2d 1513, (1978); aff'd, 46 RR 2d 621; 626 F.2d 869 (US App DC 1979) (see 403)

337. FCC is not Required to Review Changes in Entertainment Formats,'The US Supreme Ct. has upheld an FCC policy against reviewing past or proposed changes in a radio station's entertainment programming during license renewal or transfer proceedings.

   Under §309(a) and 310(d) of the Communications Act of 1934, the FCC must consider the 'public interest, convenience and necessity' when assigning broadcast licenses. The Ct. concluded that neither the language nor the legislative history compel FCC supervision of format changes, and that such supervision would not advance the welfare of the listening public, would pose substantial administrative problems and would deter innovation in radio programming. The decision reverses a Ct. of App. ruling (506 F.2d 246).

   The Ct. also found the FCC's policy did not conflict with the First Amendment rights of listeners, since the 'fairness doctrine' of Red Lion Broadcasting, 395 US 367 (1969) did not imply that the First Amendment grants individual listeners the right to have the Commission review the abandonment of their favorite entertainment programs,' FCC v. WNCN Listeners Guild, 101 S.Ct. 1266 (1981)

338. Program Length Commercials Memorandum, 26 RR 2d 1023, (1973); 44 FCC 2d 985, 29 RR 2d 469, (1974); 69 FCC 2d 682, 43 RR 2d 683, (1978), (changed, see 442)

339. Equal Employment Opportunities, 'FCC must conduct hearing when a petition to deny renewal raises substantial and material questions of fact or when renewal will not serve public interest. Where statistical disparity in minority employment substantial and licensee's minority employment is outside zone of reasonableness (flexible concept comparing employment with availability of minorities in area and recruitment policies of station) FCC conducts own inquiries, but if it cannot or does not wish to do so itself it should permit discovery by petitioners,' Chinese for Affirmative Action v. FCC and Bilingual Coalition v. FCC, 595 F 2d 621, (D.C. Cir. 1978)

340. Upgrading an Application, 'To permit a licensee to receive credit for improvement after an investigation or the expiration of the license term would undermine the basis of FCC enforcement procedures,' Trustees of U. of Penn., 69 FCC 2d 1394, 44 RR 2d 747, (1978)

341. Control and Supervision, 'The standard of adequate control and supervision is a strict one, but it is not one of strict liability for every employee peccadillo. Supervision must be reasonably diligent,' Trustees of U. of Penn., 69 FCC 2d 1394, 44 RR 2d 747, 46 RR 2d 565, (1978)

342. New Financial Qualification Standard, 'The FCC announced new financial qualification standard for radio applicants and transferees. The ability to construct or operate a new facility for three months, without relying upon advertising or any other revenue,' 69 FCC 2d 407, 43 RR 2d 1101, (1978); and three months for TV,' 72 FCC 2d 784, 45 RR 2d 925, (1980), 87 FCC 2d 200, 49 RR 2d 1291, (1981)

343. Comparative Renewal Problems, 'In 1969, Cowles, Florida, sought renewal of its license. Another firm, Central Florida, applied for same frequency. After comparative hearing between applications the FCC gave Cowles its renewal. Ct. of Appeals set aside and remanded on the grounds that the FCC had inadequately investigated anti-renewal factors and the renewal process was unclear. By determining that the licensee's past performance record was 'superior' the FCC had apparently created an irrebuttable presumption of license renewal, contrary to the full-hearing requirement of the Communications Act. The FCC then reconsidered and again ruled for Cowles. The FCC and the reviewing Ct. agreed that an incumbent licensee is entitled to some degree of renewal expectancy in a

comparative hearing. This factor is to be weighted with all the other factors, and the better the past record, the greater the renewal expectancy weight. This will prevent paper promises (see 230) by challengers from being given equal weight with proven performance; licensees will be encouraged to insure quality service and; comparing of incumbents and challenges as though new applicants would result in haphazard restructuring of the broadcast industry. The Ct. warned the FCC that renewal expectancy may not be used if doing so would be harmful to the public interest, noting that so far no incumbent television station licensee has ever been denied renewal, except WHDH, in a comparative challenge despite the filing of many such challenges,' Central Florida Enterprises v. FCC, 598 F. 2d 37 (1979), cert. dismissed, 99 S. Ct. 2189, 44 RR 2d 345, (1978), 44 RR 2d 1576 (1979); affirmed, 683 F. 2d 503, 51 RR 2d 1405, (D.C. Cir. 1982)

344. FCC-EEOC Memorandum of Understanding, 'The FCC and EEOC plan to cooperate as FCC holds that discrimination by licensee can be said to be operating against public interest. Broadcasters have unique problems and responsibilities in the area of Equal Employment,' Memorandum of Understanding, 70 FCC 2d 2320, 43 RR 2d 1505, (1978)

345. Multiple and Newspaper Ownership, 'FCC proposed, 18 RR 2d 1735, (1970), prohibiting commercial licensee owning more than one full-time station in the same market. Not passed, except for divestiture of CATV systems owned in the same market with broadcast station. Sup. Ct. upheld FCC policy grandfathering most existing cross-ownerships of newspaper-broadcasting, disallowing future cross-ownerships and requiring break-up of 'egregious' cross-ownership situations,' National Citizens Comm. v. FCC, 555 F. 2d 938, (1977); 98 S. Ct. 2096, (1978); 436 US 775, 43 RR 2d 152, (1978); 51 RR 2d 449 (1982)

346. Adequate TV Service for NJ, 'Provision of adequate service to NJ does not require construction of separate or shared NJ auxiliary studios by out-of-state (NY) licensees. No VHF stations licensed in NJ. RKO allowed to retain WOR, if moved to NJ, 1983, (see 417) 62 FCC 2d 604, 39 RR 2d 137, (1976), affirmed 574 F. 2d 1119, (1978)

347. Political Reasonable Access, 'A station denies reasonable access by not selling prime time, but does not have to sell political time within any news show,' Anthony R. Martin-Trigona, 42 RR 2d 567, 42 RR 2d 1599, (1978)

43

348. Indecent Language--Pacifica, 'Broadcast of indecent language, not necessarily obscene, can be regulated because: (1) Children have access and are unsupervised; (2) received in home--people's privacy interest involved; (3) No warning possible; (4) license power of government. §326 of Comm. Act prohibiting censorship by FCC does not limit the FCC from imposing sanctions on licensees who engage in obscene, indecent or profane language. 'We simply hold that when the FCC finds that a pig has entered the parlor, the exercise of its regulatory power does not depend on proof that the pig is obscene.' The dissent noted that the Ct. for the first time allows the government to prevent minors from gaining access to materials that are not obscene, and are therefore protected, as to the children. A work is not obscene unless 'the work, taken as a whole, lacks serious literary, artistic, political, or scientific value (Miller v. Calif. 413 US 15, 1973). The community whose standards are applied are the local communities where work is displayed or uttered. The FCC has taken the position that 18 USCA §1464 is limited to spoken words and additional legislation is needed if the FCC is to reach indecent displays on television,' FCC v. Pacifica, (Sup. Ct.) 98 S. Ct. 3026, (1978); 43 RR 2d 493, 438 US 726, (1978)

349. Money to Build Station, 'FCC does not require a legally binding commitment when a loan is used to finance a station, but a reasonable assurance the loan will be available,' 44 RR 2d 487, (US Ct. App. DC 1978)

350. Problems Defining Legally Qualified Candidate, Docket 78-103, added Section §73: 1940 to regulations; 68 FCC 2d 1049, 43 RR 2d 905, 43 FR 32790; Subsections (g) and (h) of the Communications Act of 1934, Section §312(a) (7), corrected by 43 FR 55769, 69 FCC 2d 979, 44 RR 2d 481, (1978)

351. First and Third Class Licence Requirements Dropped, FCC no longer requires stations to employ operators with third or first class licenses. Restricted Radio Telephone permit (obtainable without test) is sufficient. §73:1860; 1870; 70 FCC 2d 2371, 44 RR 2d 1521 (1979), 87 FCC 2d 44, 49 RR 2d 1453 (1981)

352. Secondary Boycott Illegal, 'NLRB has ruled that it is illegal for AFTRA union of striking radio or TV announcers to pressure advertising agencies to withdraw prerecorded 'spot' announcements from a struck station. AFTRA violated the secondary boycott and 'hot cargo' provisions of Federal labor law, which prohibit the use

of coercive tactics against the suppliers or customers of a struck business. AFTRA had contended that its tactics were lawful because sending a members' voice on tape to a struck station was the same as forcing him personally to cross a picket line,' NLRB, 240 NLRB 40, (1/29/79)

353. ASCAP/BMI Blanket License for Network TV Music legal But Not for Local TV, 'After 10 years of litigation and three previous ct. decisions, including a US Supreme Ct. decision, a Federal Ct. of App. in NY has affirmed dismissal of CBS' claim that blanket license of copyrighted music by ASCAP and BMI violates federal antitrust law. The blanket licenses, usually for one year, permit licensee to use any music controlled by performing rights society, as often as desired for either flat sum or percentage of user's revenue. CBS contended was an agreement unreasonably restraining trade. The Supreme Ct. held that blanket license was not a per se violation of the Sherman Anti-Trust Act. On remand, the Ct. of App. concluded that CBS had not proved restraint of competition. Under terms of the 1950 consent degree, ASCAP and BMI may obtain only non-exclusive licensing rights from member-composers and may not restrict or interfere with member right to issue directly to any user a non-exclusive performing rights license. However, CBS had not attempted to purchase performing rights from copyright owner. Since this right was available, blanket license did not restrain. The feasibility of getting a direct license from each individual composer was established by evidence refuting CBS' allegations of barriers to direct licensing. If CBS makes effort and encounters difficulty, then it would be entitled to obtain blanket license,' Broadcast Music v. CBS, 441 US 1 (1979); 620 F.2d 930, (2d Cir., April 3, 1980); 'Fed. Dist.Ct. in NY ruled that blanket licenses used by ASCAP and BMI with local TV stations violate anti-trust law. Restraint exists because; blanket licenses prevent price competition between music composers; they require local stations to pay for licenses to compositions they do not want; and local stations cannot reduce their music costs by reducing the amount of music they broadcast. Blanket licensee fees are based upon total revenues. Local TV stations, defined as all TV stations except the 15 owned and operated by the TV Networks do not benefit from efficiencies. In the absence of blanket licenses television producers would acquire music performance rights from composers at the same time the producers acquire synchronization rights and then pass on cost. Source licensing availability was reasoning used to support blanket license in network

case. However, networks have bargaining power necessary to obtain source licensing from producers whereas local stations do not unless blanket licenses are first eliminated. Appeal filed,' Buffalo Broadcasting Co., v. ASCAP, 546 F. Supp. 274 (SDNY 1982); permanent injunction restraining ASCAP and BMI from granting blanket license rights licenses for syndicated TV programs to local TV stations to be effective February 1, 1984, (S.N.D.Y. 1983)

354. <u>No 1st Amendment privilege prevents inquiry into the state of mind of those who edit, produce or publish, or into editorial process, in libel suits brought by public figures</u>, 'Public figure, retired Army officer Anthony Herbert, sought damages for allegedly defamatory segment on <u>60 Minutes</u>. To meet burden of proof of actual malice attempted to inquire into the state of mind of those who participated in production. Producer Barry Lando (co-defendant with Mike Wallace, CBS, Atlantic Monthly Magazine) refused to answer certain questions in deposition. District Ct. ruled defendant's state of mind was of central importance to the issue of malice. Second Circuit Ct. of Appeals reversed, but Supreme Ct. upheld as "it is evident that courts across country have long been accepting evidence going to the editorial process of the media without encountering constitutional objection." Ct. distinguished between this case and Miami Herald v. Tornillo and CBS v. DNC (see 222 and 256); saying that they involved efforts to control publication in advance and not post-publication inquiries. Principal concern to balance 1st Amendment protection of press and need to protect individuals from defamatory publications,' Herbert v. Lando, 99 S. Ct. 1635, 441 US 153, (1979)

355. <u>Cable TV Access Rules Invalid</u>, 'Supreme Ct. held FCC did not have statutory authority to adopt cable TV access rules which had been adopted in 1976, requiring system with 3,500 or more subscribers to make as many as four-channels available to public on first-come, non-discriminatory basis. In <u>Southwestern</u> (218) court held that FCC does have authority to regulate cable where regulations are reasonably ancillary to effective performance of the Commission's various responsibilities for the regulation of television. In <u>Midwest Video</u> (302) court upheld rule requiring origination of programs by systems of 3,500 subscribers or over and to maintain facilities for local production and presentation of programs. Access rules, the court said, transferred control of the content of access channels from cable operators to the public. Section §3(h) of the Communications Act

prohibits the FCC from treating persons engaged in broadcasting as common carriers. A common carrier is one who provides communications facilities to all persons who wish to use them to communicate programs or messages of their own design and choosing. The court stated that the access rules required cable to become common carriers. It was also not a frivolous argument that access rules might have violated due process of Fifth Amendment by exposing cable operators to criminal prosecution for offensive broadcasts by access users over which operators had no control,' FCC v. Midwest Video, 99 S. Ct. 1435; 45 RR 2d 581, (1978)

356. Ct. of Appeals affirms FCC renewal without hearing when station charged with violating citizens agreement, 'KCOP had petition to deny license renewal filed by association of citizens which claimed deficiency in programming and breach of agreement. FCC denied petition without holding evidentiary hearing, pursuant to Section §309(d) of Communications Act. Criticisms of quality of programming imprecise and unspecific and no material questions of fact or prima facie evidence. FCC has discretion to pursue allegations of excessive violence in programming. Ct. found that FCC decision was garbled on question of agreement breach. Agreement had been incorporated into license renewal application. These become representations to FCC and are treated as promises of future performance. FCC declined to conduct a hearing on grounds it would not arbitrate vague terms and KCOP had satisfied its obligations,' National Association for Better Broadcasting v. FCC, 591 F. 2d 812, (D.C. Cir.), 44 RR 2d 793, (1978)

357. Repeated violation of Personal Attack Rule, '$1,000 judgment against WIYN for personal attack calling organization 'subversive' and 'far left.' Attack on honesty, character or integrity. Forfeiture statute (47 USC §503 (b)), provides that each day violation is a separate offense. The lower court held 19 separate offenses (one for each day after seventh day following broadcast party not notified). Appeals court overturned, stating FCC must prove willfulness or repeated violation and each day notice not given by station does not constitute independent violations,' US v. WIYN Radio, 464 F. Supp. 101, (N.D. Ga. 1978); 44 RR 2d 1501, and 47 RR 2d 335, 614 F. 2d 495 (5th Cir. 1980)

358. Business Privilege Tax Legal on Broadcasters, 'A Pennsylvania statute authorizes City of Pittsburgh to levy tax upon ". . . all persons, transactions, occupations, privileges, subjects and personal property"

except manufacturing. Radio and TV stations sought to enjoin collection from them on grounds they were "manufacturers." Penn. Supreme Ct. held that despite complexity of changing sound and visual information into electronic signals, broadcasting is not "manufacturing." Broadcasters do not change or produce new, different, or useful articles, but merely effect "a superficial change in the original materials." Primary purpose of broadcasting was transmission of commercial messages and the sale of advertising, not translation of events into electronic impulses,' Golden Triangle v. City of Pittsburgh, 397 A. 2d 1147, (Pa. Supreme Ct. 19

359. <u>Company not public figures, and criticism of close-out</u> <u>sale is not protected 1st Amendment speech</u>, 'A slander action was brought against ABC's KGO-TV and the Better Business Bureau for quote that close-out sale was deceptive by promises of bargains not bargains at all. Trial court ruled plaintiffs were public figures and had to prove malice, citing <u>NY Times</u> v. <u>Sullivan</u>, 376 US 254 (1964), <u>Curtis</u> v. <u>Butts</u>, 388 US 130 (1967), and <u>Gertz</u> v. <u>Welch</u>, 418 US 323 (1974), which applies 'actual malice' to public officials; public figures; and to private persons who have become public figures by voluntarily injecting themselves into public controversy. Supreme Court of Calif. overruled: that conductors of sale were not 'public figures' required to prove 'actual malice'. Merely doing business with parties to a public controversy does not elevate one to public figure status. Selling goods and advertising sale because of <u>Gertz</u> and <u>Time</u> v. <u>Firestone</u>, 424 US 448 (1976) is a test of public 'controversy' not public 'interest'. Ct. balanced limited 1st Amendment interest of defendants against plaintiffs' reputation interest; '. . . a person in the business world advertising his wares does not necessarily become part of an existing public controversy. It follows those assuming the role of business critic do not acquire the First Amendment privilege to denegrate such an entrepreneur.'' Vegod Corp. v. ABC, 88 Cal. App. 3d 95; 25 Cal. 3d 763, (1979), cert. denied

360. <u>Movie for TV Depicting Subject of Public Interest Not</u> <u>Invasion of Privacy</u>, 'NBC broadcast of "Tail Gunner Joe" about the late Senator Joseph McCarthy, did not defame or invade the privacy of Roy Cohn or David Shine, former aides and advisors. Subject matter of movie still a matter of public interest and <u>unless</u> the advertising was false or published with reckless disregard for the truth, or unless the selection of actors was done in a defamatory manner, New York's Right of Privacy statute was not violated. As to balanced presentation charge

the court held this to be essentially a matter of editorial judgment and not libelous. As public figures
they would have to prove actual malice,' Cohn v. NBC,
414 NYS 2d 906, (1979), affirmed 430 N.Y.S. 2d 265,
(1980)

361. Network News Item Not Libelous Without Clear Identity,
'NBC was sued by various ranchers for statement made on
NBC Nightly News during coverage of 1973 Wounded Knee
occupation, concerning land leasing practices on Indian
Reservation. Federal Ct. of Appeals held statements not
defamatory as no direct derogatory remarks about any of
ranchers or any group of ranchers who leased land from
Indians. Summary judgment affirmed,' Glover v. NBC,
594 F. 2d 715, (8th Cir. 1979)

362. Mistaken Identification of Person as Suspect in Robbery
Not Libel as Due Care Taken, 'Station reporter named
plaintiff as suspect in robbery. In fact, the individual was not involved. Not a public figure; had not
injected himself into a matter of public interest;
although some law enforcement officers had mentioned the
plaintiff as being the suspect under investigation.
Relying primarily on Oklahoma law, the court held that
the station should have exercised that degree of care
which ordinarily prudent persons engaged in the same
kind of business usually exercise under similar circumstances. Reporter had reasonable basis, displayed
no indifference or negligence and "the need to report
matters as quickly as possible is not merely good competition but serves a paramount concern of society to
have access to information of public concern as soon as
possible." Standard of due care required of the media
had been met,' Benson v. Griffin TV, 593 P. 2d 511,
(Okl. App. 1979)

363. NBC's Broadcast of "Holocaust" Did Not Require
Presentation of Contrasting Viewpoints under Fairness
Doctrine, 'Group filed Fairness Doctrine complaint
against WNBC contending that Germany did not have a
policy of exterminating Jews in World War II. Under the
Fairness Doctrine, if a station presents one side of a
controversial issue of public importance, it must afford
reasonable opportunity for the presentation of contrasting viewpoints. FCC ruled that alleged "issue" was 30
years old and not now a controversial issue of public
importance. "In taking this action, we realize that
there may be some people who question whether or not the
Holocaust occurred. However, the complainant has provided no evidence, and indeed we are aware of none. .
. . impact does not cast doubt on the fact that the

Holocaust is a part of history." 'In re Complaint of Friedrich P. Berg, Ridgeway Group, against Station WNBC-TV, 45 RR 2d 649, (1979).

364. **Communications Act Provision Requiring Public Broadcasters to Record all Public Issue Programs Unconstitutional,** 'Court of Appeals held that Section §399(b) violates First and Fifth Amendments of Constitution. It required all noncommercial educational radio and television stations to record all broadcasts in which any issue of public importance was discussed. Purposes of provision unsatisfactory; no legitimate government interest; and difference in treatment between public and commercial broadcasters involved fundamental First Amendment rights,' Community-Service Broadcasting of Mid-America v. FCC, 593 F. 2d 1102, (D.C. Circ.), 43 RR 2d 1675, (1978)

365. **Renewal of TV License Despite Cross-ownership,** 'A citizens group filed a petition with the FCC seeking denial of renewal of WSYR-TV, Syracuse, NY on grounds station part of a group of holdings owned by Newhouse Broadcasting. Newhouse owned AM, FM, cable, two major newspapers, ALL in Syracuse. (see 345) Without a hearing FCC renewed and D.C. Appeals Court affirmed. Court ruled that group had failed to show any specific abuses attributable to common ownership, or that common ownership created economic monopolization violating the Sherman Anti-Trust Act. According to the FCC's cross-ownership rules, one of these elements must be present before FCC will consider cross-ownership in a license proceeding. At the time of renewal FCC had cross-ownership rule requiring Newhouse to divest itself of cable, but this rule was modified so as to be inapplicable to certain pre-existing systems. In a separate proceeding the Syracuse group challenged a subsequent license renewal of WSYR-TV,' Syracuse Coalition for the Free Flow of Information in the Broadcast Media v. FCC, 593 F. 2d 1170, (D.C. Cir.); 44 RR 2d 581, (1978), see 73 FCC 2d 186, 46 RR 2d 35, (1979)

366. **Supreme Court Declares Unconstitutional NY Law Requiring Rental Property Owners to Permit Cable TV Installation,** 'A number of companies compete to bring pay TV into apartment complexes; cable, Multipoint Distribution, etc. A landlord brought suit against Teleprompter and City of NY challenging constitutionality of statute which allowed cable to install facilities to service tenants and limited compensation (usually $1 unless damage could be shown). Cable used to give 5% of gross revenue from building. Sup. Ct. agreed that any

permanent physical occupation authorized by the government is a taking without regard to the public interests it may serve, even if only minimal economic impact on the owner. Remanded. Landlord still required to comply with building codes, provide mailboxes, smoke detectors, etc.,' Loretto v. Teleprompter Manhattan, 415 NYS 2d 180 (1970); 102 S. Ct. 3164, (1982); 'NY Ct. then held statute proper exercise of state's police power, provided compensation paid, subject to Ct. review'

367. Broadcaster Not Infringing Common Law Copyright in Program Idea Submitted, 'In 1959, John Szczesny, submitted to WGN an idea for a TV show consisting of filmed horse races and using numbered cards to determine "home winners." WGN acknowledged receipt of submission but stated no new program material was being solicited by the station. In 1967 the plaintiff viewed WGN's program "Let's Go To The Races," which showed films of horse races. Viewers could obtain coded winning tickets at sponsors for cash prizes. Plaintiff contended in his suit that WGN had infringed his common law copyright in his idea and had breached an implied contract for use of that copyright. (This took place before the introduction of new Copyright Act which would protect any idea put into concrete form--such as his submitted concept-- see 295) A jury found the program had been independently developed by WGN. Illinois Ct. affirmed. WGN's evidence: independent producer began to work on idea in 1955; no one from WGN spoke to producer about plaintiff's idea; denied knowledge of plaintiff's idea. Court appeal was denied primarily on lack of timely objection but noted that requiring element of novelty (originality and concreteness) as required by lower court was traditional; however, this requirement had been rejected in California (Blaustein v. Burtoń, 9 Cal. App. 3d 161 (1970)),' Szczesny v. WGN, 201 USPQ 703 (Ill. App. 1977, opinion published 1979)

368. Advertising Discounts, Price Discrimination, 'After founding of the American Association of Ad Agencies in 1917, the AAAA was successful in obtaining a standardization of a 15% discount for agencies which placed advertising for their clients. In 1956 a civil antitrust action by the Justice Department resulted in consent decrees enjoining the AAAA and other trade associations from preventing media from granting commissions to advertisers dealing directly or to house-owned advertising agencies. Among the prohibited practices were the fixing of the amount of compensation allowed or received from clients, and the practice of giving rebates of the discounts back to the clients. The media may make

independent judgments of who gets discounts. Recently, the Federal Trade Commission reversed earlier action which had required the same discounts be given to small advertisers as were given to large advertisers or agencies under the Robinson-Patman Antitrust law. Smaller advertisers are not significantly harmed by a cumulative volume discount rate structure, according to the FTC and any such order would raise prices to all advertisers; motivate media to refuse to sell to small advertisers; and would injury competition,' Ambook Enterprises v. Time, 612 F. 2d 604 (2d Cir. 1979); Times-Mirror Co. v. FTC, CCH Trade Regulation Reports, Para. 21, 937, (July 1982)

369. NBC Liable for Common Law Copyright Infringement, 'While in Africa, Dr. Burke filmed an unusual and dramatic fight between a zebra and a lioness. Burke sent film at request to naturalist Grzimek who used footage for lectures and broadcast on German public TV. Grzimek later gave film to British company which included it in production of nature program. NBC purchased nature film from British and broadcast it in 1977. Burke sued NBC. Since Jan. 1, 1978, the effective date of current Copyright Act, "common law" copyright no longer exists, and all protection is by federal statute. Prior to new Copyright Act, the creator of an artistic or literary work had the common law right to copy and profit from that work; could distribute or show it to a limited class of persons for a limited purpose without losing right. This common law copyright continued until general publication and then specific requirements had to be met to protect under 1909 Copyright Law. Burke had never applied for federal statutory copyright and NBC argued that Burke had lost his common law right because of general publication when used over German public TV. Ct. of Appeals has held that was not general publication as use only for lectures and on noncommercial TV--specific and limited. (see 489) TV broadcasting, under 1909 law does not constitute a "publication" at all. Judgment for Burke, remanded for damages assessment,' Burke v. NBC, Cert. denied, CCH Copyright Reports, Para. 25,075, (1st Cir. 1979)

370. Damages for Unauthorized Use of Names and Likenesses of "Starsky & Hutch" and "Charlie's Angels", 'Spelling-Goldberg Productions had registered the names of the shows and owned all rights to the service marks and "all rights of publicity of the stars of the shows as the characters they play." Eighteen manufacturers licensed to merchandise products; $1,800,000 for Charlie's Angels alone earned; and had granted an exclusive license for

T-shirt heat transfers. Defendants had, without a license, infringed on trademarks and rights of publicity and had competed unfairly under the Lanham Act. Damages and relief of $14,400 based on minimum of 120,000 unauthorized transfer's sold at a profit of 12¢ each. Court refused treble damages or award of attorney's fees,' Spelling-Goldberg Prod. v. Schneider, Civil No. 78-1907, (D.N.J. 1979)

371. <u>FCC Refuses to Protect Exclusivity of "Phil Donahue" show from satellite Distribution to Cable,</u> 'FCC rules had granted TV stations the exclusive right to broadcast syndicated programs in their viewing area. Syndicated programs were sold, licensed, distributed and offered to stations in more than one market for non-network broadcast, <u>not</u> including live presentations. WOTV had been granted exclusive rights by Multimedia, producer and owner of syndication rights to Donahue, to carry show on tape-delayed basis in Grand Rapids, Mich. Show was produced and broadcast live in Chicago on WGN-TV; recorded and distributed to stations like WOTV. Two cable companies in Grand Rapids began carrying WGN's broadcasts of the Donahue show via satellite-live, several days before tape of show got to WOTV. Cable operators refused exclusivity protection and WGN had not agreed that the satellite could carry their programming to cable systems, but FCC has ruled WGN's permission not necessary once signal broadcast. (see 497) In a concurring statement Commissioner Quello expressed concern over impact of order on "superstation" (term recently trademarked by Ted Turner-WTBS-TV Atlanta). Super-stations retransmit TV signals via satellite beyond their market. (see 433) Dissent: Commissioner Washburn noted WGN's signal might be sent to many markets and discourages diversity of programming. Multimedia transfered program from WGN to WBBM (which is not on satellite) when contract expired,' In re Manhattan Cable Television, Inc., 73 FCC 2d 25, 45 RR 2d 1695, (1979)

372. <u>Ct. of Appeals Upholds FCC Refusal to Renew License for Double-Billing,</u> 'FCC is not obligated to explain its decision not to renew license when stations had engaged in 5 1/2 years of double-billing with knowing participation of licensee's sole shareholder. The station would send two bills to local advertisers--one for true cost of ads and other for higher amount which local advertiser sent to national supplier for reimbursements under cooperative ad plan. Argument that conduct of CBS misleadingly advertising "winner-take-all" tennis matches was similar and posed a greater threat to public interest was not comparable. The CBS matter, according

to the court, involved a single occurance and double-billing was obvious misconduct, (see 335)' White Mountain Broadcasting v. FCC, 598 F. 2d 274, (D.C. Cir.), 45 RR 2d 681, (1979)

373. **Relationship of Lienholder to FCC Broadcast License,** 'The Utah Supreme Court has held that a Utah trial court did not impinge upon FCC jurisdiction when the court declared that the purchaser of a radio station had defaulted in its time payments, and therefore the purchaser's interest in the license and other assets was forfeited back to the seller, as provided in the purchase and sale agreement. The FCC would have to approve the license transfer thereafter, but as between purchaser and seller, the seller owned the license. If the FCC did not approve transfer, license could be terminated,' Themy v. Seagull Enterprises, 595 P. 2d 526, (Utah 1979)

374. **No Defamation as No Proof 'Actual Malice,'** 'A summary judgment was granted for WTAE-TV and consumer affairs editor and newscaster. A broadcast that steak sale ads mentioned neither grade of meat nor price per pound; that commercial grade meat was lowest grade available; and that store allowing sale on their premises terminated endorsement led to defamation suit. Steak company held to be public figure, and thus required to prove actual malice in order to recover damages. They became public figure when they voluntarily involve themselves in sale, by managing and advertising it. Split among the court whether to grant summary judgment upon a failure to prove actual malice. Under the first view, the issue of actual malice is a constitutional issue to be decided by the trial judge on the basis of actual knowledge or reckless disregard of the truth by the defendant. Under the second view, the plaintiff must raise a genuine issue as to the existence of malice. The court concluded failure to show actual malice under either test,' (also see 359) Steaks Unlimited v. Deaner, 468 F. Supp. 779, (W.D.Pa. 1979); upheld 623 F.2d 264, (3d Cir. 1980)

375. **Free Press vs. Fair Trial,** 'Supreme Ct. holds that press may be barred from a pretrial hearing of a motion to suppress evidence in Gannett; however the Constitution guarantees the public and press the right to attend criminal trials. This is not an absolute right as the judge may choose to close trial when 'overriding circumstances' are present and articulated,' Gannett v. De Pasquale, 443 US 368, (1979); Richmond Newspapers v. Virginia, 448 US 555, (1980); Chandler v. Florida, 101 S. Ct. 802, (1981)

376. Programming for Minority Audiences, 'A licensee has no obligation to divide its coverage of community problems according to the racial, ethnic or religious composition of the community. There is merit to the contention that licensee can rely on general programming to meet the specific needs of minority audiences,' Georgia Brd. of Education, 70 FCC 2d 948, 44 RR 2d 1599, (1979)

377. Pay TV Rules Amended, 'Regulation of subscription TV relaxed to allow development. Eliminated requirement that there must be four conventional stations before Pay-TV and 28 hour limitation,' Subscription Television Service, 46 RR 2d 460, (1979); 90 FCC 2d 341, 51 RR 2d 1173, (1982)

378. Pay TV Multi-Point Distribution Service is 'Broadcasting,' 'The transmission of pay TV programs which are of interest to the general public constitutes 'broadcasting' even though one cannot view without paying a fee for special equipment,' Orth-O-Vision, Inc., v. Home Box Office, et. al., 46 RR 2d 628, (SDNY, 1979); 'therefore FCC jurisdiction supercedes NY Cable TV Commission,' NY Cable TV Comm. v. FCC, 669 F.2d 58, (2d Cir. 1982)

379. Allocation of Time; Fairness Doctrine; Nuclear Energy, 'Four Calif. stations presenting editorial advertising sponsored by a utility company failed to afford reasonable opportunity for contrasting viewpoints. Although the amount of time was proportionate, the frequency and extent of presentations during peak audience listening periods showed disparity,' Public Media Center, 72 FCC 2d 776, 45 RR 2d 1751, (1979)

380. Fairness Doctrine Covers Political News Coverage When Rebroadcast Too Late, 'Debate between candidates for governor, rebroadcast two and one-half days after original broadcast was not exempt on-the-spot news coverage. 'One-day rule' governs on-the-spot treatment,' News Jersey Public B/casting Authority, 73 FCC 2d 808, 46 RR 2d 558, (1979)

381. Opinions Expressed in News Commentary Distinct From Editorial Opinion, 'Commentary by news anchorman, written by station news director is different from opinion of licensee; even if the opinion held by the news people is also held by the licensee. Commentary does not become an editorial subject to personal attack rule unless licensee authorizes commentator to speak for the station,' Let's Help Florida Committee, 74 FCC 2d 584, 46 RR 2d 919, (1979)

382. Fairness Doctrine Does Not Make Public Access Mandatory,
'A mandatory system of public access to broadcast facilities to comply with Fairness Doctrine would amount to
common-carrier status for broadcasters and is not
legal,'Handling of Public Issues under Fairness Doctrine
and Public Interest Standards, 46 RR 2d 999, (1979)

383. Qualified Candidates, 'State election laws and state
election officials' decisions prevail concerning who is
a legally qualified candidate, unless such determinations are overturned in court,' John J. Marino, 71
FCC 2d 311, 45 RR 2d 356, and 'People classified as candidates under the Federal Election Campaign Act are not
necessarily candidates under §73:1940,' National Citizens Committee for Broadcasting, 75 FCC 2d 650, 46 RR 2d
1, (1979), (see 510)

384. Lowest Unit Rate, 'Stations must provide candidates
lowest unit rate for a given class of time, but there is
no requirement to offer the cheapest class of time,'
Warren J. Moity, Sr., 46 RR 2d 399, and 'the 45-days
before the primary election rule deals only with the
lowest unit rate that may be charged, not with the dates
during which a candidate may or may not be granted
access,' Carter-Mondale, 74 FCC 2d 631, 46 RR 2d 829,
(1979)

385. Federal Candidates Access, 'Since networks are both
licensees and their affiliates' programming agents, they
are covered by political broadcasting sections of Communications Act; With respect to requests for time, a candidate must be legally qualified at time of the proposed
broadcast, but does not need to be qualified when request is made; Federal candidates desires for specific
time periods and length of time should be honored whenever possible and an arbitrary ban on the use of a particular class or length of time is not reasonable; the
Presidential nominating process is not isolated state
primary/ caucus campaigns, but a nationwide effort and
networks cannot base their acceptance or rejection of
requests upon the date of the national nominating con-
vention. Stations must honor candidates' assessment of
media needs and request for time cannot be met with just
news coverage or other exposures exempt from Sec. §315.
Each candidates' request is to be considered individually, not against backdrop of campaign as whole, or
multiplicity of candidates,' Carter-Mondale, 74 FCC 2d
631, 46 RR 2d 829; affirmed, 46 RR 2d 1711, (Ct. App.
1980); affirmed in CBS v. FCC, 101 S. Ct. 2813, 49 RR 2d
1191, (1981)

386. Political Editorial, 'Political editorial regulations in a recall election apply, even when incumbent's name is not on ballot. If an editorial endorses one over others spokesman for all those not endorsed must be given chance to reply and the original editorial does not need to be rebroadcast to balance the numerous replies against the one time endorsement,' Friends of Howard Miller, 72 FCC 2d 508, 45 RR 2d 1142, (1979)

387. What is 'News-Show' or 'Entertainment', 'Good Morning, America and Today Show are news programs for their entirety and therefore exempt from Sec. §315. The Tonight and Tomorrow Shows are basically entertainment, and are therefore not exempt from Sec. 315,' ABC, Inc., 46 RR 2d 944, (1979), (see 429)

388. Seven-Day Rule Does Not Apply to Reasonable Access Request, 'An opponent who requests time more than seven-days after another candidate for the same position has appeared must not be turned down if he request's reasonable access' and not 'equal opportunities,' Kennedy for President Committee, 80 FCC 2d 93, 46 RR 2d 1539, (1980)

389. Rule Change Narrows Fairness Doctrine by Separating From Political, 'The Personal Attack Rules-(§315(I) and §73:1920)-are amended to exempt all Sec. 315 uses of broadcast and cable facilities by candidates for public office, and to eliminate all applicability of the Fairness Doctrine to Sec. 315 uses,' Personal Attack Rules and Applicability of the Fairness Doctrine, 78 FCC 2d 457, 45 RR 2d 1635, (1979)

390. Cost of Local Programming not Important, 'The percentage of revenue devoted to local programming is not a valid criteria for judging a station's public service record,' KCOP-TV, Inc., 45 RR 2d 1063, (1979)

391. AM/FM Combinations, 'Applications creating new or transferring control of existing AM/FM combinations, filed after June 6, 1979 are subject to future FCC action which could prohibit such combination ownership. Pending applications are grandfathered,' Cross-Ownership of AM/FM Combinations, (Public Notices), 45 RR 2d 1327, (1979)

392. Public Affairs, News or Entertainment Logging, 'Public Affairs series may contain some shows devoted to entertainment--as long as those shows devoted to entertainment are logged as entertainment. Entertainment news material can be logged as news only if presented as an

integral part of a regular news program,' Service Broadcasting, 46 RR 2d 413, (1979)

393. Scheduling of Public Affairs Programming, 'Placing all public affairs programming in the overnight 'ghetto' raises the FCC's eyebrows,' Amaturo Group, Inc., 46 RR 2d 865, (1979)

394. Licensees Must be Treated Equally on Same Issue if Similar Circumstances, 'Although FCC can deal on case-by-case basis, because of lack of information of others violations, cannot single out one transgressor for denial or hearing among a number of licensees under scrutiny on the same issue (network affiliation contracts). Must explain the basis for differing treatment that are of legal significance to warrant disparity when licensees identified in same investigation,' George T. Hernreich, KAIT-TV, 72 FCC 2d 511, 45 RR 2d 963, and United TV, 46 RR 2d 655, (1979)

395. Blacks More Important Than Women, 'Ownership and Management by blacks deserves more credit in a competitive hearing than such involvement by women,' Radio Gaithersburg, Md., 72 FCC 2d 821, 45 RR 2d 1709, (1979)

396. Revocation Despite Public Service, 'In 1976, WHBI had its license revoked for numerous violations including, promoting a lottery, abdication of control to time brokers, improper logging. U.S. Appeals Court told FCC to review case, giving greater consideration to multi-language public service programming. FCC reconsidered and revoked license anyway as (1) record was vague, often not logged and not sufficient to mitigate, and (2) three other stations in market broadcast 23 languages so revocation not detrimental to the public interest,' Cosmopolitan Broadcasting, 581 F.2d 917 (DC Cir. 1978); 75 FCC 2d 423, 46 RR 2d 1285, (1979)

397. Plugola Practices, 'FCC decides not to propose a formal rule against plugola. It assumes that reasonable diligence will be used and FCC will deal with on a case-by-case basis,' Broadcast Announcement of Financial Interests of Broadcast Stations and Networks and their Principals and Employees in Services and Commodities Receiving Broadcast Promotions, 76 FCC 2d 221, 46 RR 2d 1421, (1980)

398. Newspaper-Broadcast Crossownership, 'Multiple ownership rules are not contingent upon how many signals received in market, but how local issues can be covered with diversity,' Petitions for Waiver of §73:35, §73:240 and §73:636, 74 FCC 2d 497, 46 RR 2d 684, (1979)

399. Court rules that violation of FCC's Personal Attack Rule
gives private cause of action for damages, 'In 1977,
KDKA broadcast talk show during which guest stated
motion picture director Pare Lorentz had been a member
of Communist Party. Lorentz filed suit for libel, invasion of privacy, negligence and reckless infliction of
emotional distress. Cause of action was based on KDKA's
alleged failure to comply with Personal Attack Rule
(§73:123). Defendants moved for summary judgment argu-
ing that FCC Act did not authorize private civil action;
Lorentz argued there was implied cause of action. Only
district saying, 'We find it appropriate to provide
interested citizens with a meaningful personal and practical approach to the matter of violations in giving
the right to bring suit to redress infractions of the
rule.' Case appealed and broadcaster's lost; Penn.
adopting negligence standards, 1472 F. Supp. 954 (1979),
Lorentz v. Westinghouse., 472 F. Supp. 946 (W. D. Pa.
1979); 51 RR 2d 953 (1982), (see 474, 477)

400. Protection of Idea Submitted to Producer; Elements
Needed, 'In 1964, Edgar Faris conceived an idea for a
sports quiz show for which he prepared and registered a
format. Six years later, he met with KTLA personality
to discuss possibility. Nothing came from meeting, but
some time later show, similar to and different from proposed idea was started. Faris filed suit against personality Enberg, Golden West and others, alleging breach
of express contract, breach of implied-in-fact contract,
plagiarism, breach of confidence, and breach of an
implied-in-law contract. All complaints were dismissed.
The Court of Appeals held that in order to prove
existence of an implied-in-fact contract, one must show:
that he or she prepared the work; that he or she
disclosed the work to the offeree for sale; under all
circumstances attending disclosure it can be concluded
that the offeree voluntarily accepted disclosure knowing
the conditions under which it was tendered (i.e., the
offeree must have the opportunity to reject the
attempted disclosure if the conditions were unaccept-
able); and the reasonable value of the work. In this
case no evidence submitted for sale. Court held than an
implied contract is not created just because a phone
call is returned or a request is made to read a work
unconditionally submitted. A confidential relationship
is not created just by submission. There must be evidence of communication of confidentiality,' Faris v.
Enberg, 97 Cal. App. 3d 309, (1979)

401. Libel, If Defamatory, Rather Than Slander, 'The Supreme
Ct. of Alabama has held that certain radio broadcasts

taped by a church pastor at a station constituted libel, if defamatory, rather than slander. The court relied upon decisions from other jurisdictions and upon the Restatement of the Law of Torts, Second, defining libel as: '(1) Libel consists of the publication of defamatory matter by written or printed words, or its embodiment in physical form or by any other form of communication that has the potentially harmful qualities characteristic of written or printed words.' Defamatory material broadcast by radio or otherwise is libel whether or not it is read from a manuscript,' First Independent Baptist Church of Arab v. Southerland, 373 So. 2d 647, (Ala. 1979); Gray v. WALA, 384 So. 2d 1062, (Ala. 1980)

402. Breach of Non-Competition Contract by DJ, 'Provision in employment contract was that DJ would not work in same county for station for one year after leaving. Within six months of being terminated he went to work for another station. Trial court was overturned by Alabama Supreme Court. Even though stations broadcast different music their audiences overlapped to a significant degree. Covenant not to compete was enforceable as long as three elements satisfied: (1) employer must have substantial protectible right unique in his business; (2) the restriction is relevant and reasonable to the protection of that right; and (3) there is no imposition of undue hardship on employee. In this instance, the fact that station is personalized and identified to its listeners by announcers is substantial business right. The restraint on employment for one year within county is relevant and reasonable as applied to same type of job and there was no hardship. Injunctive relief was inappropriate, but liquidating damages upheld,' Cullman Broadcasting v. Bosley, 373 So. 2d 830, (Ala. 1979); also Murray v. Lowndes, 284 S.E. 2d 10 (1982); Beckman v. Cox, 296 S.E.2d 566, (Ga. 1982)

403. Revocation of Licenses; Standard of Proof by FCC Necessary, 'Clear and Convincing standard of proof needed at agency level according to Collins v. SEC (562 F. 2d 823), applies to FCC, where loss of livelihood is involved,' Sea Island Broadcasting v. FCC, 46 RR 2d 1339, 627 F. 2d 240, (D.C. Cir. 1980)

404. Libel of Advertising Agency, 'Media Buying Service sent letters to TV stations allegedly suggesting agency breached contracts and failed to pay bills. Letters were libelous per se because they tended to injure reputation by disparaging integrity in agency's business dealings,' Matthews, Cremins, McLean, Inc., v. Nichter, 256 S.E. 2d 261, (N.C. App. 1979)

405. Copyright Damages Awarded to Iowa State University for Unauthorized Use of Student Film by ABC, 'In 1972, Iowa State offered ABC TV rights to film made by students about Olympic wrestler Dan Gable. ABC refused to buy. During Munich Olympics, two segments of 12 seconds and two and one-half minutes were used. Iowa State notified ABC of its copyright claim. ABC then used eight-seconds on "Superstars" show. Ct. awarded total damages of $15,250, plus attorney fees of $17,500 because ABC had initially denied infringements and had defended lawsuit vigorously,' Iowa State Univ. v. ABC, 475 F. Supp. 78 (S.D.N.Y. 1979); 621 F.2d 57, (2nd Cir. 1980)

406. FCC Eliminates Top-50 Policy of TV Station Ownership, 'Limitation on group ownership of stations in the top-50 markets, adopted in 1968 is eliminated. FCC concluded that multiple ownership rules were sufficient to achieve programming diversity and prevent economic concentration. Top-50 policy did not significantly affect diversity as applied only to ownership of stations in different cities, whereas rule restricting cross-ownership in the same market deals directly with diversity. Regional ownership rule restricts a party to two stations within a 100 mile radius. FCC will require, even though no rule, hearing for any application raising substantial public interest issues arising in connection with top-fifty acquisition,' Multiple Ownership of Television Stations, 46 RR 2d 1141, (1979); affirmed, NAACP v. FCC, 682 F.2d 993, 51 RR 2d 1215, (1982)

407. Right of Publicity, 'For a period of time there was considerable conflict between various jurisdictions as to the right of publicity and whether it could descend after death. These cases have generally been resolved to recognize that if a prominent person promoted and commercially exploited his name and likeness during his lifetime; that right can be inherited. Involved are considerations of fundamental fairness for an entertainer or athlete has devoted his or her life to attain celebrity status, and it would be unfair to permit a commercial enterprise to reap windfall benefits from those labors at the expense of the celebrity's heirs or beneficiaries. The ability to leave a valuable property interest to one's heirs also serves the public interest by encouraging enterprise and creativity,' Lugosi v. Universal Picures, 25 Cal. 3d 813 (1979); Gugliemi v. Spelling-Goldberg, 25 Cal. 3d 860 (1979)--no right if not exploited during lifetime. Memphis Development Foundation v. Factors, Inc., 616 F. 2d 956 (Ct. of App. 6th Cir. 1980)--right not descendible in TN; 441 F.

Supp. 1323 (W.D. TN 1977)--right survives death; Factors, Etc., Inc., v. Pro Arts, Inc., 652 F. 2d 278 (2d Cir. 1981)--not descendible. Martin Luther King, Jr., v. American Heritage, 508 F. Supp. 854 (N.D. Ga. 1981)--did not exploit during lifetime so not protected. Reversed; 296 S.E. 2d 697 (Ga. 1982); affirmed in 694 F. 2d 674 (11th Cir. 1983). Groucho Marx Productions, Inc., v. Day and Night Co., 689 F. 2d 317 (2d Cir., 1982)-right descendible. Commerce Union Bank v. Coors, 7 Med L. Rptr. 2204 (Tenn.Chanc. Ct. 1981)--right descendible. Factors, Etc., Inc. v. Pro Arts, Inc., 541 F. Supp. 231 (S.D.N.Y. 1982)--Ct. allows rehearing based on Commerce Bank v. Coors decision; belief that right is descendible in Tennessee as is in New York and California; (see 428)

408. Employment Contract is Assignable Unless Employee Fired, 'In one instance an employee's contract assigned to a new owner bound the employee for the remainder of the contract and he cannot quit and go to work for a competing station. But, where an employee is fired, the station cannot hold employee to non-competition clause as it would deprive employee of livelihood,' Evening News v. Peterson, 477 F. Supp. 77, (D.D.C.); Orion Broadcasting v. Forsythe, 477 F. Supp. 198, (W. D. Kty. 1979)

409. Federal Trade Commission Adopts Guidelines for Endorsements and Testimonials in Advertising, 'Sec. 255.1 requires endorsements that always reflect the honest opinions, findings, beliefs, or experiences of the endorser . . . and may not contain any representations which would be deceptive, or could not be substantiated if made directly by the advertiser. Ads which present experiences of consumers must be comparable to the performance consumers will generally achieve. If endorsers appear to be actual consumers, then either actual consumers must be used or the ads must disclose that the people shown are not actual consumers. §255.2 provides that any connection between endorser and seller which might materially affect weight or credibility must be disclosed, but payment to an endorser who is an expert or personality need not be disclosed as it would be expected. Violations may lead the FTC to issue a complaint,' Federal Trade Commission, Endorsements and Testimonials in Advertising, 16 CFR Part 255, (January, 1980)

410. TV Commercial Can't Copy From TV series, 'DC Comics owns copyright to Superman and has licensed its use for promotion, and, on occasion, licensed such use by a

consumer electronics retailer known as Crazy Eddie. He produced a TV commercial for his business which was nearly in every aspect copied in detail from the 'trailers' for the Superman TV series and had not obtained a license for the spot. The court found the only variation in the commercial from the trailer was Crazy Eddie's name and business purpose were substituted for Superman's name and purpose. The average lay person would instantly recognize the source. Crazy Eddie argued his commercial was a parody. The court recognized a parody is entitled to greater freedom than other uses, but the commercial was held not to be a parody and would irreparably impair Superman's licensing value. Injunction was granted,' DC Comics v. Crazy Eddie, CCH Copyright Law Reports, Para. 25,097, 205 USPQ 1177, (S.D.N.Y. 1979)

411. Exclusive Right to Trademark 'Bionic' Limited, 'In 1974, Universal produced the TV series 'The Six-Million Dollar Man,' followed by 'The Bionic Woman.' Universal applied for several trademarks. The American Footware Co. adopted the name 'Bionic Boot' and when they did a trademark search they noted the term 'bionic' had not been registered in relation to footwear and applied the trademark. The court found that Universal had not registered or applied for that specific trademark and American had priority of use. Universal could not show the term had acquired a secondary meaning so that the public associated the term with Universal or its series. Universal claimed the public would be confused as to the source but the court disagreed. The exclusive right to a trademark is derived from its actual use in the marketplace and Universal used in the area of TV entertainment and toys, so both companies could use term, if one referred to TV show and the other just used 'Bionic Boot',' American Footwear v. General Footwear, 609 F. 2d 655, (2d Cir. 1979)

412. Misrepresentation Leads to License Denial, 'Applicant, not its counsel, is responsible for complying and application is denied for misrepresentation and withholding of substantial information,' WADECO, Inc. v. FCC, 628 F.2d 122, 47 RR 2d 177, (U.S. App. DC, 1980)

413. FCC Amended Cable TV Rules Removing Blackout of Network Duplication, 'Stations, to get blackout of network duplication in their market, must prove need for protection,' Spartan, et. al. v. FCC, 47 RR 2d 1521; 619 F.2d 314, (4th Cir. 1980) (CA 4th, 1980)

414. Hoax Kidnapping of DJ Denial of Renewal, 'Failure of control by absentee licensee when promotional hoax aired about 'missing' DJ. Serious, prolonged event involved police and led to inaccurate news broadcasts,' Walton (KIKX), 47 RR 2d 1233, (1980), also WMJX, 85 FCC 2d 251, 48 RR 2d 1339, (1981)

415. Suburban Station EEO Efforts, 'Surburban stations EEO efforts will be evaluated on work force data from city and county of license and larger metropolitan area nearby,' Suburban Wash. D.C. Renewal, 77 FCC 2d 911, 47 RR 2d 417, (1980)

416. Contract for Time May or May Not Be Valid If Not Used Timely, Tanner provides promo material (jingles) for cash and use of station's commercial time which it brokers to others. Contract with KGYN, Granite Radio and KOWO among others stated use of time valid until used. In Oklahoma, Ct. ruled that spots unused were forfeited after reasonable time had passed. KGYN had made all necessary cash payments and no longer used material supplied by Tanner. In Minnesota KOWO case contract did not specify the time for performance and held reasonable time was seven-year term of the contract. In Utah, Ct. ruled that there was no time limitation and Tanner was entitled to fair market value of spots and time credits. There station still owed on contract and was still using material (see 425), 'Tanner v. Plains, 486 F. Supp. 1313, 47 RR 2d 519, (WD Okla. 1980); Tanner v. KOWO, 549 F. Supp. 411 52 RR 2d 317, (D Minn 1982); Tanner v. Granite, 49 RR 2d 219, (Utah Dist. Ct. 1980)

417. RKO-General License Revocations, (see 277) ' In 1980 FCC revoked WNAC, KHJ and WOR on basis that licensee, in cooperation with parent corporation participated in illegal trade scheme; filed inaccurate financial reports and misrepresented facts. Ct. of Appeals noted that illegal trade practice could not be retroactively applied to conduct of 15 years previous; that inaccurate financial data was insignificant and not allowing a hearing on intent was unlawful. The court noted that holding corporate licensees to a higher standard than individual owners be clarified. Court upheld FCC's WNAC revocation on basis of lack of candor. Although KHJ and WOR renewals were conditioned on Boston decision cases did not illustrate direct misconduct and, on remand, each station is entitled to distinguish its policies. FCC then ordered noncomparative hearings on RKO's remaining 13 licenses. Court then ruled that companies seeking to obtain RKO's 13 licenses are entitled to file competing applications at once. Congress passed Sec.

331, modifying the Communications Act of 1934, which states that it is FCC policy that if a licensee of a commercial VHF station agrees to reallocation of its channel to a State where there is no VHF commercial TV channel (NJ or Delaware), the FCC, nonwithstanding any other provision of law, shall issue a license for a five-year term.   RKO then moved WOR to NJ and was issued a five-year license,' 670 F. 2d 215, 50 RR 2d 821, (1981); Cong. Rec., Vol. 128, No. 113, Part II, page H6258 (1982); 685 F. 2d 708, 52 RR 2d 1, (1982)

418. Sex Discrimination in Employment by CBS, 'In 1976, former employee of KNXT-CBS, L.A. instituted class action alleging employment discrimination on the basis of sex in violation of Title VII of Civil Rights Act of 1964.   Consent decree approved by Federal District Ct. in L.A. has CBS agreeing to increase women in upper managerial and production positions when vacant through 1984; scholarship at USC for women; Career Development Training Seminar; station EEO officer; technical training for women employees, etc.   Employee who sued received $30M, but agreed to resign.   Consent decree is not an admission of violation; merits of case not tried and CBS does not have to promote or hire unqualified nor promote or hire best qualified applicant,' Cotton v. CBS, Inc., Case No.   76-2215 HP (C.D. Cal. July 9, 1980); see also Walker v. KFGO, 518 F. Supp. 1309, (D.N. Dak. 1981)

419. Unfair Labor Practice to Fire Employees Attempting Union, 'NLRB found TV station in Duluth, Minn., committed unfair labor practice in violation of 8(a) (3) and (1) of National Labor Relations Act when discharged certain employees, eliminated six o'clock news. Stations claimed low ratings but board found actions were effort to avoid pending unionization election of newsroom staff and were reprisals for union victory and unlawful,' RJR Communications, Inc., and Local 346, Teamsters, 1980 CCH Labor Law Reports, Para. 16,914, (1980)

420. Ali Gets Legal Expenses for Defense of Libel Lawsuit from ABC, 'In 1975, Muhammad Ali was critical of referee Perez in Ali-Wepner fight as Cosell pursued subject provocatively.   Perez sued Ali for libel.   Ali won but it cost $193,352 in legal expenses.   Ali, a member of AFTRA, which has a code which ABC has signed, provides that the producer of any program would indemnify performer against acts done or words spoken by Performer at Producer's request.   Ali had been paid $5M for interview and claimed his statements had been made at Cosell's

request. ABC refused to pay and Ali instituted arbitration proceedings under AFTRA collective bargaining agreement. Arbitration panel found ABC liable to Ali. The US Supreme Court has held that courts should not review the merits of arbitration decisions because they should be binding and final if agreed to in collective bargaining agreements. But, ABC appealed to Federal District Ct. Review of record found decision rational even though ABC claimed AFTRA Code did not require indemnification for ad-libs. Arbitrators had found remarks induced by Cosell; it had been taped, reviewed, edited by ABC,' ABC v. Ali, 489 F. Supp. 123, (S.D.N.Y. 1980)

421. <u>FCC Rules United Way PSA's Do Not Violate Fairness Doctrine</u>, 'ABC, NBC, CBS broadcast United Way PSA's during National Football League games. National Committee for Responsive Philanthropy filed complaint with FCC that announcements endorse only one side of controversial issue of public importance in that United Way allegedly monopolizes workplace donations, allocates funds inequitably and avoids controversial charities. FCC concluded networks not unreasonable in determining challenged announcements did not discuss directly or meaningfully possibly controversial procedures of United Way and denied request for balance,' (see 241), In re Complaint of NCRP v. ABC, NBC, CBS, 78 FCC 2d 1072, 47 RR 2d 1367, (1980); upheld Ct. of App., (1981)

422. <u>Copyright Infringement Suit of Comedy Skit Dismissed for Lack of Substantial Similarity</u>, 'The distinction between an idea and its expression was the issue when writer alleged that "egg" skit on Tony Orlando show infringed copyright to his lecture on eggs. Ct. noted that copyright protection is available only for expression of idea, and not for idea itself. Attribution to egg of human qualities is idea and sequence of events follow from common theme. Suit dismissed,' Gibson v. CBS, CCH Copyright Law Reports, Para. 25, 164, (S.D.N.Y. 1980)

423. <u>Employer Liability and Plugola</u>, 'Mutual Broadcasting System cannot be held liable for an agreement allegedly breached by employee. Generally, employer is responsible for acts of employees. A talk show host received money in exchange for his promise to promote a product. While employee might be liable for breach, the court found that employee's acts were not in futherance of his employer's business and were outside scope of employment so Mutual not responsible,' Friedman v. MBS, 380 So. 2d 1313, (Fla. App. 1980)

424. Sale and Use of Unauthorized Pay-TV Signal Decoders
Illegal, 'Pay TV industry is making legal warfare out of
unauthorized sale and use of signal decoders. Communications Act, §605, prohibits unauthorized interception
of broadcasts unless for the use of the general public.
Courts have ruled that Pay-TV is broadcast only for use
of paying subscribers; that to determine otherwise would
threaten economic vitality; and violates FCC consumer
protection policy in investment in equipment by public,'
Chartwell v. Westbrook, 637 F. 2d 459, (6th Cir., Dec.
1980); National Subscription TV v. S. & H TV, 644 F.2d
820, (9th Cir., May 1981); FCC Public Notice, Manufacturers and Sellers of Non-Approved Subscription TV
Decoders are Cautioned, (August 15, 1980); AT&C v.
Western Techtronics, 51 RR d 85, (1982)

425. Scope of Employment on Radio Programming Services
Contract, 'A former radio station employee who purchased
prerecorded music and program materials acted within
scope of employment and authority and station is obligated to pay on contract. The supplier had no notice
of, and no reason to inquire about, any limitation on
employee's authority. Station continued to use and pay
for contracted materials, thereby approving contract,'
White River Valley Broadcasters v. Wm B. Tanner Co., 487
F. Supp. 725, (E.D. Ark. 1979)

426. FCC Renewal Denial Based on Failure to Follow Programming Promises, 'KDIG-FM, now KIFM proposed to broadcast
5.38% news, 1.53% public affairs and 1.53% other exclusive of sports and entertainment. In 1971 station
sought to amend its proposal citing financial losses but
promised at least 1.1% public affairs and to increase
significantly news, religious and instructional
programming. FCC has decided station did not intend to
fulfill its promises when they had initially been made
and did not show good faith efforts as only .93% news,
no public affairs, insufficient staff, unresponsive to
problems, needs and interests of community. Ct. of
Appeals upheld FCC. Promise vs. performance inquiry is
directed toward determining whether licensee made reasonable and good faith efforts and an examination of the
licensee's efforts is as material as examination of the
fruits of the licensee's efforts,' West Coast Media, 47
RR 2d 109, (1980); 695 F. 2d 617, 52 RR 2d 1295, (1982)

427. Copyright Infringement, 'A Connecticut station broadcast
23 musical compositions without payment of ASCAP fees
and without permission of copyright holders. Station
operating at a loss was not non-profit use so court
enjoined further infringement and awarded statutory

damages of $1,000 per infringement and attorney's fees,'
Boz Scaggs Music v. KND Corp., 491 F. Supp. 908, (D.
Conn. 1980); also $54,000 damages - $26,400 attorney
fees; Rodgers v. Quests, 213 U.S.P.Q. 212, (N.D. Ohio
1981)

428. Johnny Carson Prevails in Right-of-Publicity Suit,
'Carson's right of publicity was invaded by a company
that intentionally appropriated his identity for commercial exploitation. Johnny's Portable Toilets may not
use the phrase 'Here's Johnny,' as a corporate or trade
name in connection with the advertising or sale of portable toilets,' 498 F. Supp. 71 (E.D. Mich., 1980);
Reversed Case 80-1720, (6th Cir., 1983)

429. Donahue Show Denied Exemption as News Interview Show for
Political Candidates, 'When a candidate for public
office uses a broadcast facility the station's licensee
must afford equal opportunities for such use to all
other candidates for that office unless the show is
exempt as a bona fide newscast, news interview, news
documentary or on-the-spot coverage of a bona fide news
event. Multi-media requested Donahue be considered a
news interview show and therefore exempt from §315(a).
FCC noted that show involves personal commentary, per-
mits expression by audience and a majority of guests
were of general, rather than timely, interest.' (see
387) Socialist Workers Party, 65 FCC 2d 229 (1976),
Multimedia, 84 FCC 2d 738, 48 RR 2d 1273, (1980)

430. ABC Fails to Enjoin Sportscaster From Joining CBS, 'ABC
suffered agony of defeat when sportscaster Warner Wolf
breached good faith negotiated contract to join CBS.
Court felt that Wolf had violated first refusal provision of ABC contract at CBS' instigation, however denied
injunction as court could not easily supervise the performance of a personal services contract to ABC and
first refusal right was not restrictive covenant but
three month moratorium on employment,' ABC v. Wolf, 430
N.Y.S. 2d 275, (App. Div. 1980); 438 N.Y.S. 2d 842; 420
N.E.2d 363, (NY 1981)

431. Use of Phrase in Promotional Slogan Not Trademark
Infringement, WISN Milwaukee obtained license to use 'I
Love You Milwaukee' slogan campaign. Slogan had been
registered with Patent and Trademark office as a service
mark for entertainment services. Three months before
end of campaign WOKY began to use 'I Love You' slogan
and M.B.H. Enterprises filed suit. Court ruled reluc-
tance to allow M.B.H. to appropriate the exclusive commercial use of such a common phrase despite successful

registration and cited lack of showing of confusion,'
M.B.H. Enterprises v. WOKY, 633 F. 2d 50, (7th Cir.
1980); see also Invisible v. NBC, 212 U.S.P.Q. 576,
(C.D. Cal. 1980)

432. Public TV Station May Refuse to Air Network Program, 'In
1980 PBS network ran 'Death of a Princess' about a Saudi
Arabian princess and her commoner lover who were exe-
cutied publicly for adultery. The program was critical
of Saudi religious, cultural and political life and
Saudi government protested and noted it might endanger
American citizens in Middle East. Alabama Educational
TV and Univeristy of Houston cancelled broadcast which
was challenged by subscribers and viewers of stations.
Fed. Dist. Ct. in Alabama granted summary judgment for
stations, but Fed. Dist. Ct. in Texas ordered University
of Houston to broadcast. Ct. of Appeals upheld Alabama
in that refusal to broadcast was legitimate exercise of
statutory authority and protected by First Amendment.
Another panel reversed Texas decision. Cases were con-
solidated and reheard. Resulting decision affirmed
Alabama and reversed Texas decisions. Although public
broadcast licensees, stations possess same programming
discretion as commercial broadcasters. While state is
subject to First Amendment constraints not applicable to
private licensees, FCC has determined licensees have
sole right and independent responsibility to select
programming. Public stations are not public forums and
not required to provide right of access to viewers. The
First Amendment does not preclude the government from
exercising editorial control over its own medium of
expression. In an unrelated case a class action suit
was filed against the program's producers, PBS and
others on behalf of alleged class of nearly one-billion
followers of the Islamic faith and Americans who respect
Islamic traditions. Damages of $20 billion were sought.
Court dismissed as law of defamation protects individuals, and group that sued was so large that program
could not have defamed any individual members. To permit action by such a large group would render meaning-
less First Amendment rights to explore issues of public
import,' Muir v. Alabama ETV Commission, 688 F. 2d
1033, 52 RR 2d 935, (CA 5th, 1982); Khalid v. Fanning,
506 F. Supp. 186, (N.D. Cal. 1980); Sup. Ct. appeal
denied

433. FCC Eliminates Cable TV Rules Concerning Distant Signal
Carriage Restrictions and Syndicated Program Exclusivity, 'Cable systems can now carry as many distant
signals as desired which will foster competition and add
diversity as does not affect materially the quantity of

local programming. Still required to carry local signals as well,' Cable Television Syndicated Program Exclusivity Rules, 45 Federal Register 60186 (Sept. 1980); upheld Malrite v. FCC, 652 F. 2d 1140, cert. denied. 49 RR 2d 1127, (2d Cir. 1981)

434. Trespass by TV Newsperson, 'A TV newscaster may have been guilty of trespassing when he went on private property to film a police investigation of a reported shooting incident. Remanded to trial court to determine damages caused by trespass,' Prahl v. Brosamle, 295 N.W. 2d 768, (Wisc. App. 1980)

435. Screenplay for Television Movie Did Not Infringe Book, 'Drama titled 'Murder in Texas' ruled did not infringe book 'Blood and Money' although both works recounted events surrounding death of Houston socialite Joan Hill as factual historical event. Only expression can be protected by copyright,' David Merrick v. Dick Clark, Case No. 80 Civ. 5877, (S.D.N.Y. 1980), (see 535)

436. Tax Court Denies Deduction By TV Newsperson for Clothes, Makeup and Haircuts, 'John Hynes, WCVB deducted as a business expense his wardrobe, laundry, dry cleaning, haircuts and makeup. The IRS disallowed the deductions. Tax Court upheld as Revenue Code §262 specifically denies deductions for personal, living or family expenses and burden of proof is on taxpayer. Three tests must be met for clothing to be deductible (1) required or essential, (2) not suitable for general or personal wear, and (3) in fact, not worn for general or personal use,' Hynes v. Commissioner, 80(10) CCH Standard Tax Reports, Para. 7932, (1980)

437. NBC and CBS Did Not Libel Jeweler, 'Harry Levinson, not a public figure but a jeweler of worldwide prominence was linked with 'mob boss' Anthony "Big Tuna' Accardo in numerous telecasts. Following the rule of innocent construction, adhered to in Illinois courts, the appellate ct. ruled the publications could be construed innocently as not reflecting adversely on Levinson's abilities in business and were not actionable as libel per se,' Levinson v. Time, et. al., 411 N.E. 2d 1118, (Ill. App. 1980)

438. Not Libel if Fair Comment, 'A California statute recognizes the privilege, in the absence of malice, of fair comment on matters of general public interest. KNXT showed a news report of an arrest of an auto shop owner for not giving required written estimates prior to beginning repairs. Car was also shown to be in good

working order except for broken spark plug, but repair-
man charged for $160. Ct. noted decision might have
been different if national media rather than local as
would not have been of general public interest everywhere,' Rollenhagen v. City of Orange, 116 Cal. App. 3d
414, (Cal. Ct. App. 1981)

439. CBS Required to Produce Some Out-takes From 60 Minutes,
'Supreme Ct. has refused to hear an appeal requiring CBS
to turn over to District Ct. out-takes from report on
fast-food franchises. A month after the piece was aired
a federal grand jury returned indictments for conspiracy
and fraud against the company involved and defendants
served CBS with subpoena. Appeals Ct. recognized jour-
nalists in news gathering, but has to be weighed against
defendants' need for information sought which judge
would have to view before invoking privilege. Later Ct.
ruled judge erred in release of some material to
defendants', US v. Cuthbertson, 630 F.2d 139, (3rd.
1980); Rehearing, (3d Cir. 1981)

440. TV Stations Privileged to Report, 'A qualified or con-
ditional privilege permitted stations to report legal
proceedings provided publication is fair and accurate
statement and made without malice,' Mark v. KING
Broadcasting, 618 P. 2d 512, (Wash. App. 1980) and
Mark v. Fisher's Blend Station, 621 P.2d 159, (Wash.
App. 1980); 635 P. 2d 1081, (Wash. 1981)

441. Radio Station Violated Equal Pay and Civil Rights Act,
'A former talk show hostess awarded $21M in damages and
back pay as she was paid less than a male colleague performing equal work. The disparity in salaries was sex-
based and violated the Equal Pay Act of 1963 and Title
VII of the Civil Rights Act of 1964 which entitled her
to the difference between what earned and amount should
have earned. She was also asked to perform certain
clerical tasks the male host was not required to perform
and then was fired in retaliation for her refusal to
perform such work,' Futran v. Ring Radio, 501 F. Supp.
734, (N.D. Ga. 1980)

442. FCC Eliminates Regulations on Programming Minimums,
Commercial Maximums, Logs, and Changes Ascertainment
Requirements for Radio, 'Noting the growth of radio stations the FCC has decided to rely upon market-place forces to achieve balanced programming and in determining
commercial levels. In the area of programming, radio
stations, which had guidelines (see 291), will now be
asked to offer programming responsive to public issues
and each station may take into account the services
provided by other radio stations in the community rather

71

than providing something for everyone. Formalized ascertainment requirements will give way to ascertainment procedures which assure that all significant segments of a community are contacted regarding problems, needs and issues and a list setting forth five to ten issues that the radio station covered during the year must be maintained. Limits on commercials have been eliminated (see 190) with the expectation that audiences, advertisers and individual station owners will act to curb abuses or excesses. Thus, is cleared the way for program-length commercials previously disapproved (see 259, 338). Program log requirements have been eliminated as a paperwork burden on radio stations, but public files containing relevant program information will be required. These rules presently only affect commercial radio stations,' 73:24(R) (5); (30); (Y) (1); 112; 282; 1800; 1810; 1840; 3526; Federal Communications Commission, Deregulation of Radio, 46 Federal Register 13888, 84 FCC 2d 968, 49 RR 2d 1, (Feb. 1981, effective April 3, 1981)

443. Radio Station May Not Broadcast "Away" Games Violating Rights Given to Another Station, 'Wichita State won injunction against KWKN preventing them from broadcasting away games in Wichita area as exclusive rights given by State to KAKZ. KWKN tried to get away games by signing contracts with schools with which Wichita State was to play, but ct. ruled State's opponents had no right to broadcast their games in Wichita,' Wichita State University v. Tri-City Broadcasting, District Ct. of Sedgwick County, Kansas, Case No. 81-C-130, (1981)

444. Can TV Stations Broadcast Video Tapes Entered into Evidence?, 'Nixon v. Warner Communications, 435 US 589, (1979) (see 328) recognized presumption in favor of public access to judicial records. Richmond Newspapers v. Virginia, 65 L. Ed. 2d 973, (1980) held that absent an overriding interest, the trial of a criminal case must be open to the public. Ct. ruled upon application of NBC that Abscam trial tapes entered into evidence may be copied and televised; however, the Fifth Circuit refused to allow the media to copy tapes admitted into evidence at the trial of the speaker of the Texas House of Representatives which came from another FBI operation. KSTP in Minnesota sought to copy and televise three hours of videotape received in evidence about the kidnapping of the wife of a clergyman which had been taped by the kidnapper and which included repeated sexual rapes of the victim. There the ct. denied the station request as no public interest would be served as in the case where political corruption was involved,' US v. Myers, 635 F.2d 945, (2d Cir. 1980); Application of

KSTP, 504 F. Supp. 360, (D. Minn. 1980); Belo Broadcasting v. Clark, 654 F. 2d 423, (5th Cir. 1981)

445. **Failure to Program to Unmarried Adults not Basis for License Denial,** 'All five Washington, D.C. TV stations refused to carry dating service program so company filed petition to deny license renewal. FCC held and Ct. affirmed that no particularized local need as single adults in D.C. are no more in need of finding a date than single adults elsewhere,' Walker v. FCC, 627 F. 2d 352, 47 RR 2d 361 (D.C. Cir. 1980)

446. **Legal Expenses Incurred by Broadcaster in Defending an FCC License Revocation Proceeding are Tax Deductible,** 'Inaccurate filings, false information led to license revocation. $46M in legal fees for hearings deductible,' BHA Enterprises v. Commissioner, 74 T.C., No. 46, (1980)

447. **FCC Denies License Renewal, Affirmed on Basis of Lack of Veracity,** 'FCC denied license renewal for WSWG-AM and FM after investigation based on complaints by citizens group. Substantial shortfall in amount of time station devoted to non-entertainment; lack of good faith effort to carry out programming representations proposed in 1970; lack of candor in dealings with FCC; no effort to comply with EEO affirmative action requirements and even fired some black employees. Format change was considered only as evidence of station's lack of veracity,' Leflore Broadcasting v. FCC, 636 F.2d 454, 47 RR 2d 901 (D.C. Cir. 1980)

448. **Contempt Citation Against TV Reporter for Refusing to Reveal Source,** 'Walter Roche of WBZ-TV refused to reveal confidential sources consulted for investigative report on local judges. Ct. held sources would be identified during other testimony by other witnesses and order not oppressive, unnecessary or irrelevant. Object was to use interviews to reveal inconsistent statements made by witnesses,' In the Matter of Roche, 411 N.E. 2d 466 (Mass. Sup. Judicial Ct. 1980)

449. **Ct. of Appeals Upholds FCC that Carter News Conference Exempt From Equal Time,** 'Then-President Carter held a news conference on the eve of the New Hampshire primary and Ct. of Appeals held that telecast was exempt from equal opportunity requirements of §315 as on-the-spot coverage of a bona-fide news event. The FCC is only required to consider whether or not the broadcaster intends to promote the interest of a particular candidate in presenting such coverage. Then, four days

before the Illinois 1980 primary a press conference and speech by Carter was covered. The FCC affirmed the Broadcast Bureau's decision that neither §312(a) (7) nor the fairness doctrine entitled Kennedy to free responsive time when time was available for purchase. The Ct. of Appeals again upheld the FCC noting that while §315(a) sets forth a right of equal opportunity when there has been a prior use by another candidate; §312(a) (7) is not dependent upon prior use but requires the broadcaster to provide reasonable access to a candidate or to sell the candidate time at prescribed rates. The fairness doctrine claim was denied as Kennedy had not identified the particular controversial issue involved and there was no evidence that broadcasters had failed to present contrasting viewpoints on the economy,' Kennedy for President Comm. v. FCC, 636 F. 2d 417, 636 F. 2d 432; 47 RR 2d 1521, 1537, (D.C. Cir. 1980)

450. Unauthorized use of Chaplin Films by CBS, 'Day after Chaplin died, Dec. 26, 1977, CBS broadcast half-hour retrospective comprised 40% of compilation done of footage from copyrighted Chaplin films. Sued; CBS defended on basis of 'fair use'. Ct. found CBS could have used public domain material; that excerpts were quantitatively substantial and qualitatively great overall; had been denied previously such use; was not sufficiently newsworthy in themselves for exemption as original compilation was used in 1972 Academy Awards show. Award by jury for $12,280 in statutory damages; $300M punitive; $300M for unfair competition,' Roy Export Co. v. CBS, CCH Copyright Law Reports, Para. 25, 212, 208 USPQ 581, (S.D.N.Y. 1980); affirmed 672 F.2d 1095, (2d Cir. 1982); Sup. Ct. denies appeal

451. Lea Act, §506 of Communications Act Repealed, 'The 34-year old amendment which prevented unions from coercing broadcasters to hire and maintain staff they did not need was repealed by Congress (H.R. 4892). Provision was in reaction to 1946 featherbedding by American Federation of Musicians,' P.L. 96-507, 12/8/80

452. Extended License Terms, Lottery for Licenses, Prohibition for Payment to Withdraw Applications, Deletion of License Fees; Passed by Congress, 'Communications legislation included in 1981 budget bill extended license term to five years for television stations, seven years for radio. A lottery procedure was established which the FCC, at its discretion may use for initial grants of licenses. Protection for licensees from frivolous competing applications by prohibiting payment to other applicants in exchange for withdrawal of their

74

applications included along with deletion of license fees earlier proposed. The FCC also authorized for a two-year period. To provide Congress with an opportunity for regular and systematic oversight of the FCC's implementation of Congressional policy,' 8/13/81--Signed by President; Lottery Selection rejected,' 89 FCC 2d 257, 50 RR 2d 1503 (1982); 'Congress then passed new lottery system under which selection between applicants may be made, so long as the qualifications of the applicant thus selected are subsequently reviewed and approved by the FCC,' Cong. Rec., Vol. 128, No. 155, Signed by President, (1982)

453. <u>Same Title May Cause Reverse Confusion</u>, 'A summary judgment is not possible when two films have the same title, as liability may be imposed by jury if they find the use results in confusion as to the origin of plaintiff's product. Claim of misappropriation of an idea requires (1) novel idea, (2) disclosure of idea made in confidence, and (3) idea adopted and used by defendant,' Capital Films v. Charles Fries, 628 F. 2d 387, (5th Cir. 1980); see Narwood v. Lexington, 541 F. Supp. 1243, (S.D.N.Y. 1982)

454. <u>Suit Challenging Network Production of all Documentaries Dismissed</u>, 'Twenty-six independent producers sued for antitrust, First Amendment and Civil Rights ABC, NBC, CBS. Charged that in-house documentary production froze independents out of market, monopolized, denied access. Court dismissed, technically, as did not constitute state action; TV industry defies traditional antitrust analysis; percentage of market insufficient for networks to control prices or exclude competition; affiliates may take or reject product. If proof that independents can produce at one-half cost and as high a quality may be inter-network conspiracy, but needs further proof,' Levitch v. CBS, 495 F. Supp. 649, (S.D.N.Y. 1980); Ct. of App. upholds (1983)

455. <u>Volunteer On-air Talent Access Not a Right</u>, 'After volunteer producer for non-commercial FM started sexual and racial harassment proceeding station refused use of facilities. Volunteer brought action claiming deprived right of access under Civil Rights Act of 1964 and violation of First Amendment. Court dismissed; access to broadcast media not constitutional or statutory right and station not public accommodation,' Bridges v. Pittsburgh Community B/casting, 491 F. Supp. 1330, (W.D. Pa. 1980)

456. Pay TV Operation Blocked by Justice Department, 'Planned 1981 Pay-TV operation of Premiere by Columbia, MCA, Paramount, 20th Century-Fox and Getty Oil may constitute price-fixing and group boycott violating Sec. 1, Sherman Act. Government showed reasonable likelihood Premier was concerted action to make films available only to own corporation thereby refusing to deal with, and to boycott, other services, thereby restraining competition,' U.S. v. Columbia, 507 F. Supp. 412, (S.D.N.Y. 1980)

457. Cable System Cannot Cablecast Ohio State Football, 'Warner Amex CUBE, Columbus, Ohio sought order to allow cablecast of Ohio State Football games. NCAA had sold exclusive rights to ABC, but previous negotiations and threat of antitrust suit had allowed ten earlier sold-out games to be carried. ABC then refused to give up exclusivity on games not sold out and Warner filed second antitrust suit. Court ruled that must show irreparable harm with inadequacy of money damages for injunction and Warner failed as within their power to still carry sold-out games and buy tickets of those games not sold out. Warner did buy out seats and did show games,' Warner Amex v. ABC, 499 F. Supp. 537, (S.D. Ohio 1980)

458. Court Enjoins City Ordinance Restricting Cable System Expansion, 'Case that will have wide-ranging effect on city home rule struck down city ordinances placing a permanent geographical limitation on cable system expansion. City can be held liable for violation of antitrust law in restraint of trade by refusing to allow competition between cable companies. Case concerns control over the quantity and quality of communication which may not be of such local concern as to justify exercise of sovereign authority by city. Exercising pervasive controls would violate First Amendment and lose claim of antitrust exemption. Court found, under present technology more than one cable company can be on same poles without adversely affecting public ways,' Community Communications v. City of Boulder, 630 F. 2d 704, (10th Cir. 1980); 496 F. Supp. 823, (D. Colo. 1980); upheld by Supreme Court, 70 L. Ed. 2d 810, 50 RR 2d 1183, (1981)

459. Amended Public File Rule, §73:3526, 'TV licensees are not required to place new statement of program service in public file at renewal time if statement on file is current,' 87 FCC 2d 1127, 50 RR 2d 704, (1981)

460. Contract Must be Performed, 'TV station which had en-
tered into contract to carry some basketball games with
TV syndicator and which failed to do so must perform,'
William B. Tanner v. Briarcliff, 50 RR 2d 737, (1981)

461. Bona fide News Interview Program Political Exemption,
'TV news interview show exempted from equal opportunities when two candidates get into argument for two of
30 minutes during which candidate did not respond to
questions. Not loss of control by licensee,' Tucker v.
KNXT, 50 RR 2d 768, (1981); and 'rebroadcast of news
interview show after six months, in regularly scheduled
hour, but during election campaign does not deprive show
of exempt status as still newsworthy, controlled by station, not unreasonable,' Robert Hanna, 88 FCC 2d 346, 50
RR 2d 781, (1981)

462. Political Action Committee Access, 'Since federal candidates access is personal right no such right is afforded Political Action Committees. Broadcaster obliged
to give free response time to candidates if PAC obtains
time,' 89 FCC 2d 626, 51 RR 2d 233, (1982)

463. Denial of Renewal of One Out of Seven Stations Enough,
'Sufficient remedial and deterrent effect to deny one
license out of seven where misconduct limited and individual who did misconduct no longer with licensee,'
Faulkner Radio, 88 FCC 2d 612, 50 RR 2d 814, (1981)

464. State Law on Public Broadcasting Not Preempted by
Federal Law, 'NJ Sup. Ct. holds Sec. 315 does not pre-
empt state statutes requiring public broadcasting to
promote full discussion of issues, consistent with
balance, fairness and equity in state race for governor,' McGlynn v. NJ Broadcasting Auth., 439 A. 2d 54, 50
RR 2d 867, (1981)

465. Short-Term Renewal, 'Licensee used station to further
private interests in anti-competitive manner,' E. Boyd
Whitney, 86 FCC 2d 1133, 49 RR 2d 1240, (1981)

466. Renewal Denied, 'Majority stockholder unlawfully transferred control, made misrepresentations, willfully violated technical rules, lacked candor,' Stereo Broadcasters, 87 FCC 2d 87, 49 RR 2d 1263; Reconsideration
denied, 50 RR 2d 1346, (1981)

467. News Distortion-Slanting Defined, 'Mere inclusion of
incorrect information cannot lead to conclusion deliberate and petition for full hearing against TV network
denied,' Yellow Freight v. FCC, 49 RR 2d 1663; 656 F.

2d 600, (1981), 'station editorial on conduct of mayor
not news-slanting as no evidence of deliberate falsification and editorials did not relate to honesty, integrity or like personal qualities so not personal
attack,' Mayor Maier v. WTMJ, 50 RR 2d 73, (1981); 53 RR
2d 377, (1983)

468. Sales Reps May Have More Than One Client Per Market,
'FCC repeals policy which had barred sales rep firms
owning radio or TV license from representing rival station in same area,' 87 FCC 2d 668, 49 RR 2d 1705, (1981)

469. CATV Cross-Ownership Rule Waived, 'CBS permitted to own
cable systems if aggregate number of suscribers less
than one-half of one percent of total of US subscribers,' CBS, 87 FCC 2d 587, 49 RR 2d 1680, (1981)

470. Newspaper Cross-Ownership Abuse, 'Practice of newspaper
with local license to list programs out-of-channel sequence and give itself preferential photos constitute
cross-ownership abuse,' KHQ, 87 FCC 2d 705, 50 RR 2d 21,
(1981)

471. Prohibition Against Retransmission, 'Reminder by FCC
that licensees and cable systems cannot retransmit
without permission summarized contents or texts of
messages transmitted by others,' Retransmission, 50 RR
2d 76, (1981); and 'ESPN Cable Network enjoined from
cablecasting highlights of Boston Red Sox and Bruins
games without consent of either team as not 'fair use'
under Copyright Act, video taped from WSBK which offered
to sell use. Although only 2 minutes in length from
complete game court stated it was the quality of use and
since were highlights was substantial as networks had
paid for such use,' New Boston Television, v. ESPN,
Civil Action 81-1010-Z, (D. Mass. 1981)

472. Lottery, 'The fact that proceeds of lottery held at
local fair were given in part to local civic and chari-
table organizations did not absolve licensee, but war-
ranted reduction in fine,' Smith Broadcasting, 87 FCC 2d
1132, 50 RR 2d 356, (1981)

473. Waiver of Network Definition, §73:658, 'Network definition is any organization offering interconnected programs on regular basis for 15 or more hours per week to
at least 25 affiliated TV licensees in 10 or more states
waived to permit interconnected religious programming of
up to 30 hours per week,' Christian B/casting Network,
87 FCC 2d 1076, 50 RR 2d 359, (1981)

474. **No Private Cause of Action in Personal Attack,** 'Federal District Ct. may hear both state and federal claims in state libel case combined with personal attack charge even if personal attack claim fails so long as federal claim not frivolous. However one cannot obtain damages based on FCC rule violation,' Lechtner v. Brownyard, 50 RR 2d 609 (WD Pa. 1981); 679 F. 2d 322, 51 RR 2d 953, (1982); and same result, Cyntje v. Daily News, 53 RR 2d 299, (6th D.C. 1982)

475. **Licensing of Hopalong Cassidy Films for TV Enjoined as Infringement of Copyright in Cassidy Books,** '1935, late Clarence Mulford granted right to make films based on books. Copyrights to films expired and company sought to license 23 for TV exhibition as public domain material. Federal District Court ruled exhibition would violate copyright in books as substantial similarity,' Filmvideo Releasing v. Hastings, CCH 25, 222, (S.D.N.Y. 1981); affirmed 668 F.2d 91, (2d Cir. 1981)

476. **ABC Exclusive Right to Televise Sports Event Upheld,** 'ABC obtained exclusive rights for 1981 World Figure Skating Championships to be held in Hartford. CBS affiliate brought suit charging agreement represented unconstitutional restriction on freedom of press as called for local stations not to broadcast footage until ABC finished entire broadcast if they wished entry into arena where event staged. If arena were privately operated, such a contract provision is valid, however, since not private state action existed and attention directed to capacity in which city was functioning. Court ruled city not operating as government but in proprietary manner and restrictions were not arbitrary, minimal, and allowing local TV coverage would diminish commercial value to ABC,' Post Newsweek v. Travelers, Skating Club and City of Hartford, 510 F. Supp. 81, (1981)

477. **Radio Station's Refusal to Air Hypnotic Political Ads Not Subject to Damages,** 'Candidate sought to purchase time for political ads using hypnotic techniques. Station requested exemption from FCC from any obligation to present, but FCC refused to issue a ruling. Station rejected ads and candidate sued for damages for violating Sec. 315 and First Amendment. Federal Court of Appeals dismissed on grounds Sec. 315 did not create private cause of action for damages and no governmental action was involved giving rise to First Amendment. Should have sought action from FCC as Congress' intent for FCC supervision,' Belluso v. Turner Communications, 633 F. 2d 393, (5th Cir. 1980)

478. Docu-drama OK Despite Inaccuracies, 'In absence of showing contract violated and of clear and convincing evidence of irreparable injury injunction against showing denied for ficionalized film about Guardian Angels. In another case of famous Scottsboro rape trial NBC thought one of participants was deceased. After broadcast she wrote NBC considered broadcast libelous but NBC proceeded to rebroadcast. Federal District Court in Tennessee ruled that NBC had not negligently broadcast any untruths and had not broadcast with malice as she was public figure. Movie was not completely accurate. After petitioning Supreme Court for hearing appeal was settled out of court,' Sliwa v. Highgate, No. 24070/80 (N.Y. Sup. Ct. 1980); Street v. NBC, 7 Media Law Reporter 1001, (6th Cir. 1981)

479. Poor Ratings Reasonable to Reassign Newsperson to General Reporting, 'TV anchorman sought order to re-assign as anchor from general reporting reassignment. Alleged violated Fair Labor Standards Act, which makes it illegal for employer to retaliate against employee who files charges or participates in labor dispute. Court denied injunction because felt he would fail to prove action was because of discriminatory motive. Station contended reassignment was due to ratings and unfavorable consultant's report. Court refused to interpret ratings or report and stated belief that news director and station manager thought ratings were too low,' Haines v. Knight-Ridder, CCH Labor Law Reports, Para. 33,976, (D.R.I. 1980)

480. Copyrighted 'Be a Pepper' Commercial Infringed by Sambo's, 'Federal District Court in Dallas enjoined showing of Sambo's commercials, based on finding that copied essence of copyrighted Dr. Pepper commercial and jingle, 'Dr. Pepper v. Sambo's, 517 F. Supp. 1202, (N.D. Tex. 1981)

481. Demonstration Did Not Create Unreasonable Risk, 'The producer, syndicator and broadcaster of the Mickey Mouse Club TV Show were found not liable for injuries sustained by an 11-year old boy who attempted to duplicate a sound effects demonstration which required placing a BB pellet inside a balloon, which he swallowed. The demonstration did not create an unreasonable risk of harm and was not an invitation to act in such a way as to pose a clear and present danger of injury,' Walt Disney v. Shannon, 276 S.E. 2d 580, (Ga. 1981); see also, DeFilippo v. NBC, 446 A.2d 1036, (R.I. 1982)

82. Not Proven NBC Incited Violent Act, 'In a case where it was alleged that a rape scene in movie 'Born Innocent' motivated a similar attack on a nine-year-old girl in San Francisco the court granted a nonsuit on grounds that the jury would not be able to determine whether NBC had incited the violent act. Plaintiff conceded NBC did not encourage or advocate violent acts, so broadcast was protected speech. Court refused to impose liability on basis of simple negligence as would lead to selfcensorship and seriously inhibit broadcasters in airing controversial programs.' Olivia N. v. NBC, 126 Cal. App. 3d 488, (1981); Cal. Sup. Ct., US Sup. Ct; appeal denied.

83. Greatest American Hero Does Not Infringe Superman, 'Since expression of ideas was dissimilar and only theme or general idea had any similarities, does not infringe, 'Warner Bros. v. ABC, 654 F. 2d 204, (2d Cir. 1981); 523 F. Supp. 611; 530 F. Supp. 1187, (S.D.N.Y. 1982)

84. CBS Wins Libel Suit, '60 Minutes interviewed the wife of Richard Alfego, who had taken their children from the custody of his ex-spouse in violation of the child custody order. Alfego sued that although not named or shown his identity was obvious and his reputation was injured. Court acknowledged that news must be substantially complete and accurate and not distorted, but not every fact and detail sympathetic to every side need be presented. Wife's charges were opinion and not libelous so long as not based on undisclosed falsehood, so dismissed,' Alfego v. CBS, 7 Media Law Reporter 1075, (D. Mass. 1981)

85. Libel, 'At WFBR, Baltimore, D.J. Johnny Walker stated humorously, following looting by blacks during blizzard, that a local black TV commentator was seen entering a hospital for a bad knee, caused by carrying a TV during the blizzard. The newsman sued, and although a public figure the jury awarded $30,000 from Walker, and $35,000 punitive damages from the station. In affirming the award the appelate court rejected the general rule that limits situations in which punitive damages may be awarded against an employer, when the remarks have been ad-libbed,' Embrey v. Holly, 429 A. 2d 251, (Md. App. 1981)

86. Communications Act Provision Limiting Commercial Radio Operator Licenses to United States Citizen is Declared Constitutional, 'A D.J. and a radio station engineer challenged requirement that only US citizens can hold

Radio Operator licenses. Although D.J.'s are not required to be licensed it was alleged career opportunities would be limited as many smaller stations require on-air personnel to perform additional technical functions which require an operator's license. §303(1) upheld as immigration is an exclusive federal interest, political in nature. The national interest in providing an incentive for aliens to become naturalized, or providing the President with an expendable token for treaty negotiating purposes is sufficient to justify requirement,' Campos v. FCC, 650 F. 2d 890, (7th Cir. 1981)

487. Libel--Animal Cruelty, Trespass, 'Cases involved alleged cruelty to animals. KSL broadcast report of cruelty to horses. Court ruled for KSL on grounds of general interest, privilege and lack of malice shown, Utah Sup. Ct. remanded as KSL liable if shown departed from standards which exist, or ought to exist, in news media industry. WMC-TV broadcast report on starving cattle. Fed. Ct. of App. ruled that owner was private and that he had burden of proof reports were false. Trial court had erred in ruling station had to prove truth of story. In a third case, reporters entered home with Humane Society investigator, took pictures even though protested by owner. Court ruled was trespass as reporters have no special immunity or special privilege to invade rights and liberties of others, Seegmiller v. KSL, 626 P. 2d 968; Wilson v. Scripps-Howard, 7 Media Law Reporter 1169 (6th Cir.); Anderson v. WROT-TV, 441 N.Y.S. 2d 220, (N.Y. Sup. Ct. 1981)

488. City Loses Libel Suit Against ABC, 'There have been relatively few reported cases of libel actions taken by cities. The Village of Grafton, Ohio, filed against ABC when a crawl was used on 'The Killing Ground' documentary which listed 54 locations of hazardous chemical waste dumps. Grafton was on the list. The court ruled the statement was privileged because made about a city; the city had no reputation to be defamed as did a person; and the information came from a federal agency though erroneous,' Grafton v. ABC, 435 N.E. 2d 1131, (Ohio App. 1980)

489. Star Trek Not Public Domain, 'Between 1966 and 1968, Star Trek was distributed without a copyright notice and a company claimed it had entered public domain. Court ruled this was not a publication under 1909 © Act, in effect until 1978, as license agreements restricted access,' Paramount v. Rubinowitz, Case CV 81-0925, (E.D.N.Y. 1981)

490. **Indecency Statute for Cable TV Overboard**, 'A Utah statute banning indecent, although not necessarily obscene, material on cable is unconstitutionally overbroad as invaded area of free speech by failing to incorporate any reference to contemporary community standards,' Home Box Office v. Wilkinson, 531 F. Supp. 987, (D. Utah, 1981); upheld D. Ct. (1982)

491. **Cable Operators Need Not Carry Scrambled Pay-TV Signals,** 'Subscription TV stations petitioned FCC to require cable operators to carry scrambled signals. FCC refused to require carriage as no evidence needed for economic success of STV; would impose burden on cable operators; and could be done by contract,' WWHT v. FCC, 656 F. 2d 807, (D.C. Cir. 1981)

492. **NAB Code Provisions Ruled Violation of Antitrust**, 'Since 1952, the NAB trade association has sponsored a TV Code. The government challenged the Code's multiple product, time and program interruption standards. The multiple product standard prohibited the advertising of two or more products or services in a single commercial if the spot was less than 60 seconds. Time standards limited the amount of commercial material to be broadcast each hour to 9½ minutes per hour in prime time, plus ½ minute for promotional announcements, and 16 minutes at all other times. Independent stations were allowed more time and children's programs were limited as to commercial time allowed. Standards also limited the number of consecutive interruptions of the program and announcements per interruption. The court ruled that the multiple product standard was a per se violation of Sec. 1 of the Sherman Act, and ordered a trial on the time and program interruption standards. The NAB ceased enforcing the code upon the courts decision and appealed. A consent decree was agreed upon;' US v. NAB, 51 RR 2d 175, 553 F. Supp. 621, (DDC 1982)

493. **Equal Access to Justice Act**, 'Rules are adopted providing for the award of attorney's fees and other expenses to qualified parties who prevail over the federal government in certain administrative and court proceedings,' Subpart K, §73:1501-73:1530, 50 RR 2d 1338, (1982)

494. **Stereo Broadcasting**, 'FCC authorizes AM stations to provide stereo broadcasts but abandons its attempt to select a single approved transmission system, leaving to the marketplace the determination. Minimal technical standards are established to prevent interference,' AM Stereophonic B/casting, 51 RR 2d 1, (1982)

495. Conflict of Interest of Public Affairs Host--Political, 'A licensee's failure to determine, prior to broadcast of interviews with political candidates that the host was serving as campaign treasurer for one of the candidates did not amount to intentional discrimination in violation of §73:1940,' Phyllis Cowan, 89 FCC 2d 382, 51 RR 2d 104, (1982)

496. Financial Report, Form 324 Eliminated, 'Lack of public interest for the information is given for elimination of financial report data,' Annual Financial Report, 51 RR 2d 135, (1982)

497. Satellite Retransmission of NY Mets Games on WOR-TV Does Not Infringe Copyright, but Substitution of Teletext Signal of WGN-TV Does, 'Eastern Microwave retransmits WOR signal to cable systems, and Mets owner objected, contending violation of Sec. 106 of Copyright Act. Held retransmission exempt under Sec. 111(a)(3) as EMI is passive common carrier; does not convert or control signal. However, when United Video, a passive carrier, retransmitted WGN signal and replaced vertical blanking interval Teletext with Dow Jones Teletext, this was held not passive. WGN intended material to be an integral series of related works, even if not viewed simultaneaously. Teletext, if not intended to be viewed in conjunction with program not protected and viewer utilization does not deprive of protection. Ct. felt technological advances motivated reform of Copyright Act which requires it to use flexibility in decision,' Eastern Microwave v. Doubleday Sports, 691 F.2d 125; WGN v. United Video, 693 F.2d 622 (1982); clarified, 692 F.2d 628, 52 RR 2d 1693, (1983); Sup. Ct. appeal denied

498. Ex Parte, 'Fine of $6,000 for contact by one party without notice to other or giving opponent opportunity to be heard is ruled not unreasonable nor excessive,' Desert TV, 88 FCC 2d 1413, 50 RR 2d 1283, (1982)

499. Short-term Renewal, 'KGGM, Albuquerque for not meeting needs of Latin-American audience,' New Mexico Broadcasting, 50 RR 2d 340, (1982)

500. Renewal Denied, 'Peoria radio station denied license renewal due to misrepresentations regarding changes in ownership and control of the corporate licensee,' Peoria Community Broadcasters, Inc., and Central Illinois Broadcasting Co., 79 FCC 2d 311, 48 RR 2d 1164, (1982)

501. Political editorial violation, 'Although FM apparently violated political editorial, public and political file

inspection rules, no action as not flagrant nor intentional,' WJFD, 50 RR 2d 1413, (1982)

502. Local-Public Notice changed, 'Requirement that applicants submit proof of publication of local notice of applications removed and replaced by single certification of compliance with notice requirement, 51 RR 305, (1982)

503. Comparative applicants, 'Turning attention to subtleties when comparing ownership and management between applicants, review board affirms FM award,' Bradley, Hand and Triplett, 89 FCC 2d 657, 51 RR 383, (1982)

504. Community size determinant, 'FCC review board favors license for station in larger, unserved community over smaller, served community,' Cornwall, 89 FCC 2d 704, 51 RR 2d 389, (1982)

505. Low Power TV, 'FCC authorizes low power TV as primarily rural and fill-in providing valuable local service and specialized programming. The imposition of multiple ownership restrictions is rejected to encourage participation by experienced broadcast operators,' Low Power, 51 RR 2d 476, (1982)

506. License renewal denied, 'Reversing Adm. Law Judge, FCC holds that one man owned-and-operated classical music FM station license should be denied. Various grounds cited, including failure to conduct community survey and to broadcast for community needs,' Simon Geller, 90 FCC 2d 250, 51 RR 2d 1019, reconsideration denied, 52 RR 2d 709, (1982)

507. Direct Satellite to Home Authorized, 'FCC establishes nonlocal broadcast service from satellite direct to home. Multiple ownership restrictions rejected in favor of minimilist regulatory approach to encourage rapid development, 'DBS, 90 FCC 2d 676, 51 RR 2d 1341, (1982)

508. FCC Reduced in Size, Commissioners cut from seven to five members as of July 1, 1983 to streamline by decreasing size and cost,' 97-21, Second Session, August 18 (1982); and FCC bureaus reorganized, with Broadcast Bureau and Cable TV Bureau compressed into four new divisions: Audio Services; Enforcement; Policy and Rules; and Video Services, (Nov. 1983)

509. NonCommercial Educational Stations Promotional Announcements Expanded.' Spots for program-related materials sold by non-profit organizations and to raise funds for station or non-profit performing arts organizations in

connection with programs furnished allowed; so long as spots do not interrupt other regular programs,' Educational Promotional Annoucements, 90 FCC 2d 895, 51 RR 2 1567, (1982)

510. Legally Qualified Candidate Only if State Certified, 'FCC affirms that not legally qualified candidate for equal opportunity purposes unless certified under applicable state law,' Mayor Bergin, 90 FCC 2d 813, 51 RR 2d 1535, (1982)

511. UHF-TV Only to Channel 70, 'FCC eliminates requirement that TV sets receive UHF Channels 70 through 83 and provides for licensees operating on those channels to transfer to lower frequencies,' UHF-TV Reception Improvements, 90 FCC 2d 1121, 51 RR 2d 1628, (1982)

512. Editorializing by NonCommercial Stations Unconstitutional?, 'Held unconstitutional Sec. 399 of Communications Act to prohibit noncommercial stations from editorializing as no compelling governmental interest for restriction on free speech. Relatively small percentage of governmental funding. Public interest served by Fairness Doctrine requiring balanced presentation,' League of Women Voters v. FCC, 547 F. Supp. 379, 52 RR 2d 311 (1982); Supreme Ct. will hear appeal, (1983)

513. Fairness Doctrine Weighted by Overall Programming, 'FCC rejects request that individual program or series of programs must comply with Fairness Doctrine. Compliance weighted by reference to overall programming. Balancing frequent paid commercials of one side against presentation of opposing view in less frequent but more substantial programming, particularly news, is not imbalance,' American Security Council, 52 RR 2d 419; Citizens for a RadioActive Waste Policy, 52 RR 2d 481, (1982)

514. Interim Operators Which Broadcast Lottery Not Disqualified, 'Difficulty of interim operation by antagonistic applicants rendered effective supervision of employees too difficult to warrant disqualification for broadcast lottery occuring during religious programming (see 316),' Gilbert Broadcasting, 91 FCC 2d 450, 52 RR 429, (1982)

515. Cable System 'Must-Carry' Local Station Even If Last Channel Available, 'Sole empty channel must go to local religious station even if subscribers uninterested,' and 'deleting must-carry signal with subsequent saturation of system is at operator's own risk,' New Milford Cablevision, 52 RR 2d 617 (1982); Rockland Cable, 53 RR 2d 253; KSDK, 53 RR 2d 283, (1983)

16. **Antitrust 'Block-Booking' Action May Proceed Against NBC,** 'Producers of 'Bonanza' and 'High Chaparral' brought antitrust action against NBC and purchaser of syndication rights, NTCA. Claim conspiracy to require buyers to take exhibition rights to other, less desireable programs to get desireable series. This tying arrangement is called block-booking. Dist. Ct. ruled producers had no standing to sue, but Ct. of Appeals reversed. The _per se_ nature of the violation, if proven, would be illegal and affected producers who were in the target area of potential injury,' Aurora Enterprises v. NBC 524 F. Supp. 655; 688 F. 2d 689; 52 RR 2d 693, (1982) (see 176)

17. **Networks May Decide President's Speech Bona fide News Event,** 'FCC declines to question network's pre-address decision that Reagan's last minute plea for support of policies and Republican Party scheduled shortly before mid-term election of 1982 was a bona fide news event,' Democratic National Committee, 91 FCC 2d 373, 52 RR 2d 713, (1982)

18. **District Ct. Cannot Determine Validity of FCC Rule Where Declaratory Judgment Action,** 'In a case where FCC rule conflicts with a provision of a franchise agreement between a city and a cable operator the appropriate conduct for the district ct. is to recognize the primary jurisdiction of the FCC and stay proceeding pending resolution of validity by the agency,' City of Peoria v. GECCO v. FCC, 690 F. 2d 116, 52 RR 2d 787, (1982)

19. **Lack of Candor Issue Need Not Be Raised as Separate Issue,** 'FCC must be able to rely upon representations made before it in hearing process, and failure to provide complete and accurate information may always be examined during the hearing even if not designated as separate issue,' William M. Rogers, 52 RR 2d 831, (1982)

20. **Short-term Renewal,** 'Network clipping, single unintentional instance of lack of candor, issuance of memo pertaining to local tennis club that was arrears in advertising payments not to cover in sports programming, serious exaggeration of station coverage area in promotional coverage maps overridden by forty-eight years of service and affirmative steps to correct practices upon discovery,' Gross Telecasting, 52 RR 2d 851, (1982)

21. **Diversification of Ownership of Primary Importance,** 'Review Board of FCC reemphasizes primary importance of diversification of ownership in comparative hearing,' Communications Properties, 52 RR 2d 981, (1982)

522. Minority Ownership, 'Female participation, while not as significant as other minority participation (see 395), merits more than a slight preference, and where things are equal can be determinative. Issue must be certified to be considered. Female minority 100% integrated ownership wins over 100% local ownership. Minority policy is not dependent upon proof that minority-owned station will specifically program to meet minority needs (see 376). In an effort to increase opportunities for minority ownership the FCC issued a policy statement supplementing 1978 Policy Statement (68 FCC 2d 979, 42 RR 2d 1689),' North Carolina Radio Service, 52 RR 2d 993; Horne Industries, 52 RR 2d 1009; Waters Broadcasting, 52 RR 2d 1063; Minority Ownership in Broadcasting, 52 RR 2d 1301, (1982)

523. Three-Year Ownership Rule Eliminated, 'In 1962 FCC adopted rule requiring license to be held for at least three years or face hearing for trafficking. Eliminated to allow unfettered marketplace forces; however, the amount of funds receivable in sale (see 55) of a construction permit is restricted and a one-year holding period is required for construction permit obtained through comparative hearing,' 52 RR 2d 1081, (1982)

524. Sale of Equipment Allowing Unauthorized Reception Illegal, 'Manufacture and sale of equipment allowing unauthorized interception of Multipoint Distribution Service of pay service is violation of Sec. 605 of Communications Act and permanent injunction granted (see 424),' Home Box Office v. Advanced Consumer Technology, 549 F. Sup. 14 (S.D.N.Y. 1981); same result in American Television and Communications v. Manning, 651 P. 2d 440 (Colo. App. 1982); and American Television and Communications v. Western Techtronics, 529 F. Supp. 617, (D. Colo. 1982)

525. Station's Requesting Nonduplication Protection Must Specify Cable Systems Carrying, 'Declaratory ruling granted requiring stations requesting nonduplication of network programming or sports shows to specify the cable systems on which protection is to be provided,' Rule Making Proposal to Substantiate Requests for Carriage Or Nonduplication, 52 RR 2d 1327, (1982)

526. WABC-TV License Renewed Despite Deceptive Programming, 'Station staff members broadcast letters purporting to be from viewers but written by staff, ficticious interviews and questions supposedly from studio audience. License informed FCC upon disclosure, instituted corrective procedures, dismissed or forced to resign those

involved. FCC admonished licensee for failure to exercise reasonable diligence, supervision and control to insure that no matter that would decieve or mislead public is broadcast. License renewed but full Commission would review next renewal application,' American Broadcasting Company, 52 RR 2d 1378, (1982)

527. Directors Guild Members Need Not Work for HBO; Exempt from Antitrust, 'From 1973 to 1978, the Directors Guild waived its requirement that members work only for signatories of Guild Agreement to enable HBO and other pay channels to become established. In 1978 Guild sought collective bargaining agreement from HBO. When terms were refused, Guild ordered members not to work for HBO. HBO sued alleging Guild members were independent contractors and Guild's order was illegal restraint of trade. Broad range of concerted labor activity is exempt if union able to establish acts in self-interest and apart from non-labor group. Actor's Equity upheld in licensing agents and regulating their fees; (101 S.Ct. 2102 (1982). Guild was held exempt also from antitrust laws and HBO had not shown violation or loss or damage to its business,' Home Box Office, v. Directors Guild, 531 F. Supp. 578, (1982)

528. Termination for Just and Sufficient Cause, 'News Reporter at WJKW-TV Cleveland terminated for 'just and sufficient cause.' Arbitration hearing held where evidence presented and firing upheld. Appealed, remanded, appealed and decision upheld on basis bargaining agreement was ambiguous and arbitrator could determine,' American Federation of Television and Radio Artists v. Storer, 660 F. 2d 151, (6th Cir. 1981)

529. Federal Grant of Public Broadcasting Construction Funds Not Appealable, 'A decision by National Telecommunications and Information Administration of Department of Commerce to grant federal funds for construction of public broadcast station not subject to review by Federal Ct. of Appeals. Two universities contended grantee had misrepresented information. The statute authorizing the Secretary of Commerce to distribute such grants is in the Communications Act of 1934, but, act does not provide for judicial review other than of FCC,' Xavier University v. NTIA, 656 F. 2d 306, (5th Cir. 1981)

530. Independent Producers May Copyright Works Paid for by Federal Government, 'A TV series commissioned by the Federal Government, produced by a public TV station, broadcast by PBS is not public domain notwithstanding

Sec. 105 of 1976 Copyright Act which provides that there is no protection for any work of the U.S. Government. The production was not prepared by a government employee; would not deprive the public of access; and did not conflict with First Amendment interests. The Ct. proceeded on the assumption that an assignment to the government had taken place although series not assigned and no governmental agency had a copyright interest. Government was not precluded from receiving and holding copyrights transferred to it by assignment,' Schnapper v. Foley, 667 F. 2d 102, (D.C. Cir. 1981), Sup. Ct. declined appeal, (1982)

31. CBS 'Guns of Autumn' Did Not Defame Hunters, 'Two documentary films broadcast in 1975 did not defame Michigan United Conversation Clubs. Programs were not 'of and concerning' the MUCC or individual members. They were not shown, described or identified,' Michigan United Conservation Clubs v. CBS News, 665 F. 2d 110, (6th Cir. 1981)

532. Invasion of Privacy and Right of Publicity Claims Against ABC, 'ABC's 20/20 segment, narrated by Geraldo Rivera, reported on alleged arson-for-profit scheme. Rivera stated 20/20 had uncovered circumstantial evidence and then interviewed manager of building alleged to have been burned for profit. Under Illinois law, it is libel per se to impute a criminal offense to an individual. Seven statements were made about the manager, which when viewed in context charged him with such criminal activity that even in the form of opinion are not constitutionally protected. Manager was also private figure who had not thrust himself to the forefront of any particular public controversy,' Cantrell v. ABC, 529 F. Supp. 746, (N.D. Ill. 1981)

33. Mental Patient's Consent to Filming Invalid, 'New York's Civil Rights Law applied when CBS documentary portrayed mentally incompetent patient who had signed consent form. Ct. ruled he was not competent or capable to grant such consent as form must be witnessed by a physician who has interviewed and examined the patient. A psychologist is not a physician,' Delan v. CBS, 445 N.Y.S. 2d 898, (N.Y. Sup. Ct. 1981)

534. Damages for Airing Commercial After Employment Agreement Expired, 'In 1973 agreement signed with performer for commercial to be used in 1974. Screen Actor's Guild put company on notice that term of employment contract had expired after that use. In 1975 commercial was used again. $1,000 compensatory damages and $15,000 punitive

damages were awarded,' Welch v. Mr. Christmas, Inc., 454 N.Y.S. 2d 971; see also Dzurenko v. Jordache, 451 N.Y.S. 2d 102, (App. Div. 1982)

535. Producer Must Repay Advance for Failing to Produce Mini-Series, 'David Merrick was paid $916,666 to produce 'Blood and Money' for CBS. Under the Rights Agreement CBS agreed to pay total of $1,250,000 for his right, title and interest and to budget $10 million for the project. Merrick hired a writer and director who were committed to other projects and one year later Merrick was told project could not be completed on date in Production Agreement. CBS was not informed. Their agreement provided that if photography did not begin by August 1979 the deal would terminate, with rights reverting to Merrick but CBS committed to pay balance provided no breach of contractual obligations. CBS and Merrick agreed to delay, but Merrick then repudiated oral modification of agreement. Ct. ruled that oral modification was upheld by actions and later repudiation constituted breach of contract and ordered return of advance and monies paid to his agents. Writer and Director may retain their fee and physical property rights to screenplay belong to CBS, but other rights revert to Merrick,' (see 435) CBS v. Merrick, Case CV 79-4822-DWW, (C.D. Cal. 1982)

536. 'Good Faith' Negotiation Clauses in TV Rights Contracts, 'The International Skating Union contracted exclusive TV rights to Candid Productions for 16 years. In 1980 the ISU granted TV rights to CBS and Candid contended ISU did not bargain, as required, in good faith as they had signed with CBS before negotiating. Ct. ruled that promise to negotiate was vague and uncertain and unenforceable,' Candid Productions v. ISU, 530 F. Supp. 1330, (S.D.N.Y. 1982); however, 'First refusal rights to televise sporting events are essential in the broadcast industry, for without them a network is placed in the position of promoting an event and enhancing its value without sufficient security to prevent the future benefit from being reaped by another broadcaster. Thus, when CBS refused French Tennis Open deal requiring it to promote Wimbledon or pay additional fee and NBC agreed since it had rights to Wimbledon; Ct. agreed was odious and unconscionable demand and not bonafide proposal. Preliminary injunction given pending immediate trial, 'CBS v. French Tennis Federation, (NY Cty., Special Term, Jan. 1983)

537. Misleading Survey in TV Commercial Violates Lanham Act, 'Bristol-Myers ran a TV commercial in which it reported

91

a consumer-survey comparing 'Body on Tap' with competitive products. Vidal Sassoon, Inc., sued, contending that 900 women, as reported, did not participate in product-to-product comparison; 1/3 were 13 to 18 years old and may not be 'women'; and only 1% statistically insignificant difference between top four ratings. Fed. Dist. Ct. granted motion for preliminary injunction to halt commercial on grounds that it was ambiguous and misleading violating Sec. 43(a) of the Lanham Act. Decision upheld on appeal,' Vidal Sasson, Inc., v. Bristol-Myers, 213 U.S.P.Q. 24, (2d Cir. 1981)

538. 'WKRP' Episode Did Not Infringe Copyright Despite Similarities, 'Distinction between unprotectible 'idea' and its protectible 'expression' at issue when 1976 four-page radio script and sales proposal copyrighted which featured staff of fictional radio station involved in remote broadcast from business when interrupted by armed robber. WKRP, broadcast by CBS in 1978 also featured episode involving remote broadcast from business interrupted by armed man. Script never submitted to MTM and CBS, but issue became question of substantial similarity. Ct. relied upon abstractions test; essence of infringement lies in taking not a general theme, but particular expression in treatment, details, scenes, events and characterizations. WKRP episode not actionable infringement because it is only an idea, and handling of scenes, details and characterization were not substantially similar. Implied contract requires direct submission,' Giangrasso v. CBS, 534 F. Supp. 472, (E.D.N.Y. 1982)

539. ABC Did Not Misappropriate 'Exclusive Story' on Cause of Elvis' Death, 'Larry Seller's told Geraldo Rivera in 1978 he had exclusive story of cause of Elvis Presley's death. Insisted Rivera sign agreement that Sellers owned copyright and required ABC to credit him. Sellers agreed not to give or sell story to any other network or reporter. Two theories were given; that doctor and bodyguard had slowly replaced medication with placebos causing cardiovascular failure; alternatively, murdered to prevent Presley from seeking repayment of loan. Rivera informed Sellers could not use story without verification. Sellers called once but did not divulge further information. Nine months later Rivera conducted two-month investigation and broadcast two-hour special which stated Presley died of interaction of prescription drugs. Sellers sued for misappropriation, breach of contract and copright infringement. Although Sellers did mention this 'third' theory it was only in passing and background. A vague or indefinite contract will not

be enforced under NY law. The idea used was neither specific enough, nor novel or unique enough to support misappropriation or copyright claims,' Sellers v. ABC, 668 F. 2d 1207, (11th Cir. 1982)

540. 'SuperStation WTBS Allowed to Broadcast NCAA Football in 1982, But Not National Baseball Championship Games,' Dispute over TBS right to broadcast NCAA football arose when NCAA altered exclusive affiliation with ABC offering two networks rights and offered cable or pay series on a trial basis. In 1982, NCAA signed with Turner for two-year supplemental series. Turner does not operate cable or pay system, but TBS is originator, over satellite, of cable programming. ABC affiliate in Atlanta and ABC sued on basis that they had contract with NCAA based on understanding supplemental series would be carried on cable or pay only; not conventional over-the-air station. CBS contract with NCAA did carry provision allowing one over-the-air station to carry series after contract signed with Turner. ABC had attempted to obtain specific provision prohibiting any over-the-air coverage for supplemental series. Ct. agreed that WSB-TV Atlanta and ABC would suffer irreparable harm and the NCAA had breached its contract with ABC. However, ABC had been dilatory in seeking relief; Turner had substantially changed its position in reliance on its NCAA contract; schools in supplemental series would be harmed, therefore, TBS could carry 1982 games, but were enjoined broadcasting games in 1983 through 1985. To alleviate damage to WSB, NCAA ordered to permit broadcast of two University of Georgia and two Georgia Tech games in addition to regular 1982 games to be carried by ABC,' Cox Broadcasting v. NCAA, C-89120, (Georgia Superior Ct. 1982). However, Turner, which owns both Atlanta Braves and TBS wished to broadcast National League Baseball Championship games under exception to ABC's rights which grants each club participating in series the right to permit its local flagship station to broadcast series in the team's home market. WTBS, ruled Ct. would be damaging to ABC as its signal is not just in home market, but carried by cable systems reaching 20 million homes in U.S. Injunction granted,' ABC Sports v. Atlanta National League Baseball Club, C-82-6104, (S.D.N.Y. 1982)

541. NCAA Football TV Network Contracts Violate Antitrust Law, 'In 1952 the NCAA adopted by majority vote a plan that declared the NCAA was the exclusive representative of all member schools for the purpose of selling TV rights to football games. Colleges are not permitted to make own contracts with networks or individual stations.

93

Rules also limit how many times on TV and amount of money from TV. Major football schools formed College Football Association in disatisfaction with minority powers and in 1981 negotiated a lucrative offer from NBC while NCAA was negotiating with ABC,CBS and Turner. NCAA made public statements that violation of NCAA rules would be dealt with and the Universities of Georgia and Oklahoma filed suit to obtain injunction barring NCAA from disciplinary action. Temporary order was issued, but CFA members opted out of NBC contract. The ct. has since ruled that since the vast majority of NCAA schools do not play football on TV or at all and vote to restrict the TV rights of the minority; and that the majority have voted to obtain a substantially larger portion of TV money; the NCAA has fixed prices and restricted the output of its members. These practices are illegal per se under antitrust law. The ct. also held the plan was illegal under the rule of reason and had no redeeming pro-competitive benefits. A Federal Court of Appeals has stayed the order pending appeal,' Board of Regents of University of Oklahoma v. NCAA, 546 F. Supp. 1276, (1982)

542. FM Radio Assignment Policy Changed, 'FCC's first prior-ity in assigning FM stations will be to assure the availability of at least one full-time station for as many people as possible. FCC will then attempt to pro-vide either a first local or second non-local signal depending on which would reach greater audience. No further reservation of channels to community (see 558) and relaxation of policy to allow competing application to obtain a second channel in community if available, thus avoiding comparative hearings,' In the Matter of FM Assignment Policies and Procedures, 90 FCC 2d 88, 51 RR 2d 807, (1982)

543. Is Liquor Advertising State Ban UnConstitutional or Legal?, 'In Mississippi statutes prohibiting alcoholic beverage advertising were ruled unconstitutional as violation of First Amendment and Equal Protection Clause. Ct. determined that commercial speech is pro-tected only if lawful activity and not misleading unless the government restriction seeks to implement a substan-tial governmental interest; directly advances that interest, and; reaches no further than necessary to accomplish the limited objective. Liquor advertising, stated the ct., involved lawful activity which was not misleading and did not artificially stimulate consump-tion. Thus, a complete prohibition was not rational to promote temperance as it only penalized advertising ori-ginating in the state,' Lamar Outdoor Advertising v.

Mississippi State Tax Commission, 539 F. Supp. 817, (S.D. Miss. 1982); however 'State of Oklahoma was allowed to prohibit by statute the advertising of the sale of alcoholic beverages. The prohibition could be upheld either as a direct exercise of the State's Twenty-First Amendment authority to control liquor within its boundaries, or as an exercise of its ancillary authority to protect citizens against potential harm by reducing sale and consumption. It was noted that Oklahoma had a referendum introducing the statutory scheme and a judicial repeal of one segment of the total alcohol law would be impermissible,' Oklahoma Telecasters Association v. Crisp, 53 RR 2d 903, (10th Ct. App. 1983)

544. Sale of TV Series to Syndicator and Simultaneous Re-run by Network Upheld, 'MGM, producer of 'Chips' sold exclusive local run to McGraw-Hill. NBC, which had original license to broadcast certain number of times announced network re-run schedule. McGraw-Hill sued on basis of no exclusivity as contracted. Ct. issued decision same day NBC was to begin re-run that McGraw-Hill had not demonstrated probability of success of suit on merits; and did not show irreparable injury. NBC would suffer hardship if injunction requested was granted,' McGraw-Hill v. MGM, 537 F. Supp. 954, (S.D.N.Y. 1982)

545. Miami Dolphins Stop TV Station From Carrying Home Games, But Radio Station May Sue To Retain Astro Games, 'Professional basketball, baseball and hockey are exempt from some provisions of antitrust law and are permitted to sell TV rights as single package, unlike college sports (see 541). The teams may also black-out home coverage of games to keep ticket sales high. A TV station 96 miles from Miami was to carry Dolphin games, outside 75-mile radius of NFL rule. However, new powerful transmitter would penetrate 75-mile limit and Dolphins refused TV coverage. Ct. ruled that should be based on signal penetration, rather than station location and station not allowed to carry,' WTWV v. NFL and Miami Dolphins, 678 F. 2d 142, (11th Cir. 1982); however, 'KYST's contract to carry Astros Baseball games was cancelled and Houston Sports entered into a contract with KENR. The Ct. considered whether radio broadcasting is such a part of baseball that it participates in the exemption from antitrust laws and concluded it is not. The unique characteristics and needs of baseball are not involved in a broadcast contract. Extending the baseball exemption to this particular situation is unrealistic, inconsistent and illogical. The issue raised was whether the Ct. could rule on an antitrust violation and breach of contract and therefore denied

motions to dismiss,' Henderson v. Houston Sports, 541 F. Supp. 263, (S. D. Tex. 1982)

546. If Capable of Defamatory Meaning, No Summary Judgment Possible, 'Appeals Ct. overturned lower ct. decision which had granted summary judgment, as inappropriate. In 1977, ABC broadcast documentary 'Sex for Sale' about effects of sex businesses on local communities. In voice-over commenting on street prostitution accompanying visual was three women walking down local street. Suit brought by one of women. Since her appearance was capable of defamatory meaning; no privilege; not public figure it is up to jury to decide whether broadcast was understood to be defamatory,' Clark v. ABC, 684 F. 2d 1208, (6th Cir. 1982)

547. Unauthorized Taping Off-Air By School District Not Fair Use, 'An educational cooperative did large-scale off-air videotaping of copyrighted films and distributed them to schools in NY. The Board argued it was making fair use and repeated showings permitted time-shifting to allow more flexible viewing for teachers and students. Since taping interfered with marketability of the copyrighted works (Learning Corporation of America no longer allows telecast of its educational films because of declining film sales believed due to such taping); taping was massive and highly sophisticated; licensing agreements are available from educational film companies for taping; taping was substantial and verbatim; was not fair use and permanent injunction granted, plus damages,' Encyclopedia Britannica Educational Corp., v. C.N. Crooks, 542 F. Supp. 1156, (W.D.N.Y. 1982)

548. TV Screen-Credit Breach Nets Actor $1.8 Million, 'MGM-TV agreed in 1976 to give William Smithers up-front billing; that no other performer would get better compensation in series 'Executive Suite.' For this most-favored credit arrangement Smithers agreed to less than his usual fee. After airing it was learned his agreement was changed in unsigned long form contract which he declined. Threat to blacklist was evidence of tortious breach of contractual duty of good faith and fair dealing. Damages for breach of contract, tortious breach, fraud, punitive damages for emotional distress totaled $1.8 million,' Smithers v. MGM, C-65508, (Cal. App. 1983)

549. Homeowner Has No Privacy Rights when Pirating Signal, 'Using external visual and electronic inspection of antenna to determine if homeowner is pirating the signal is no violation of First Amendment right to privacy,'

Movie Systems, Inc., v. Heller, 52 RR 2d 1483, (D. Minn. 1982)

550. Right to Refuse Advertisements Only On Reasonable
Policy Statement on Minority Ownership of Cable TV Facilities, 'FCC expresses intention to use tax cer- tificate authority to promote additional minority ownership in the cable field,' 52 RR 2d 1469, (1982)

551. Right to Refuse Advertisements Only On Reasonable Grounds, 'Ct. held that no absolute right to reject com- mercials, reasonable grounds such as technical quality, obscenity, libelous content, etc. Therefore, station should not have rejected commercials containing price comparisons where prices could not be checked after broadcast of first annoucement,' Sam's Style Shop v. Cosmos Broadcasting, 696 F. 2d 128, 52 RR 2d 1533, (5th Ct. App. 1982)

552. Sec. 312 of Communications Act Implementation Case-by- Case, 'Sec. 312 states that a station must not deny access to any candidate for federal office, regardless of what form that access takes. The FCC affirms its use of a case-by-case, complaint activiated approach to implementation of the reasonable access provisions. Were the FCC to abandon consideration of individual complaints in favor of a policy based on overall review at the time of licensee renewal, the timely resolution of access disputes would be impossible. Congress also intended such enforcement as it included the access pro- visions in the revocation section of the Act,' Reason- able Access Implementation, 53 RR 2d 89, (1983)

553. Religious Broadcasters Rights May be Infringed to Investigate--Renewal Denial, 'In a civil action arising from the stormy stewardship of licensee Faith Center Church, the Ct. of Appeals rejected the claims that investigation of the president and pastor of his per- sonal church donations by the FCC, disclosure of the investigation to the press and public, and sharing of the information with state law enforcement authorities violated his First Amendment and civil rights. Ct. agreed that the investigation of his personal donations (in the context of investigating solicitation on broad- cast stations) violated his First Amendment right to exercise his religion freely, since his faith requires that his donations remain secret in order to retain their sacred character. However, the FCC's duty to pro- tect the public from diversion or misuse of funds soli- cited through the broadcast media are sufficiently com- pelling to justify these infringments. Ct. also reject- ed civil rights claims, holding that mere sharing of

information does not suggest conspiracy. Allegation that FCC action marked a single step in violation of Establishment Clause of First Amendment was rejected,' Scott v. Rosenberg, 53 RR 2d 127 (9th Ct. App. 1983); continued refusal to comply with discovery order causes FCC to deny renewal of station; Faith Center, 53 RR 2d 797, (1983)

554. Public Notice Regarding Transferability of Broadcast Licenses, 'Any station whose renewability appears to be affected by misconduct of joint licensee will be designated for hearing at the same time as the original station. Any stations not affected by the alleged conduct will be freely transferable. The FCC also affirmed its authority to revoke the licenses in one service on the basis of egregious violations of the rules of another service,' Public Notice, 53 RR 2d 126; Bernard Winner, 53 RR 2d 215, (1983)

555. FCC and Public TV Station Need Not Provide Captions for Handicapped, 'Ct. of Appeals had held that FCC, in renewal, had to consider whether in public interest for public TV station not to have complied with Sec. 504 of Rehabilitation Act of 1973 which requires non-discrimination for handicapped in any federally assisted activity. Supreme Ct. ruled that while a public TV station has the duty to comply the FCC may find the licensees' efforts adequate since no adverse finding by Dept. of Education which was the proper agency to consider discrimination under Rehabilitation Act. The FCC has no enforcement responsibilities in relation to that law and there was no need to treat public stations more stringently than commercial stations,' 74 L. Ed 2d 705, 53 RR 2d 271, (US Sup. Ct. 1983)

556. Ct. Order Prohibiting Criminal Trial Coverage Prior Restraint, 'When a one sentence order, not limited to time or geographic area prohibited a TV station from broadcasting a news segment concerning a criminal trial the Ct. alternatives to prior restraint were considered; and defendents only asked for segment to be withheld until after the trial, in that area,' US v. McKenzie v. CBS, 53 RR 2d 301, (5th Ct. App. 1983)

557. No violation of Personal Attack Rule in Religious Cult Program, 'Not identifiable group,so no personal attack in program on religious cults which charged deceptive practices, brainwashing and human indecency,' Disciples of the Lord Jesus, 53 RR 2d 319, (1983)

558. FCC Abolishes Suburban Policy, Berwick Doctrine and De Facto Reallocation Policy, 'The Suburban Policy, enacted by FCC in 1965, was to discourage applicants from filing applications for small communities near large cities but to identify with larger community. Burden was on applicant to show they really wished to serve suburban area. The Berwick Doctrine applied the same public interest considerations to FM and TV as to AM by requiring an evidentiary hearing determining whether programming would be for larger or smaller community specified as community of license. The Defacto Reallocation Policy affected only FM and TV when a channel assignment for one community was to be used to establish a service to another community. One had to request removal of channel from one city and show effective use to provide service to another unless one could show station to be licensed to unlisted community would be within 10 miles (Class B or C FM and all TV) of a community listed in the Table of Assignments. Now applicants need only submit petition for rulemaking to add unlisted community to Assignment Table,' 53 RR 2d 681, (1983)

559. FTC Changes Requirements in Advertising Grocery and Gasoline Games, 'The FTC regulates contests and advertising that is broadcast. Grocery stores and gasoline stations were required to include in ads exact number of prizes in each catagory, odds, geographic area covered, number of outlets participating and termination date of game. Remember, to keep from being a lottery-no consideration. FTC has agreed to exempt marketers and users of games-of-chance promotions from the necessity of disclosing full prize and odds in broadcast advertising. FTC also no longer requires TV to disclose both aurally and visually. Other businesses not regulated as were grocery stores and gasoline stations,' FTC, 16 CFR 419, (1983)

560. Approval of Application Withdrawal Payment if Not Frivolous, (see 452); 'FCC approved withdrawal of competing application settlement agreement, under recently amended Sec. 311(c) (3) of Communications Act where circumstantial evidence suggested original application was not mere sham directed toward achieving a profitable settlement,' Cedar Creek Radio, 53 RR 2d 745; Rule Amendments, 53 RR 2d 823, (1983)

561. Sales Representative Firm Obtains Damages for Breach of Contract, 'The Katz Agency acting as the exclusive national advertising representative for a broadcast station was ruled entitled to damages for breach of contract. The station was sold, without notice to Katz,

and the new owner cancelled their contract without giving a required one year's notice,' Katz v. Evening News, 53 RR 2d 815, (1983)

562. Not Selling Advertising to Other Stations In Market May Violate Antitrust, 'The FCC's statutory mandate does not require it to enforce the antitrust laws directly, but they must deny licenses if violation occurs and may consider potential violation. Exercising that authority, the FCC admonished a TV station which had refused to sell advertising to a local FM station where that TV station had previously sold time to other FM stations in that market including its own. The TV station was held to have discriminated in an improper attempt to influence or penalize the other licensee and by refusing to permit it to advertise over their TV station had attempted to gain a competitive advantage for its own FM station,' Midwest Communication, 53 RR 2d 993, (1983)

563. Accusation of Fiscal Irresponsibility Is Not Personal Attack, 'FCC ruled that a paid ad in which a U.S. Congressman was described as fiscally irresponsible was not a personal attack, particularly since the Congressman was given an opportunity to purchase equal time for a response,' Hon. Les AuCoin, 53 RR 2d 1024, (1983)

564. Filming U.S. Currency in Advertising Counterfeiting?, 'The filming of U.S. currency and obligations for advertising purposes is a criminal offense according to 18 USC 474, 504. Filming may be done for the purposes of philatelic, educational, historical or newsworthy purposes. The Supreme Ct. will rule on whether the federal government may ban or regulate photographs or artwork depicting U.S. currency. A federal ct. in NY ruled that barring magazines from doing so constituted overbroad subject matter regulation that interfered unduly with protected speech,' Regan v. Time, Inc., 539 F. Supp. 1371, (1982); appeal pending, (1983)

INDEX

1

3

4

9

11

12

13

14

18

20

Political Candidates:

--access	245,268,330,347,383,385,386, 387,388,429,449,462,517,552
--advance script	108,258
--appearance in person	141,206
--burden of proof on	146,350,510
--cancellation of talk	104
--cancellation of other program	54
--censorship of	67,104,107,157,216,258,389
--charges for time	157,268,293,347,384
--Communist	102
--defamation by	138,145,216,389
--defining	350,383,510
--dramatic skit by	102
--equal opportunity for	54,179,206,227,268,303,347, 380,388,449,517,563
--equality in facilities	206,268,347
--equality in time	157,206,227,268,303,347,386, 387,429
--FCC rules	146,228,242,330,389,501,552
--Federal Candidates	245,268,293,383,385,449,517, 552
--Federal Election Act	245,268,293,383
--format controlled by	24,258,303,429,461
--for same office	71
--free vs. paid time	245,347,449,563

28

Public Access	52,53,58,81,90,184,222,224, 235,239,241,255,317,355,376, 379,382,421,455,462,557
Public Disclosure	205,271,409,495,526
Public Figure	263,311,354,359,360,362, 374,407,437,478,485
Public Interest Groups	212,237,262,266,271,279,280, 282,300,303,304,307,318,319, 320,337,339,345,356,382,383
Public Issues, discussion	42,52,56,80,86,88,136,150, 184,235,238,239,240,241,244, 255,256,263,265,267,270,274, 275,292,300,305,310,317,321, 348,363,364,393,421,513
Public Service Requirement	56,246,284,285,331,390,392, 393,396,442
Public Standing	212,243
Public Utility, not a	14,53,270,382
Qualified Candidate	(see Political)
Racetrack Broadcasts	69,92,185
Racial Intolerance	34,68,233
Radio Formats	337
Radio Price-Fixing	143
Rape, Privacy of	188,286,444
Rate-Card Agreement	143
Ratings, Use of	299,479
Reasonable Access, Political	347,385,388,449,517,552
Rebroadcasts	20,106,134,471,525,540,544